Power Puzzles

Three volumes in one

Power
Puzzles

Three Volumes in One

Philip Carter and Ken Russell

BARNES
&NOBLE
BOOKS
NEW YORK

This volume was previously published as three separate volumes:
Power Puzzles, *Power Puzzles 2*, and *Power Puzzles 3*.

About Mensa

Mensa is a social club for which membership is accepted from all persons with an IQ (Intelligence Quotient) of 148 or above on the CATTELL scale of intelligence. This represents the top 2% of the population. Therefore one person in 50 is capable of passing the entrance test, which consists of a series of intelligence tests.

Mensa is the Latin word for *table*. We are a round-table society where all persons are of equal standing. There are three aims: social contact among intelligent people; research in psychology; and the identification and fostering of intelligence.

Mensa is an international society with 110,000 members of all occupations: clerks, doctors, lawyers, policeofficers, industrial workers, teachers, nurses, and many more.

Enquiries to: MENSA FREEPOST
Wolverhampton WV2 1BR
England

MENSA INTERNATIONAL
15 The Ivories,
6-8 Northampton Street,
London N1 2HV
England

AMERICAN MENSA LTD.
2626 East 14th Street
Brooklyn, NY 11235

About the Authors

Philip Carter is a Justice of the Peace and an Estimator from Yorkshire. He is Puzzle Editor of *Enigmasig*, the monthly newsletter of the British Mensa Puzzle Special Interest group.

Ken Russell is a London surveyor and is Puzzle Editor of *British Mensa*, a magazine sent to its 43,000 British members monthly.

Acknowledgments

We are indebted to our wives, both named Barbara, for checking and typing the manuscript, and for their encouragement in our various projects.

Power
Puzzles
1

1 "X" Puzzle

Find twenty-two words in the grid, each must have at least one X in it. Words may be in any direction but always in a straight line.

D	I	O	L	Y	X	X
E	X	A	M	E	Y	I
X	A	L	S	L	L	P
T	I	Y	E	X	E	H
E	E	N	X	O	M	O
R	E	X	A	C	T	I
X	Y	P	T	U	X	D

(Solution 4)

2 Warehouse

A warehouse has to be built at one of the mile points along a road so that its weekly delivery miles are kept to a minimum.

A   B   C   D

A requires   8 deliveries per week
B requires   4 deliveries per week
C requires   7 deliveries per week
D requires   6 deliveries per week

Where should the warehouse be built?

(Solution 8)

3 Alphabet Crossword

Complete the grid by using all twenty-six letters of the alphabet.

A B C D E F G H I J K L M
N O P Q R S T U V W X Y Z

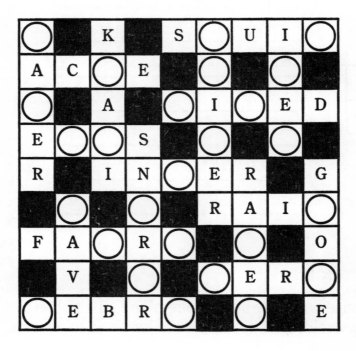

(Solution 11)

4 Reverse Anagram

If we presented you with the words MAR, AM, and FAR and asked you to find the shortest English word which contained all the letters from which these words could be produced, we would expect you to come up with the world FARM.

Here is a further list of words:

BEAT, ROUTE, BRAIN, MINT

What is the shortest English word from which all these words can be produced?

(Solution 16)

2

5 No Blanks

The blank squares have been removed from this crossword.
Letters have been inserted in their place. You have to find the
blank squares.

S	C	A	L	A	R	A	R	E	M	A	N	D
E	R	R	I	C	E	P	A	P	E	R	E	I
M	I	T	T	E	N	A	M	E	T	R	E	S
I	O	I	O	R	E	V	U	E	O	I	D	I
C	A	S	T	A	W	A	S	L	O	V	E	N
O	L	T	E	G	A	T	E	H	O	E	D	V
N	O	O	N	E	W	I	F	E	Z	S	R	E
D	O	C	O	T	E	M	I	N	E	T	I	S
U	P	O	N	P	L	A	C	E	S	O	F	T
C	A	V	E	D	O	N	O	R	T	I	T	M
T	R	E	P	A	N	O	M	E	A	L	I	E
O	E	R	E	M	E	D	I	A	T	E	E	N
R	O	T	T	E	R	O	C	R	E	D	I	T

(Solution 21)

6 Fair Play

In a game of thirty-six players that lasts just fifteen minutes,
there are four reserve players. The reserves alternate equally
with each player, therefore, all forty players are on the sportsfield
for the same length of time. For how long?

(Solution 23)

7 Anagrammed Synonyms

In each of the following, study the list of three words. Your task is to find two of the three words which can be paired to form an anagram of one word which is a synonym of the word remaining. For example:

LEG - MEEK - NET

The words LEG and NET are an anagram of GENTLE, which is a synonym of the word remaining, MEEK.

1. BIDS - SEE - TOO
2. VEERED - WEAK - TAN
3. SIT - HIND - POORER
4. OUT - KISS - SCALE
5. POST - SLAP - AIDE
6. TREE - ART - EBB
7. WHET - MUTE - TAILS
8. DRAIN - ONCE - ACT
9. SIN - EAT - GET
10. SANE - VICE - SKEW

(Solution 27)

8 1984

The digits 0, 1, 2, 3, 4, 5, 6, 7, 8, 9 can be arranged into an addition sum to add up to almost any total, except that nobody has yet found a way to add up to 1984.

However, nine digits can equal 1984 by an addition sum. Which digit is omitted?

(Solution 32)

4

9 Round the Hexagons

Can you work out what should be the contents of the bottom hexagon?

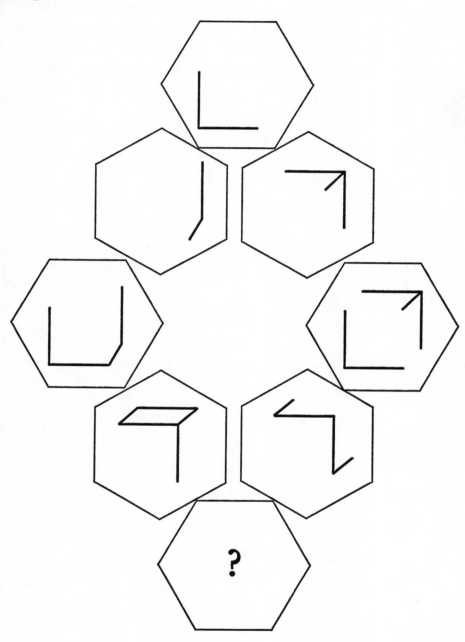

(Solution 36)

10 Hexagon

Fit the following words into the six spaces encircling the appropriate number on the diagram so that each word correctly interlinks with the two words on either side (you will see that each word has two consecutive letters in common with the word on its side). (NOTE: To arrive at the correct solution some words will have to be entered clockwise and some counterclockwise.)

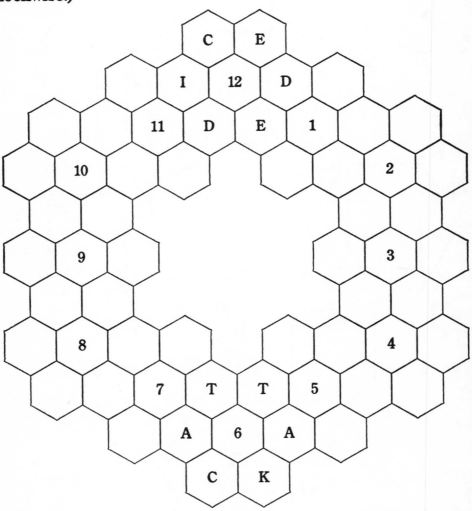

ADROIT – DEFERS – GERUND – ROTATE – REMARK – TAGGED – ~~ATTACK~~ – ~~DECIDE~~ – URGENT – MALADY – WIDENS – DIVIDE

(Solution 40)

11 Circles

Which of these fit into the blank circle to carry on a logical sequence?

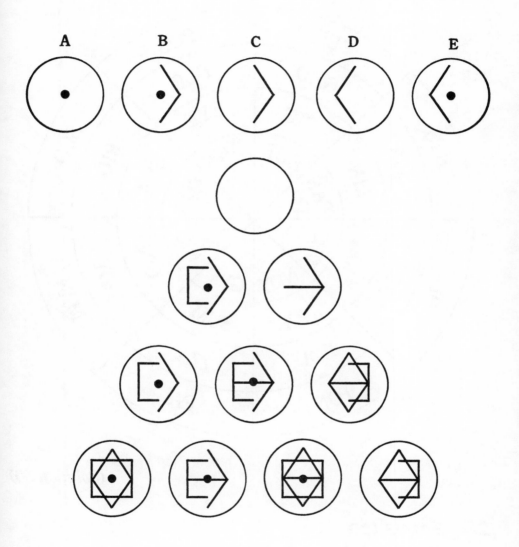

(Solution 44)

12 Target Crossword

Find sixteen 6-letter words by pairing up the thirty-two 3-letter bits.

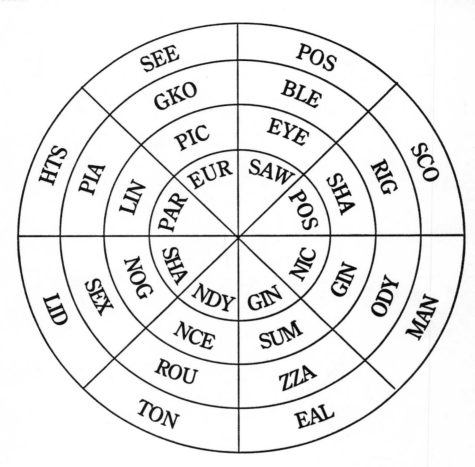

(Solution 50)

13 Sequence

What number comes next in this sequence?

101, 65, 131, 116, 131, 1021, ?

(Solution 54)

14 No Repeat Letters

The grid below contains twenty-five different letters of the alphabet. What is the longest word which can be found by starting anywhere and working from square to square horizontally, vertically, or diagonally, and not repeating a letter?

J	N	B	D	I
X	E	R	V	G
P	O	C	U	Q
S	K	T	W	L
Y	H	M	A	F

(Solution 58)

15 Word Circle

Complete the fifteen words below so that two letters are common to each word. That is, reading across, the same two letters that end the first word also start the second word, and the two letters which end the second also start the third word, etc. The two letters that end the fifteenth word also are the first two letters of the first word, to complete the circle.

..AR..	..EE..	..NA..	..NU..
..SU..	..TT..	..GA..	..PH..
..MI..	..BU..	..VI..	..EL..
..ND..	..IG..	..FE..	

(Solution 61)

16 Missing Square

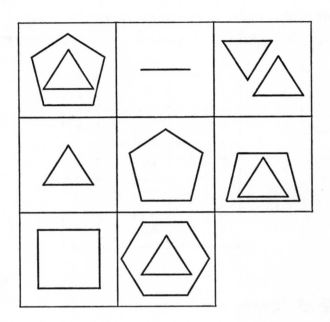

Which of the following is the missing square?

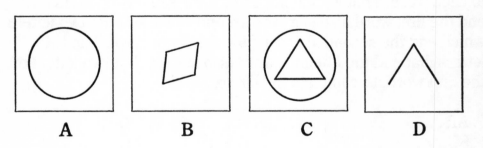

A   B   C   D

(Solution 66)

10

17 Logic

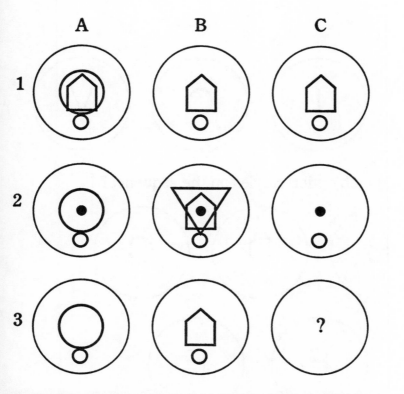

Logically which circle below fits the above pattern?

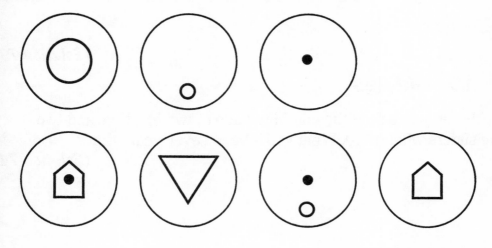

(Solution 70)

11

18 Sequence

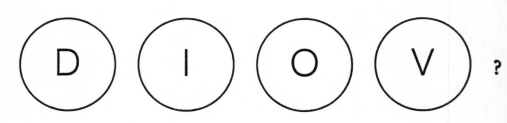

Which option carries on the sequence?

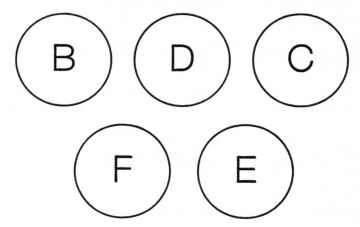

(Solution 79)

19 Old Age

In ten years time the combined age of two brothers and two sisters will be 100. What will it be in seven years time?

(Solution 74)

20 Word Search

Find twenty words to do with D R I N K S.

Words run backward, forward, vertically, horizontally, and diagonally, but always in a straight line.

E	S	U	E	R	T	R	A	H	C
N	E	Y	V	E	Z	L	O	A	O
I	R	N	A	Z	C	C	P	X	I
D	E	W	I	O	K	P	K	N	N
A	G	F	H	D	U	C	I	A	T
N	A	O	G	C	A	T	H	E	R
E	L	O	C	R	R	C	L	O	E
R	R	I	R	A	G	M	S	E	A
G	N	A	M	O	I	E	L	U	U
O	R	A	N	G	E	A	D	E	M

(Solution 83)

21 Letters Sequence

Which two letters come next in the following sequence?
TO, NE, US, RN, ER, RS, ?

(Solution 87)

22 Bracket Word

Place two letters in each bracket so that these finish the word on the left and start the word on the right. The letters in the brackets, read downwards in pairs, will spell out a 10-letter word.

ME (..) AS
UN (..) UT
SA (..) NE
MO (..) IN
LE (..) GO

(Solution 91)

23 Odd One Out

Which is the odd one out?

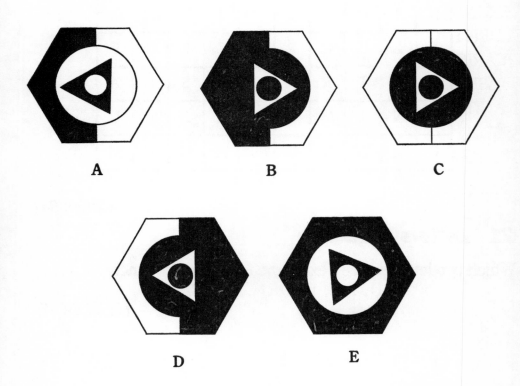

A   B   C

D   E

(Solution 95)

14

24 *Word Power*

In column (A) is a list of words. The problem is to rearrange them so that their initial letters spell out a quotation. To make the task easier, refer to the definition in column (B) and put the correct word with that definition in the answer column (C). When all the words have been correctly placed in column (C), the quotation will then appear reading down the initial letters.

(A) Words	(B) Definitions	(C) Answers
KOHL	Unearthly, weird	——————
ESCULENT	A rare word for edict	——————
TOLU	Refreshment with food and drink	——————
GERUND	Uproot	——————
ELDRICH	A cosmetic powder	——————
VICARIOUS	With great strength	——————
UKASE	Penniless	——————
INANITION	Delegated	——————
AMAIN	Edible	——————
ODALISK	A noun formed from a verb ending -ing	——————
REFECTION	Female slave in a harem	——————
IMPECUNIOUS	A female swan	——————
EXTIRPATE	Exhaustion	——————
TERMAGANT	An aromatic balsam	——————

(Solution 99)

25 Greek Cross to Square Puzzle

Draw two lines which will dissect the Greek Cross into four congruent (same size and shape) pieces which can then be arranged to form a square.

(Solution 103)

26 Appropriate Anagrams

Find the appropriate anagrams of these words and phrases.

PARADISE REGAINED

SAINT ELMO'S FIRE

SAUCINESS

SEMOLINA

TOTAL ABSTAINERS

WAITRESS

THERAPEUTICS

THE MONA LISA

MEDICAL CONSULTATIONS

A SENTENCE OF DEATH

(Solution 107)

27 Jumble

Beginning always with the middle letter "V," spell out eight 11-letter words traveling in any direction. Each letter (except for the "V") can only be used once.

I	T	Y	E	R	I	S	L	Y
L	C	U	T	A	O	U	Y	L
I	I	L	A	C	X	A	U	S
T	M	R	E	I	E	T	I	O
P	A	S	E	**V**	A	C	I	A
I	H	R	I	E	E	C	N	T
Y	S	C	E	R	N	N	T	I
O	E	O	S	U	T	A	I	O
R	E	M	N	O	I	T	L	N

(Solution 111)

28 Four Integers

ABCD represents four integers such that the following arrangements are square numbers. What integer does each letter represent?

CABA
DCBA
DACB

(Solution 114)

17

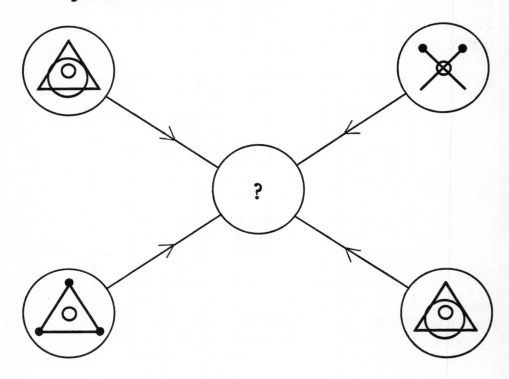

Each line and symbol which appears in the four outer circles is transferred to the center circle according to these rules:

If a line or symbol occurs in the outer circles:

once	it is transferred
twice	it is possibly transferred
three times	it is transferred
four times	it is not transferred

Which of the circles A, B, C, D, or E, shown opposite, should appear at the center of the diagram?

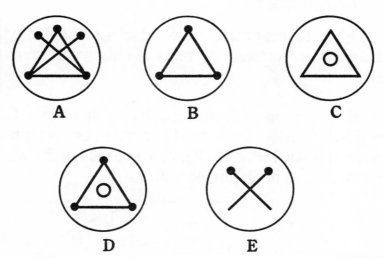

(Solution 116)

30 Cheeses

Six cheeses of different sizes are placed on stool A. How many moves will it take to move the cheeses one by one to stool C? A cheese must not be placed on a cheese smaller than itself.

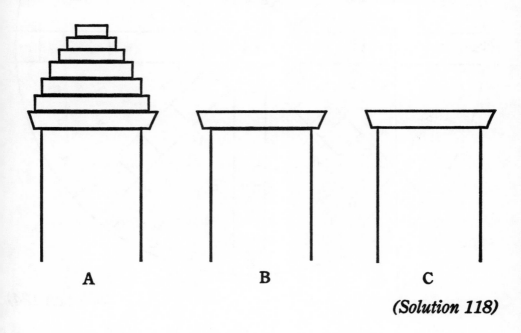

(Solution 118)

31 The Gallopers

The name given to this puzzle is the old fairground name for the roundabout ride on horses, now more familiarly known as the carousel.

Complete the words in each column, all of which end in G. The scrambled letters in the section to the right of each column are an anagram of a word which will give you a clue to the word you are trying to find, to put in the column.

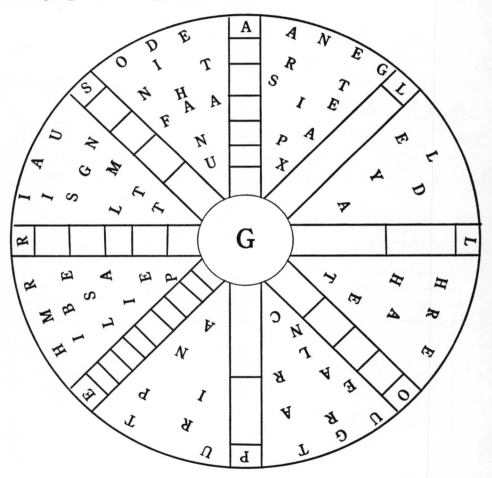

(Solution 124)

20

32 Analogy

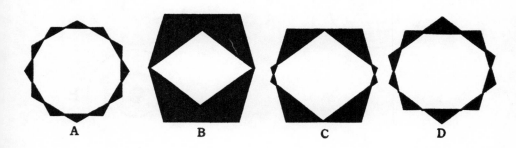

(Solution 129)

33 Birds

The twenty-five words can be paired up to make twelve birds with one word left over. Which is the word?

GREBE	WARBLER	DOVE	WATER	PIGEON
CARRIER	PEACOCK	HAWK	PETREL	SNOW
NIGHT	MUSCOVY	WILLOW	BLACK	OUSEL
COCKATOO	HOUSE	GOOSE	OWL	MARTIN
STORMY	DUCK	TAWNY	TURTLE	CRESTED

(Solution 133)

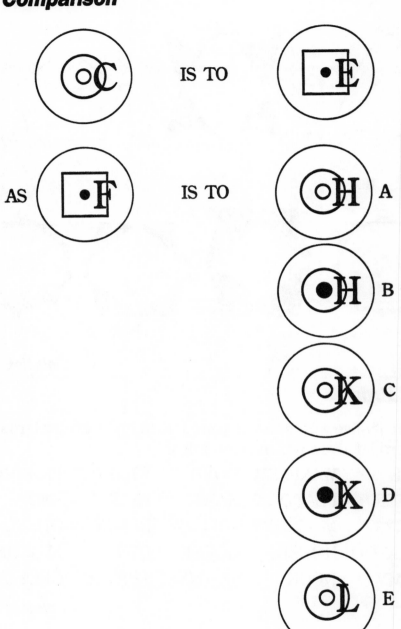

IS TO

AS

IS TO

A

B

C

D

E

(Solution 121)

35 Knight

Using the knight's move as in chess, spell out the message. You have to find the starting point.

AS	IT	OWN	PEOPLE'S	ARE
BUT	OTHER	ARE	HARD	OUR
FIND	SILLY	BELIEVE	PROBABLY	THOUGHTS
THAT	THEY	WE	AS	TO

	x		x	
x				x
		Knight		
x				x
	x		x	

(Solution 135)

23

36 Series

Write down the tenth term of

$$6, 18, 54, \ldots$$

And find a formula for quickly working out the answer.

(Solution 138)

37 Division

Divide the grid into four equal parts, each of which should be the same shape and contain the same nine letters which can be arranged into a 9-letter word.

N	T	G	E	O	O
N	U	Y	N	S	S
Y	U	R	R	Y	E
R	G	O	S	U	G
E	Y	S	O	T	U
T	G	E	T	R	N

(Solution 142)

38 Three Animals

Use all the letters in the sentence below only once to spell out the names of three animals.

ALL HERE NAME A POT PLANT

(Solution 146)

39 Equilateral Triangle

Draw in the largest possible equilateral triangle so that it does not touch another triangle and does not overlap the sides of the grid.

(Solution 151)

40 Directional Numbers

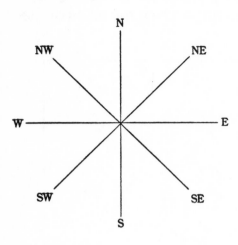

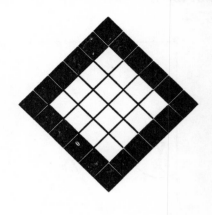

Fit all the numbers below into the grid. Each number must travel in a straight line in the direction of a compass point and start and finish in a shaded square.

217932	28778	6884	632
482912	34981		984
834252			
911763			
864131			
882122			
982711			
276966			
417644			
924492			

(Solution 157)

41 Find a Word

Trace out a 13-letter word by moving along the lines. You need to find the starting letter and must not cross a letter twice.

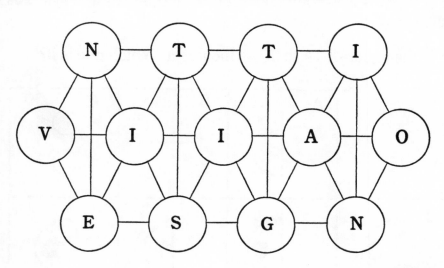

(Solution 1)

42 Synonym Circles

Read clockwise to find two 8-letter words which are synonyms. You have to find the starting point and provide the missing letters.

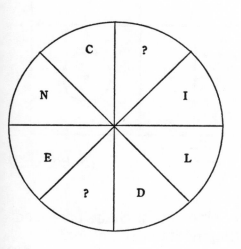
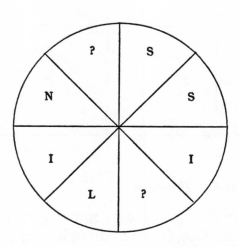

(Solution 5)

43 Grid

Each of the nine squares 1A to 3C should incorporate all the lines and symbols which are shown in the outer squares A, B, or C and 1, 2, or 3. Thus 2B should incorporate all the lines and symbols in 2 and B.

One of the squares, 1A to 3C, is incorrect. Which one is it?

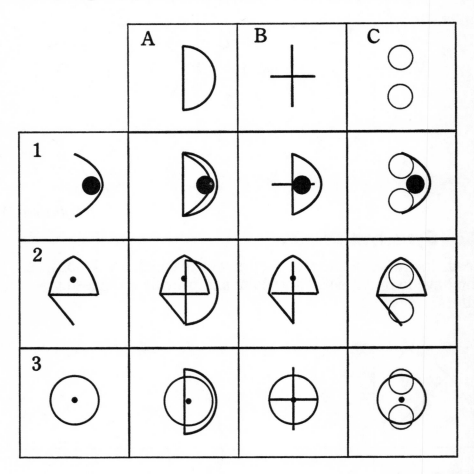

(Solution 9)

44 Chairs

In how many ways may eight people sit on eight chairs arranged in a line, if two of them insist on sitting next to each other?

(Solution 13)

28

45 Double-Bigrams

A bigram is any sequence of two consecutive letters in a word, for instance IG in the word BIGRAM, and a double-bigram is such a sequence which occurs twice in succession, such as IGIG in the word WHIRLIGIG.

Below we list several double-bigrams. Can you complete the words in which they occur?

••• POPO ••••••
••• LOLO ••
••• ENEN •••
••• VIVI ••
•• LALA •••
•• TITI ••
•• BIBI ••
••• WAWA •
•• OTOT •••
•• ODOD •••••••
• NINI •••••••
••• ININ •
••• DIDI ••
• ATAT ••••

(Solution 17)

46 Number

What number is missing from the grid?

8	12	6
3	20	6
3	9	?

(Solution 20)

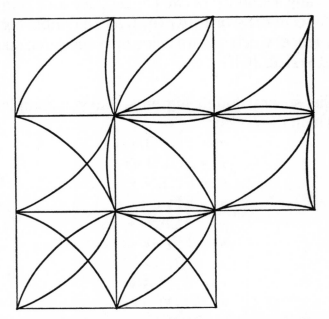

Look across each horizontal line of boxes and down each vertical line of boxes and choose the missing square from the options below.

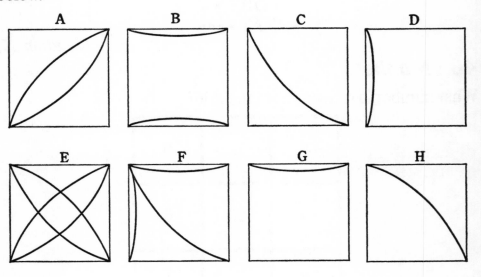

(Solution 25)

48 Anagrammed Magic Square

Using all twenty-five letters of the sentence below only once, form five 5-letter words which when placed correctly in the grid will form a magic word square where the same five words can be read both horizontally and vertically.

CARTER'S NORTHERN FACE SAFEST

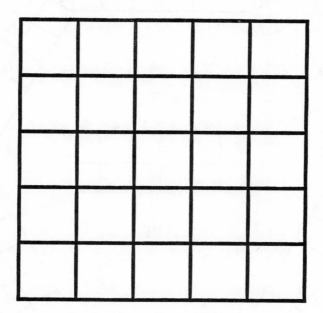

(Solution 29)

49 Stations

There are eight stations from town A to town B. How many different single tickets must be printed so that one may book from any station to any other?

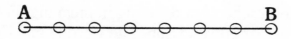

(Solution 33)

31

50 Hexagram

Solve the six anagrams of FISH. Transfer the six arrowed letters to the key box and solve this anagram to discover a key seventh.

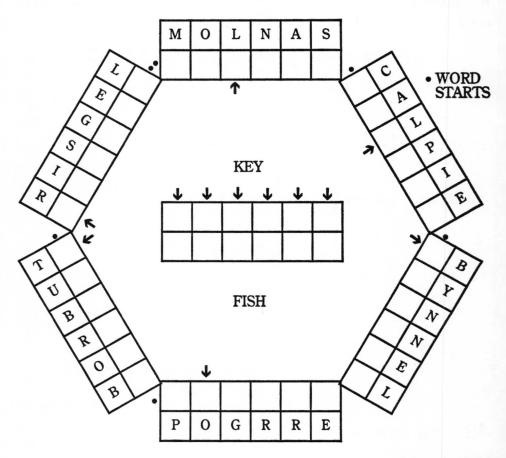

(Solution 37)

51 Homonym

A homonym is a word having the same sound and perhaps the same spelling as another, but differing in meaning. For example, Cleave and Cleave or Sun and Son. The words I and Eye are examples of a pair of homonyms in which none of the letters in one word appear in the other. Can you find another pair of homonyms which have this feature?

(Solution 41)

52 Circles

Which of these fit into the blank circle to carry on a logical sequence?

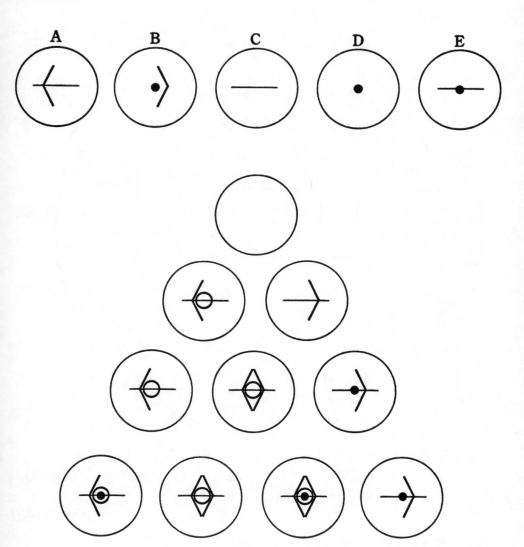

(Solution 46)

53 Pentagram

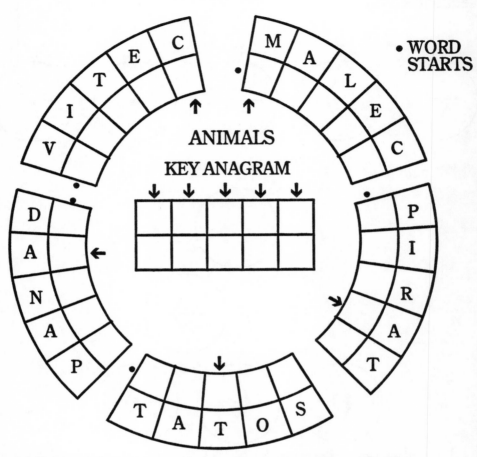

ANIMALS

ANIMALS
KEY ANAGRAM

• WORD STARTS

The five 5-letter words have been jumbled. Solve the five anagrams of ANIMALS and then transfer the arrowed letters to the key anagram to find a sixth.

(Solution 48)

54 Something in Common

What do the answers to the following clues all have in common?

A small container   A European monetary currency
To enter abruptly   An inside covering
To strike smartly   To walk long and far
Easily damaged   Broker

(Solution 51)

55 Octagons

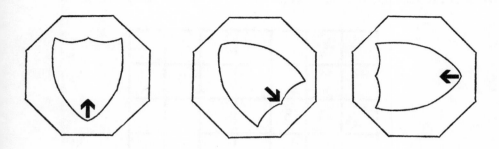

Which octagon comes next in the above sequence?

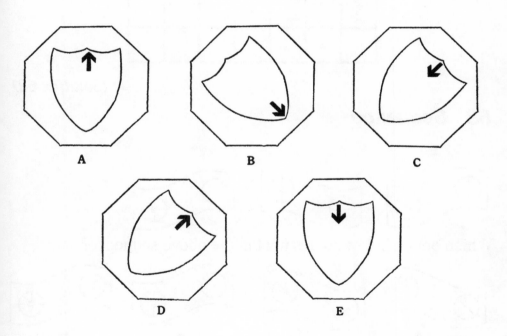

(Solution 55)

56 Cards

Permutation = Arrangements
How many 4-card permutations can you make in a pack of 52
playing cards?

(Solution 59)

57 Number Logic

Where, logically, would you place the number 1 in this grid?

					9	
		8				
				7		
	6					5
3			4			
	2					

(Solution 63)

58 Sequence

Which option below comes next in the above sequence?

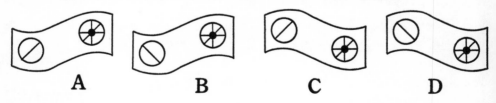

A   B   C   D

(Solution 67)

The answers are all 9-letter words and will be found in the grid one letter on each line in order.

C	G	P	R	M	D	F	M	O
B	A	E	U	E	A	U	L	A
S	C	S	J	A	B	N	R	L
E	L	G	T	K	U	I	A	S
C	A	S	U	I	Y	J	E	M
C	V	U	F	T	L	T	B	T
H	A	E	O	A	O	I	O	E
O	U	O	E	E	N	N	N	N
T	T	N	R	A	P	E	R	T

Clues:
1. To go stealthily
2. A soldier armed with hand fire-arms
3. Small ribbed melon
4. Seducer
5. Paving stone
6. Dried hemp
7. Reclining
8. Argument against
9. To gad about

(Solution 71)

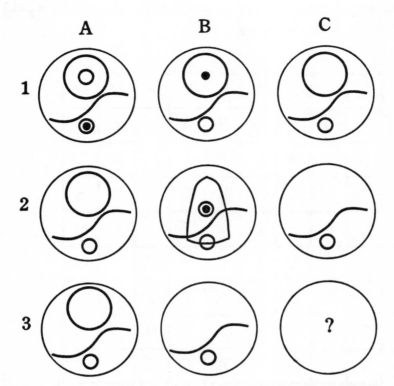

Logically which circle below fits into the above pattern?

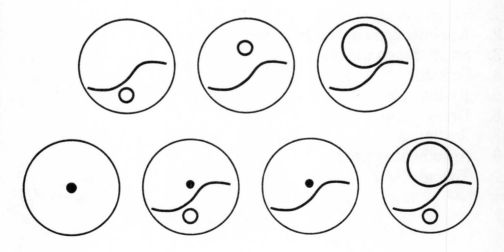

(Solution 75)

61 Pyramid

Spell out the 15-letter word by going into the pyramid one room at a time. Go into each room once only. You may go into the passage as many times as you wish.

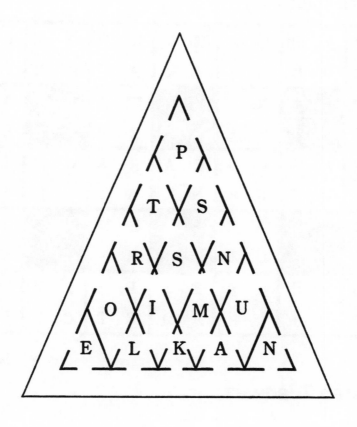

(Solution 78)

62 Sequence

ANDY, AMY, DES, DEAN, RUTH, RAY

What name below completes the above sequence?

TERRY, JANE, ALEC, BETH, TRUDY

(Solution 80)

63 Clueless Crossword

In each square there are four letters. Your task is to cross out three of each four, leaving one letter in each square, so that the crossword is made up in the usual way with good English interlocking words.

F P Q T	J C U L	H A N U	M O E R	R B A T	O A E D	R S F L
P U L E		N O P E		U A E R		A L E O
L E I A	E A N P	P D G A	E A N K	R S A T	O N I E	L K I M
E O T B		A E O N		E M S N		I A C E
K D P E	R U I A	D R S E	E S A D	P I R T	I E C N	D C K G

(Solution 84)

64 Three Triangles

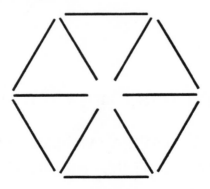

Move the position of only four matches to make three equilateral triangles.

(Solution 88)

65 Alternative Crossword

In the upper grid, the crossword letters have been replaced by numbers. Select the correct letter for each number from the three alternatives given, and enter the letter into the blank grid to make a crossword.

2	6	5	5			1	3	6	7
4		6	7	5	6	7			6
3	7		2	3	2			5	2
6	3	7		5			6	5	2
	2	2	1	3	2	2	2		
3	2	5		5			2	2	8
7	7		5	7	1			7	5
5		7	3	5	2	2			6
7	5	5	4			3	5	5	2

1	A B C
2	D E F
3	G H I
4	J K L
5	M N O
6	P Q R
7	S T U
8	V W X
9	Y Z

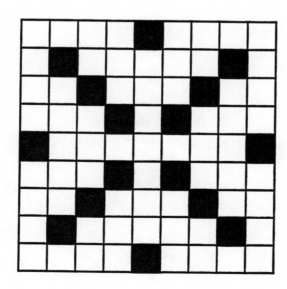

(Solution 93)

41

66 Circles

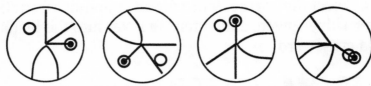

Which circle continues the sequence?

A   B   C   D   E

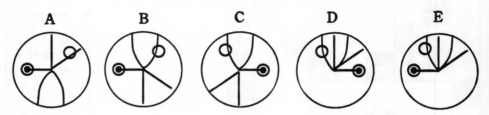

(Solution 96)

67 Square Roots

Does the number 6 2 4 9 7 3 2 3 have a square root composed of integers?

i.e. $\sqrt{144} = 12$, answer in integers

$\sqrt{141} = 11.874342 \ldots \rightarrow 00$

(Note: Integers = whole numbers)

(Solution 100)

68 Wine

A man can drink a bottle of wine in $2\frac{1}{2}$ hrs.
His wife can drink a bottle of wine in $1\frac{1}{2}$ hrs.

How long would it take for the pair of them drinking at their respective rates to finish the wine between them?

(Solution 104)

69 Alternative Crossword

In the upper grid, the crossword letters have been replaced by numbers. Select the correct letter for each number from the three alternatives given, and enter the letter into the blank grid to make a crossword.

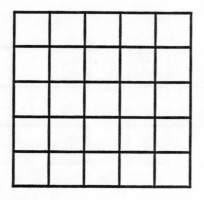

7	8	1	3	2
3	1	6	2	5
5	8	5	4	5
6	2	5	3	7
7	6	1	2	2

1	A	B	C
2	D	E	F
3	G	H	I
4	J	K	L
5	M	N	O
6	P	Q	R
7	S	T	U
8	V	W	X
9	Y	Z	–

(Solution 108)

43

70 Anagrammed Phrases

All the following are anagrams of well-known phrases. For example, SO NOTE HOLE = ON THE LOOSE.

1. SINGLE GLIDE LOSE PET
2. HUG TIGHT VETO POSE
3. BOTH ONES GET QUIET
4. HALF YELLOW ANT
5. YES LOOP A SAND FLAT

(Solution 112)

71 Work it Out

What number should replace the question mark?

(Solution 117)

44

72 Cryptogram

This is a straight substitution cryptogram where each letter of the alphabet has been substituted for another.

CLUNK CK AZQC UX CLUNNKZ LUMYN,

CYKZ CK XKK UN CLUNNKZ CLUNK;

PSN CYKZ CK XKK UN CLUNNKZ CLUMYN,

CK AZQC 'NUX ZQN NYKZ CLUNNKZ LUMYN;

TQL CLUNK NQ YDFK UN CLUNNKZ LUMYN,

GSXN ZQN PK CLUNNKZ LUMYN ZQL CLUMYN;

ZQL BKN XYQSJV UN PK CLUNNKZ LUNK,

PSN CLUNK – TQL XQ 'NUX CLUNNKZ LUMYN.

(Solution 122)

73 Sequence

Which of the following comes next in the above sequence?

(Solution 126)

74 Sequence

RAYON, EPAULET, WORTH, ?

What word below continues the above sequence?
ITINERARY, ROMANCED, CARDIGAN, REEF, CHANCE

(Solution 130)

75 Threes

Can you group these into sets of three?

ROOKS   WHALES   PIGS
MACHINE GUNS   ACTORS   HIPPOPOTAMUSES
SCOUTS   OXEN   WASPS
HYENAS   SEALS   SWINE
PEAS   BABOONS   MICE
WOLVES   PENGUINS   CIGARETTES

(Solution 136)

76 Common

What do these words have in common?

1. BIBBER
2. PRACTICAL
3. BADLY
4. BARCELONA
5. RAGGED
6. EDITOR
7. TWENTY
8. ACROSS

(Solution 139)

77 Scales

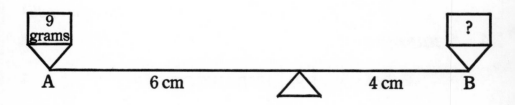

What value weight should be placed on the scales at B to balance the scales?

(Solution 143)

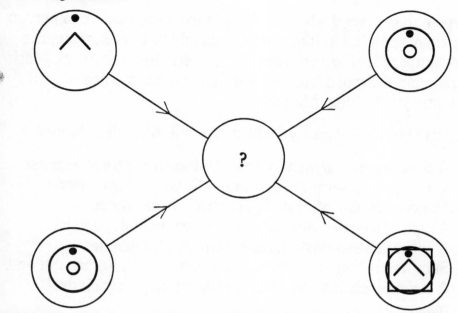

Each line and symbol which appears in the four outer circles is transferred to the center circle according to these rules:

If a line or symbol occurs in the outer circle:
once	it is transferred
twice	it is possibly transferred
three times	it is transferred
four times	it is not transferred

Which of the circles A, B, C, D, or E, shown below, should appear at the center of the diagram?

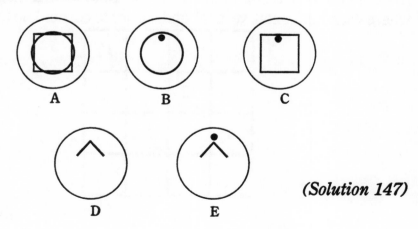

(Solution 147)

47

79 Eponyms

An eponym is a word which is derived from the name of a person because of their invention, action, or product. For example, the word "ampère" is derived from the French physicist André Marie Ampère and the word "mausoleum" after the tomb of a 4th-century B.C. king, Mausolus.

Can you identify the eponyms from the following definitions?

1. A close-fitting garment, from a 19th-century trapeze artist.
2. Very harsh, after a 7th-century B.C. Greek lawmaker.
3. Nonconformist, after a 19th-century Texas rancher.
4. A type of sweater, after a 19th-century British general.
5. A spiritual relationship, after a Greek philosopher.
6. Sumptuous banquets, after a 1st-century B.C. Roman general.
7. A strict disciplinarian, after a 17th-century French drill master.
8. Dull-witted, after attempts to ridicule followers of an 11–12th-century Scottish theologian.
9. Spellbind or enchant, after an 18–19th-century German physician.
10. Crafty or deceitful, after a 15–16th-century Florentine statesman.

(Solution 152)

80 Magic "34"

Arrange the remaining digits from 1 to 16 to form a magic square where each horizontal, vertical, and corner-to-corner line totals 34.

			16
	12		
4			
		8	

(Solution 2)

81 Square Numbers

Each horizontal and vertical line contains the digits of a 4-figure square number. All digits are in the correct order but not necessarily adjacent. All digits are used only once.

4	4	9	4	8	1	9	2
1	1	6	2	8	1	3	2
2	7	8	9	5	4	1	6
3	9	6	3	0	4	1	0
6	2	0	0	9	4	4	1
5	6	3	0	2	2	3	5
5	4	1	4	7	7	6	6
6	3	1	3	9	4	6	9

(Solution 6)

82 Middle Letters

Find the complete words that contain these middle letters.

SSB*
ISERL
ZZYW*
NGIP
NKEYD
USTJ*
RFETC
TEDDF
ISYC*
PPLEG*

* These words are hyphenated

(Solution 10)

83 Sequence

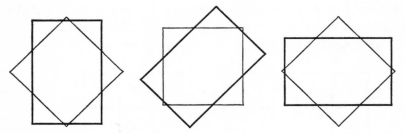

Which of the options below continues the above sequence?

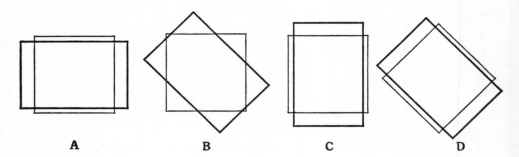

A   B   C   D

(Solution 14)

84 Baby

How heavy was the baby at birth? asked the mother.
The nurse replied 12.96 lbs, divided by 1/4 of his own weight.

How much did the baby weigh?

(Solution 18)

85 Names

What have the following names got in common?

STAN, TINA, MARK, DAN

(Solution 22)

86 Do-It-Yourself Crossword

Place the pieces in the grid in order to complete the crossword.

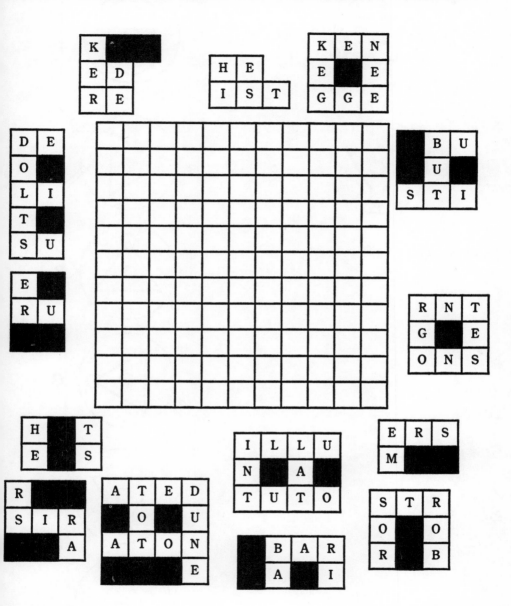

(Solution 26)

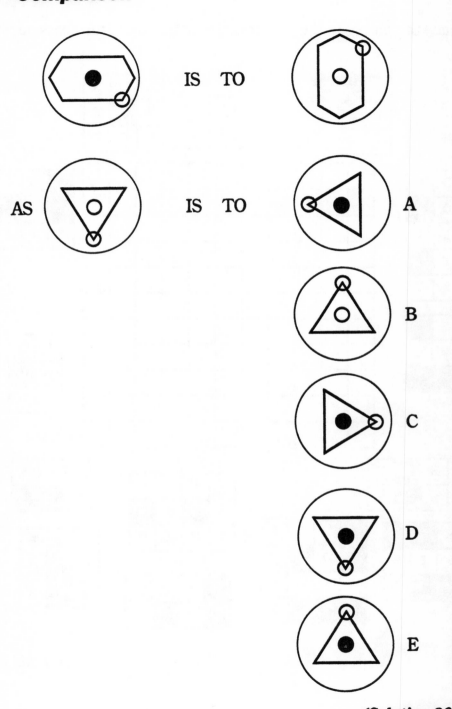

IS TO

AS

IS TO

A

B

C

D

E

(Solution 30)

88 The Puzzling Puzzle

Start at the middle square and work from square to square horizontally, vertically, or diagonally to spell out six puzzling words. Every square must be visited only once and every square is used. Finish at the top right-hand square.

U	N	O	S	M	E	T	→
N	C	T	E	Y	R	N	
R	D	Y	R	M	I	E	
N	U	M	★	W	D	L	
I	E	D	O	E	B	M	
M	G	A	R	X	O	E	
A	P	A	P	R	L	B	

(Solution 34)

89 Bath

You are trying to fill a bath with both taps full on, but have accidentally left out the plug. Normally the hot water tap takes eight minutes to fill the bath and the cold water tap takes ten minutes. However, the water empties out through the plug hole in five minutes. How long will it take for the bath to fill?

(Solution 38)

90 Circles

What should be the contents of the circle with the question mark?

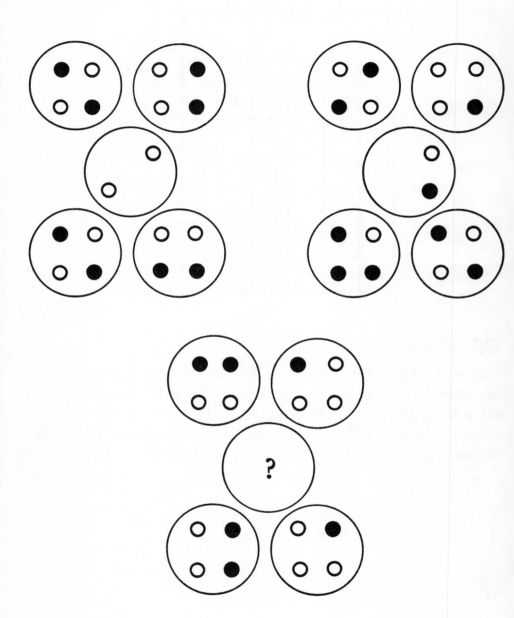

(Solution 43)

91 Fish

Change one letter of each answer to obtain the name of a fish.

		ANSWER	FISH
1.	CORRECT	_ _ _ _ _ _	*_ _ _ _ _
2.	KINE	_ _ _ _ _ _	_*_ _ _ _
3.	ARTILLERYMAN	_ _ _ _ _ _	_ _ _ _ _*
4.	SMALL CHILD	_ _ _ _ _ _	*_ _ _ _ _
5.	STUPID PERSON	_ _ _ _ _ _ _	*_ _ _ _ _ _
6.	RESENTMENT	_ _ _ _ _ _	*_ _ _ _ _
7.	ENGINEER	_ _ _ _ _ _	*_ _ _ _ _
8.	VISION	_ _ _ _ _	*_ _ _ _
9.	AMMUNITION	_ _ _ _ _ _	*_ _ _ _ _

(Solution 47)

92 Odd One Out

Which is the odd one?

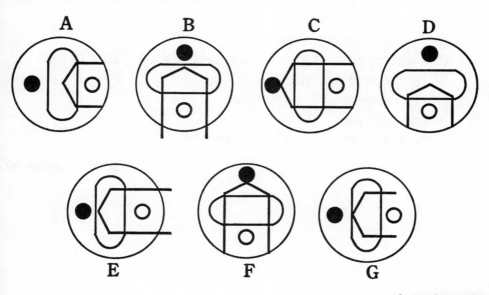

(Solution 52)

55

93 Nursery Rhyme Crossword

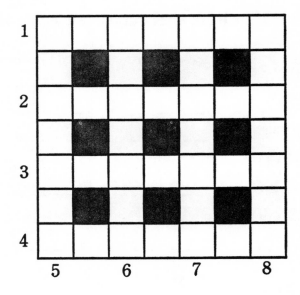

In the narrative are eight clues. Find them, solve them, and then place the answers in the grid.

4. The longed for number, four and twenty **blackbirds,**
3. were dealt with, by being baked in **a pie**
2. they tried to reinstate it,
8. the birds gave out a song
5. that deserved being called a dainty dish, to place before the king who was called
1. His Greatness
6. by the buffoons
7. who arrived on a wheeled footboard.

(Solution 57)

94 Network

Find the starting point and travel along the connecting lines in a continuous path to adjacent circles to spell out a 14-letter word. Every circle must be visited only once.

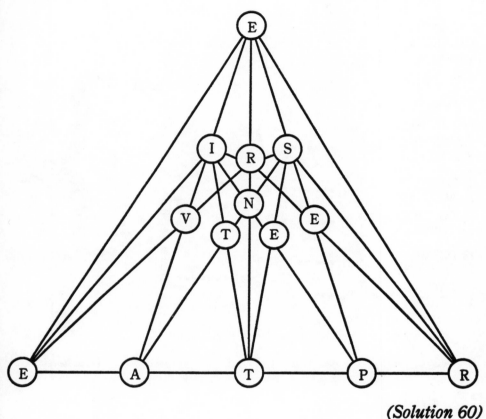

(Solution 60)

95 Find Another Word

BELOW, ORE, ROWER

Which word below goes with the three words above?
BOAT, LONG, SHORE, CARRY, WIND

(Solution 64)

96 Connections

Each pair of words, by meaning or association, leads to another word. Find the missing words 18–30. The number of letters in the missing words are indicated by the dots.

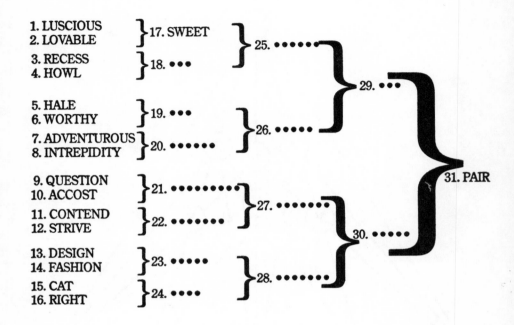

1. LUSCIOUS
2. LOVABLE
} 17. SWEET
3. RECESS
4. HOWL
} 18. •••

25. ••••••

5. HALE
6. WORTHY
} 19. •••
7. ADVENTUROUS
8. INTREPIDITY
} 20. ••••••

26. ••••••

29. •••

9. QUESTION
10. ACCOST
} 21. •••••••••
11. CONTEND
12. STRIVE
} 22. ••••••••

27. •••••••

13. DESIGN
14. FASHION
} 23. ••••••
15. CAT
16. RIGHT
} 24. ••••

28. •••••••

30. ••••••

31. PAIR

(Solution 69)

97 Ending

Find a 3-letter word which when placed on the end of these words make new words.

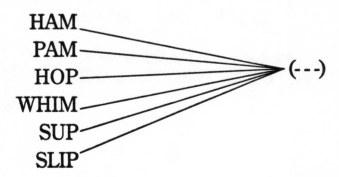

HAM
PAM
HOP
WHIM
SUP
SLIP

(- - -)

(Solution 72)

Which option below continues the above sequence?

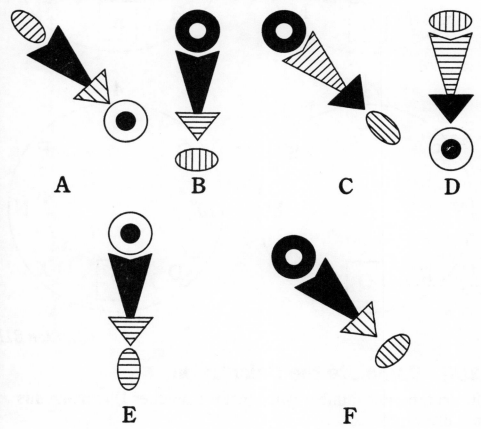

A   B   C   D

E   F

(Solution 76)

99 Safe

In order to open the safe, you have to rotate the wheels to find a 4-letter word.

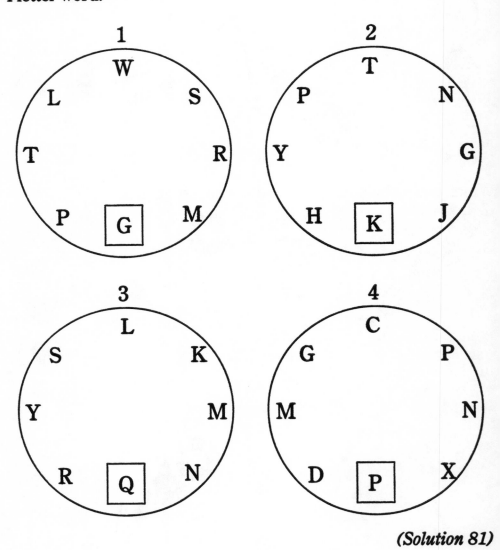

(Solution 81)

100 Complete the Calculation

Insert the same number twice (not the number 1) to make this calculation correct.

$$6 \div 6 = 6$$

(Solution 85)

101 Grid

Each of the nine squares 1A to 3C should incorporate all the lines and symbols which are shown in the outer squares marked A, B, or C and 1, 2, or 3. Thus 2B should incorporate all the lines and symbols in 2 and B.

One of the squares, 1A to 3C, is incorrect. Which one is it?

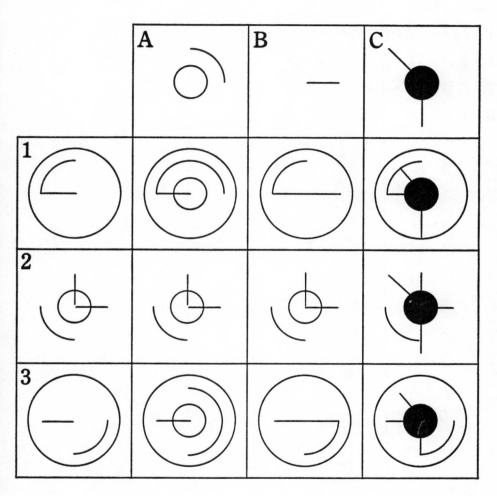

(Solution 89)

102 Connections

Insert the numbers 0–10 in the circles opposite, so that for any particular circle the sum of the numbers in the circles connected directly to it equals the value corresponding to the number in that circle, as given in the list.

Example:

$1 = 14$ $(4 + 7 + 3)$

$4 = 8$ $(7 + 1)$

$7 = 5$ $(4 + 1)$

$3 = 1$

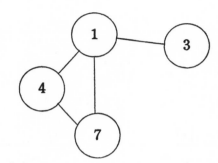

$0 = 8$

$1 = 4$

$2 = 18$

$3 = 25$

$4 = 16$

$5 = 7$

$6 = 11$

$7 = 17$

$8 = 29$

$9 = 13$

$10 = 22$

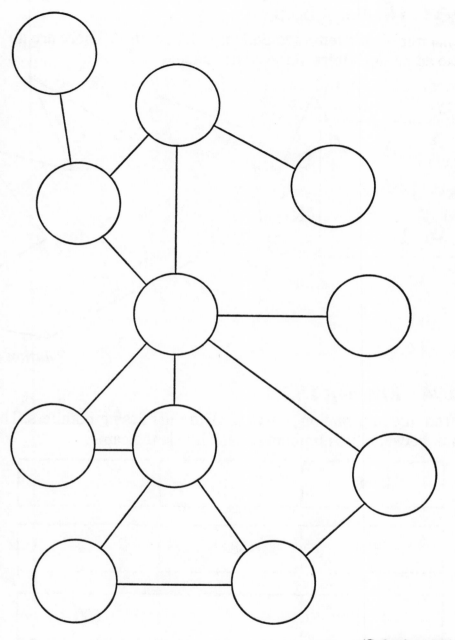

(Solution 98)

103 No Neighbors

Unscramble the letters to find an 18-letter word. There are no two adjoining letters in the same shape.

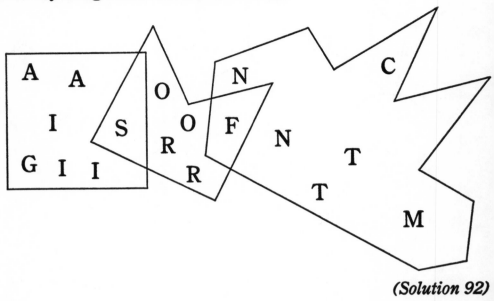

(Solution 92)

104 Missing Links

From the information provided fill in the missing numbers. The link between the numbers in each line is the same.

2798		

4389	3827	

4051		800

(Solution 101)

105 Occupations

These thirty-six 3-letter bits can be grouped to form twelve 9-letter words which are all occupations.

PRO	KER	BAL	NOT
ATH	PUP	KEE	OST
HYP	EOP	MAJ	HER
EER	ZOO	IST	ORD
IST	PLO	PET	GON
GEO	LOG	PER	UGH
OMO	FES	POO	NER
ROP	EMA	SOR	IST
MAN	HAR	IER	DOL

(Solution 106)

106 Sea Level

If you were standing on top of a 50-foot-high cliff, how far would you be able to see out to sea?

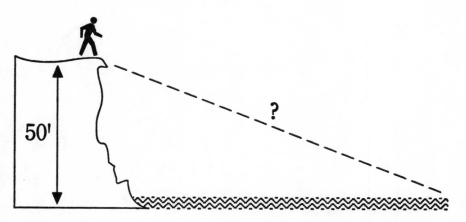

(Solution 109)

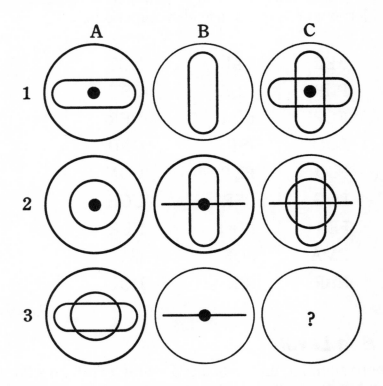

Logically which circle below fits into the above pattern?

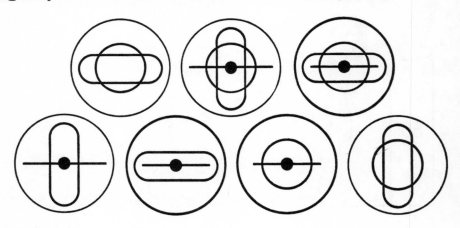

(Solution 113)

108 Quotation

Rearrange the words to form a quotation. The boxed letters spell out the name of the quotation's author.

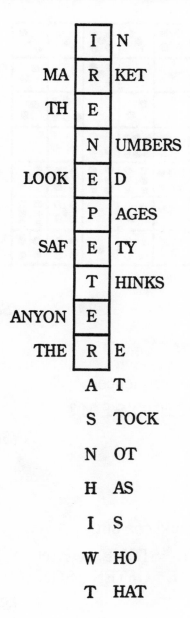

I N

MA R KET

TH E

N UMBERS

LOOK E D

P AGES

SAF E TY

T HINKS

ANYON E

THE R E

A T

S TOCK

N OT

H AS

I S

W HO

T HAT

(Solution 120)

109 Dominoes

Draw in the lines of the twenty-eight dominoes, which are from 0–0 to 6–6.

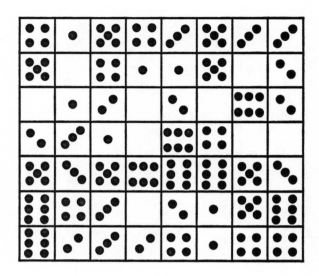

(Solution 123)

110 Letter Sequence

What letter comes next in this sequence?

TENTDTTSFM?

(Solution 127)

111 Odd One Out

Which of these words is the odd one out?

TEN   ONE   STONE   OPEN
TENT   TOE   OFTEN   SON

(Solution 131)

112 Missing Number

What number should replace the question mark?

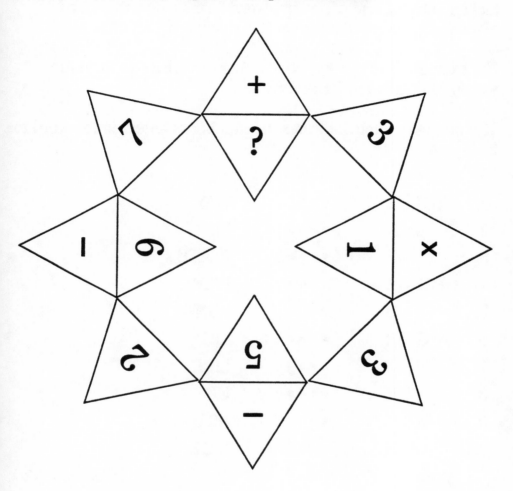

(Solution 134)

113 *Middle Words*

In each of the following insert a word in the bracket which when tacked onto the end of the first word forms a new word, and when placed in front of the second word forms another word.

For example: ARC (•••) RING. Answer: HER – to form the words ARCHER and HERRING.

The number of dots indicates the number of letters in the word to be inserted.

1.	GRUB	(••)	WAY
2.	MAR	(••••)	PIN
3.	OF	(••••)	PLATE
4.	ORANGE	(••••)	PILE
5.	SO	(••)	SON
6.	STAR	(••••)	LET
7.	DIGIT	(•••)	LIER
8.	WAR	(••••)	UP
9.	WRIT	(••)	ART
10.	MOB	(•••)	RICE

(Solution 140)

114 Track Word

Work around the track to find a 15-letter word. You have to provide the missing letters and find the starting point. The word might appear reading clockwise or counterclockwise, and the overlapping letter appears twice.

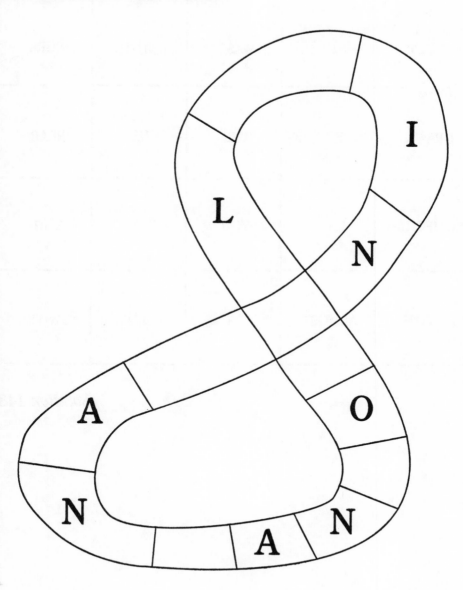

(Solution 144)

115 *Quotation*

Rearrange the words to read out a quotation by Will Rogers.

CAN'T	IT	WAS	MINUTE	SURE
DRAWN	UNDERSTAND	THE	BE	READ
SOMETHING	BY	YOU	UP	YOU
YOU	ALMOST	A	CAN	LAWYER

(Solution 148)

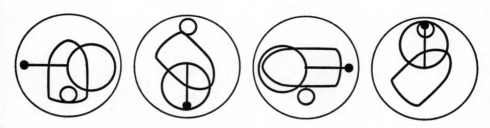

Which option below continues the above sequence?

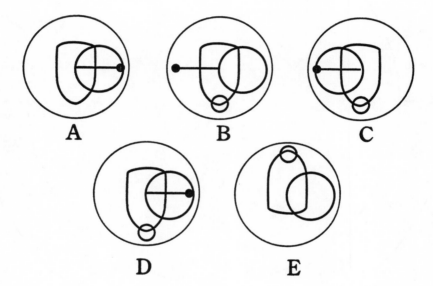

(Solution 153)

117 Quotation by Mark Twain

Find the quotation. Start at "I".

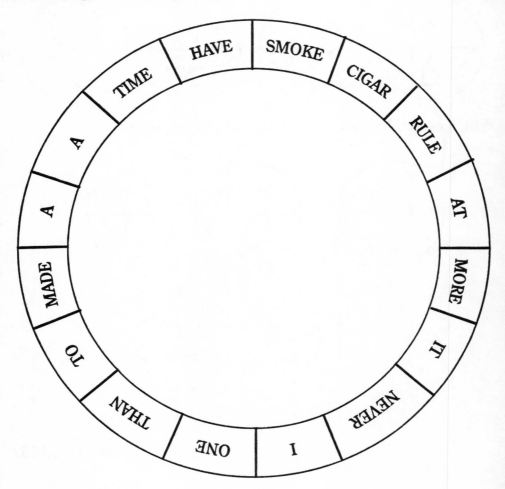

(Solution 156)

118 · Spots

When spots are placed on the circumference and then joined, regions will be formed.

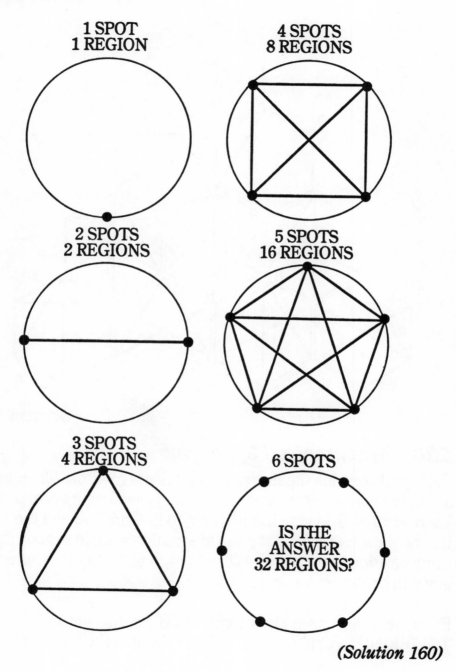

1 SPOT
1 REGION

4 SPOTS
8 REGIONS

2 SPOTS
2 REGIONS

5 SPOTS
16 REGIONS

3 SPOTS
4 REGIONS

6 SPOTS

IS THE
ANSWER
32 REGIONS?

(Solution 160)

119 The Hexagonal Pyramid

Work out the contents of the top hexagon.

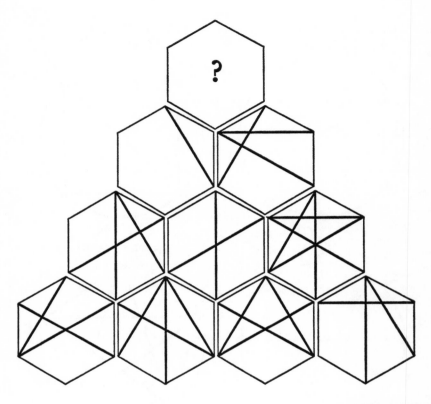

(Solution 158)

120 Synchronized Synonyms

Each grid contains the letters of eight 8-letter words. All letters are in the correct order and each letter is used only once. Each word in Grid One has a synonym in Grid Two and the letters of each of the eight pairs of synonyms are in exactly the same position in each grid. Clues to each pair of synonyms are given in no particular order.

Example: The answers to the clue VAST are the words TOWERING in Grid One and GIGANTIC in Grid Two.

Find the remaining seven pairs of synonyms.

D	D	S	L	D	C	I	I
A	A	(T)	W	E	S	S	X
T	I	I	I	L	(O)	T	O
L	E	A	T	N	R	R	N
D	E	D	(W)	A	L	(E)	U
D	L	O	C	U	L	T	T
A	(R)	E	O	(I)	E	(N)	E
R	W	O	D	S	(G)	R	R

Grid One

P	P	D	W	G	S	S	R
C	I	(G)	E	O	O	E	L
D	C	O	E	H	(I)	N	L
I	E	C	I	D	V	S	E
U	E	I	(G)	T	L	(A)	E
S	V	H	R	E	U	N	A
L	(N)	E	D	(T)	R	(I)	S
R	E	O	Y	D	(C)	E	R

Grid Two

Clues: VAST, SLICK, CHIEF, LONE, TWISTER, DIARY, FORBID, BREADTH

(Solution 159)

121 Brain Strain

Insert the missing numbers so that the calculations are correct, both across and down. All numbers to be inserted are less than 10 (there is no zero).

	+		−		=	9
+	■	+	■	+	■	×
	+		−	6	=	
−	■	÷	■	−	■	÷
	+	4	−		=	
=	■	=	■	=	■	=
6	÷		+		=	

(Solution 3)

122 Circle

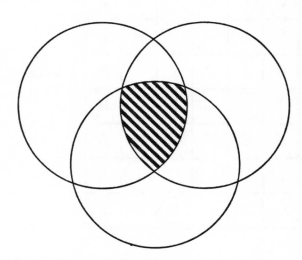

Approximately how much of one circle is shaded?

(Solution 7)

123 "E" Frame

All vowels are "E" and are not shown. All consonants are shown and all are used once only. "42" means four consonants and two vowels.

DOWN

	1	2	3	4	5	6	7	8	
1	R	L	S	P	T	L	D	T	42
2	Y	P	L	S	D	T	L	P	52
3	B	B	B	P	D	H	W	L	42
4	K	J	R	N	S	N	N	T	42
5	L	D	N	P	L	S	N	S	52
6	N	R	L	K	R	T	N	B	42
7	W	R	C	R	F	B	D	M	32
8	N	T	H	T	M	R	F	M	32
	42	42	42	42	42	42	42	42	

ACROSS

Clues:

Across

1. Arid land
2. Walked carefully
3. Duck-like feet
4. Small house
5. Never ceasing
6. Dog's house
7. Put off
8. Go in

Down

1. Happening every seven days
2. Threefold
3. Man addicted to lewdness
4. Condiment
5. Nothing more
6. A worshipping place
7. Yellow flowering plant
8. Symbolic representation

(Solution 12)

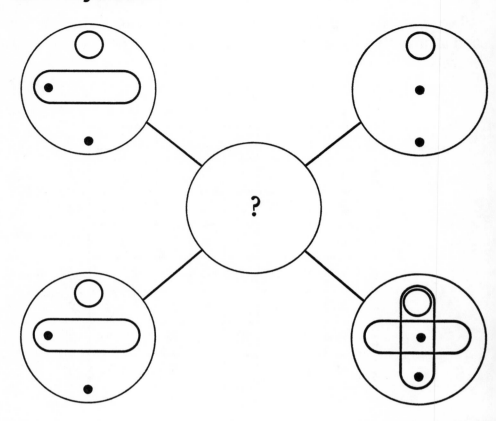

Each line and symbol which appears in the four outer circles is transferred to the center circle according to these rules:

> If a line or symbol occurs in the outer circle:
> once   it is transferred
> twice   it is possibly transferred
> three times   it is tranferred
> four times   it is not transferred

Which of the circles A, B, C, D, or E, shown opposite, should appear at the center of the diagram?

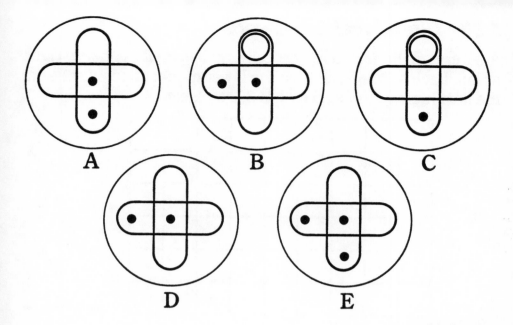

(Solution 15)

125 Add a Letter

Find a letter in place of "?" so that when it is added to each of the 5-letter sets and rearranged, 6-letter words will be formed.

The 6-letter words are names of plants and trees.

?	C	H	E	W	S
	C	H	U	M	S
	G	O	N	E	R
	C	H	O	R	E
	S	E	E	M	S

(Solution 19)

126 Directional Crossword

Answers run horizontally, vertically, or diagonally, either to right or left. Each solution starts on the lower number and finishes on the next higher number, i.e., 1 to 2, 2 to 3, etc.

1 / 5						4
10		13		12		7
	17				15	
	18				14	
			16			
11		8			9	6
3						2

1. Mislead
2. Anti-perspirant
3. Stormy
4. Wave passing around the earth
5. Learned
6. Talk over
7. Ship
8. Mechanical man
9. Controllable
10. Descriptive term
11. Leaves for smoking
12. Exposed
13. Girl's name
14. Gilbert and Sullivan's "____men" guardians
15. Hotchpotch
16. Musical instrument
17. Make a mistake

(Solution 24)

127 Quartering a Square

Divide the square into four quarters. Each quarter should be the same size and shape and contain the same four symbols.

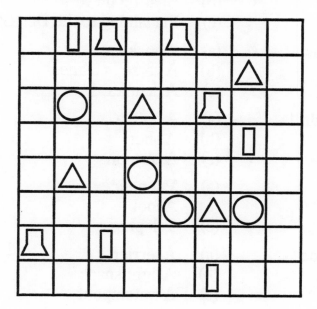

(Solution 28)

128 Concentration

A B C D E F G H

What letter is two to the right of the letter immediately to the right of the letter four to the left of the letter two to the right of the letter four to the right of the letter immediately to the left of the letter which comes midway between the letter two to the left of the letter "C" and the letter three to the left of the letter "F"?

(Solution 31)

129 Polling Day

At a recent election a total of 23,968 votes were cast for the four candidates, the winner exceeding his opponents by 1026, 2822, and 6428 votes respectively.

How many votes were received by each candidate?

(Solution 35)

130 Alternatives

Select the correct meaning from the three alternatives.

1. Canicular
   - (a) Oval-shaped
   - (b) Bearing flowers
   - (c) Pertaining to the Dog-Star

2. Dipsas
   - (a) A snake
   - (b) A verse of 5 lines
   - (c) A drunkard

3. Escadrille
   - (a) A flotilla
   - (b) A shoe
   - (c) A platoon

4. Fon
   - (a) Phonetic
   - (b) A fool
   - (c) Telephone

5. Griffon
   - (a) A terrier
   - (b) A light snack
   - (c) A waterspout

6. Ikebana
   - (a) Flower arranging
   - (b) Exercise routine
   - (c) A waterfall

7. Lempira
   - (a) Monetary unit of Honduras
   - (b) Circular motion
   - (c) A drug

8. Mazzard
   - (a) Skull
   - (b) Drizzle
   - (c) Food

(Solution 39)

131 Ten-Digit Number

Write down a 10-digit number such that:
The 1st digit indicates the total number of 1's
The 2nd digit indicates the total number of 2's
The 3rd digit indicates the total number of 3's, etc., to the 10th
digit, which indicates the total number of zeroes.

(Solution 42)

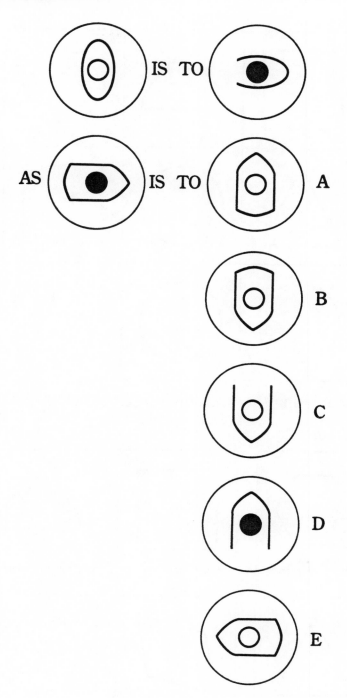

IS TO

AS

IS TO

A

B

C

D

E

(Solution 45)

85

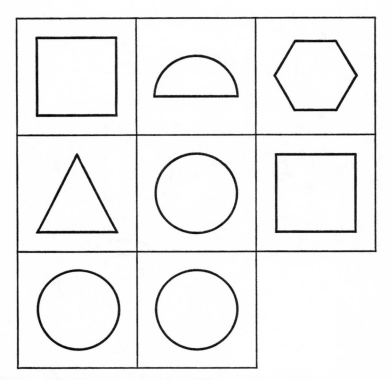

Choose the missing square from the options below.

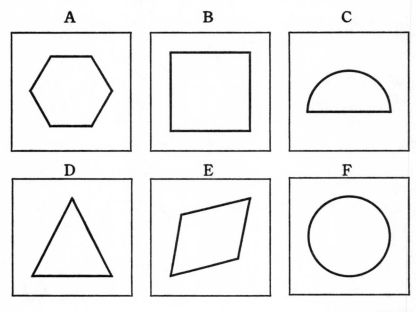

(Solution 49)

134 Found in the USA

All the following are anagrams of things which can be found in the USA.

1.   MINUTE BATH STEEP GRID LIE
2.   AND TRY NO CHANGE
3.   SKATE ALERT GAL
4.   NUN I'M STRAY COOK
5.   HAIL GAME NICK
6.   I HE SHE WE TO HUT

(Solution 53)

135 Odd One Out

Which is the odd one?

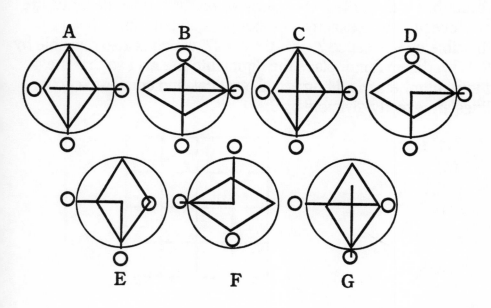

(Solution 56)

136 Anagram Theme

Arrange the fourteen words in pairs so that each pair is an anagram of another word or name. The seven words produced will have a linking theme. For example, if the words TRY and CREASE were in the list, they could be paired to form an anagram of SECRETARY and the theme could be PROFESSIONS.

AGE	AURA	DIN	END	
FLAN	GAIN	GRAIN	HAY	SEW
IRE	NEAT	RAIL	RUNG	SIT

(Solution 62)

137 Nines

A number is divisible by 9 exactly when the sum of its digits are also divisible by 9 exactly. For example, the number 7866 is divisible by 9 because 7 + 8 + 6 + 6 = 27, which is also divisible by 9. With this in mind, place the digits into the grid so that the 4-figure numbers in all horizontal, vertical, and corner-to-corner lines are exactly divisible by 9.

1, 1,
2,
3, 3, 3,
5, 5,
6, 6, 6,
7,
8, 8, 8,
9.

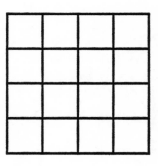

(Solution 65)

138 Missing Letters

Fill in the missing letters to make ten occupations.

1.   • N • T • M • S •
2.   • T • N • M • N
3.   • O • T • W • I •
4.   • I • E • T • R
5.   • A • A • N • R
6.   • I • T • C • A •
7.   • S • E • E • T •
8.   • I • L • N • S •
9.   • E • C • N • R •
10. • A • F • T • E •

(Solution 68)

139 Sequence

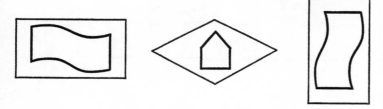

Which option below continues the above sequence?

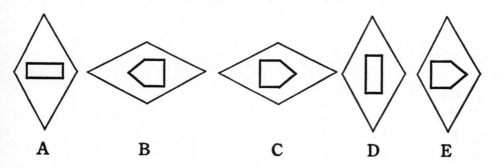

A   B   C   D   E

(Solution 73)

140 Niners

Solve the eight clues.

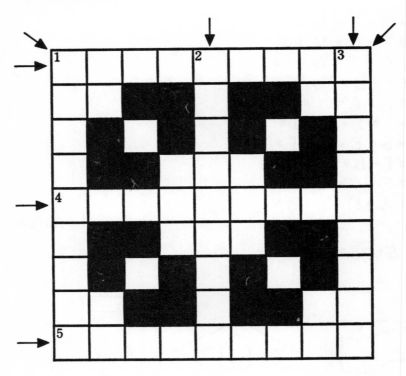

Clues:

Across

1. Declarer
4. Ramp or bridge
5. For boiling water

Down

1. Revolutionist
2. Frankness
3. Of a definition

Diagonal

1. Chargeable
2. Coming into renewed life

(Solution 77)

141 Safe

The safe can only be opened by pressing the buttons in the correct order, following the directions on each button. The last button is marked (0). You have to find the 1st button.

N

	A	B	C	D	E
1	3S	3S	1E	3S	3W
2	1N	1E	2E	3W	3S
3	2E	1W	2N	1N	1W
4	1S	1N	2E	1W	1N
5	1E	3N	1E	0	2W

W   E

S

(Solution 82)

142 Song

This verse of an old song has had all of its vowels removed and is written in groups of five. See if you can reconstitute it and make it into its words.

LLRND	THMLB	RRYBS
HTHM	NKYCH	SDTHW
SLTHM	NKYTH	GHTTW
SSCHF	NPPGS	THWSL

(Solution 86)

143 Pyramid Word

Solve the five clues, place the five words in the pyramid, then rearrange all fifteen letters to find a 15-letter word.

- abbreviation for pound sterling (1)
- the ratio of the circumference of a circle to its diameter (2)
- weapon (3)
- family of ruminant animals (4)
- convey in a vehicle (5)

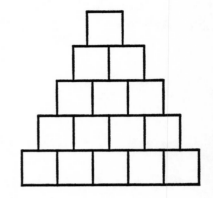

(Solution 90)

144 Middle Word

Place a word in the brackets which means the same as the words or phrases outside the brackets.

1. A Chinese idol (- - - -) Fate
2. Triangular sail (- - -) To balk
3. Branched candleholder (- - - - -- - -) Rotating firework
4. Wolverine (- - - - - --) One who eats to excess
5. Stuffing (- - - -) Buffoonery
6. Young deer (- - - -) To flatter
7. Polecat (- - - ---) Search out
8. Polecat (- - - - -) Vetch
9. Darling (- - - - - -) Lathe-head
10. Broken piece (- - - - -) Beetle's wing case

(Solution 94)

145 Cross-Alphabet

Insert the letters of the alphabet only once each into the grid to form a crossword. Clues are given, but in no particular order.

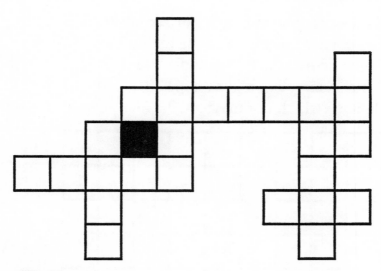

Clues:
- correctly
- side post of a door
- vessel in which consecrated host is preserved
- beast of burden
- adored
- speedy
- swagger
- Turkish cap

(Solution 97)

146 Number Sequence

What number comes next in this sequence?

1, 8, 70, 627, 5639, ?

(Solution 102)

147 Multiple Magic

Fill in the remaining numbers from 1 to 81 to form a multiple magic square to produce:

1. A 3 × 3 inner core where each horizontal, vertical, and corner-to-corner line totals 123 (a magic 123)
2. A 5 × 5 inner core which is a magic 205
3. A 7 × 7 inner core which is a magic 287
4. A whole 9 × 9 which is a magic 369

		63						
81								1
		36		45				
	18							
	72							
						27	56	
				9				

(Solution 105)

148 Three Squares

Using only six matchsticks create three squares of equal size. This one calls for a bit of lateral thinking.

(Solution 110)

149 *Plan in Works*

Change one letter from each word to make, in each case, a well-known phrase, for example:

    PET RICE QUACK = GET RICH QUICK

1.   GO PUT IN FIRE
2.   PIN HARDS TOWN
3.   BOOK HERS
4.   PULL AT PITCH LATER
5.   FASTS ON LINE
6.   TALL IF FIRM
7.   GO SICK SHE MUST
8.   SET START
9.   RUM TUM
10. FOE IN MY
11. NOW GO SAD
12. SO CRY BUT

(Solution 115)

150 *Odd One Out*

Which is the odd one?

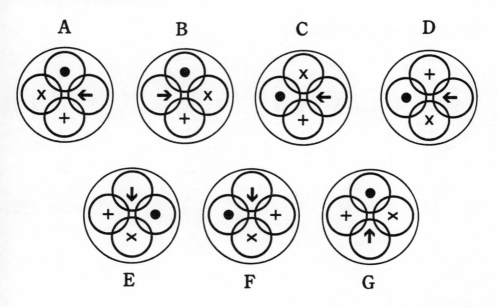

(Solution 155)

95

151 Trios

Complete the words to find, in each set, three words which are synonyms. For example:

IN • • N •   = INVENT
• • I • IN • • •   = ORIGINATE
• • • I • N   = DESIGN

1.   A • • • • T • • • T
     • A • • AT • • •
     A • T • • AT • • •

4.   G • A • • • • • •
     • • A • • • • G
     • • • GA • •

2.   • • SS • • • O •
     • O • • • • S • O •
     • • SO • • • • O •

5.   • • • • IT • • •
     I • IT • TI • •
     • • • • T • • • • IT

3.   • • V • • E
     • EVE • E •
     VE • E • • • • E

6.   • W • • E •
     • • • E • • W • • E
     WE • • E

(Solution 154)

152 Number

Which number should go in D?

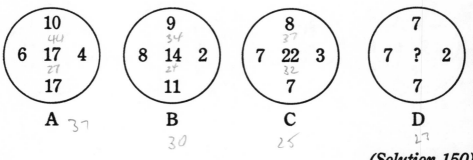

(Solution 150)

96

153 Brackets

Place a word in the brackets that when added on to the end of the first word forms a new word or phrase, and when placed in front of the second word also forms a new word or phrase.

1.	RAIN	(- - - - -)	READER
2.	LAMP	(- - - - -)	HOUSE
3.	HORSE	(- - - -)	GROUND
4.	HORSE	(- - - -)	HAND
5.	FLINT	(- - - -)	SMITH
6.	CROSS	(- - - -)	LAND
7.	BRUSH	(- - - -)	WOOD
8.	DRAGON	(- - -)	FISHING
9.	DREAM	(- - - -)	LOCKED
10.	BALL	(- - - - -)	LESS

(Solution 149)

154 Magic Square

The answers to the five clues are all 5-letter words, which when placed correctly in the grid form a magic word square where the same five words can be read both horizontally and vertically.

Clues (in no particular order):
- In Roman times the ninth
  day before the Ides
- An appointed meeting
- Anguish
- Stiffness
- To bestow

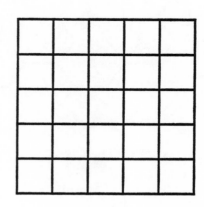

(Solution 145)

155 1 - 2 - 3

Fill in the last line to a regular rule.

$$1$$
$$11$$
$$21$$
$$1211$$
$$111221$$
$$312211$$
$$13112221$$
$$---------?$$

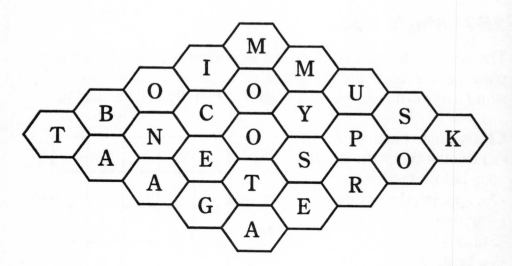

(Solution 141)

156 Honeycomb

Reading in any direction, find sixteen animals. Letters may be used more than once in the same word.

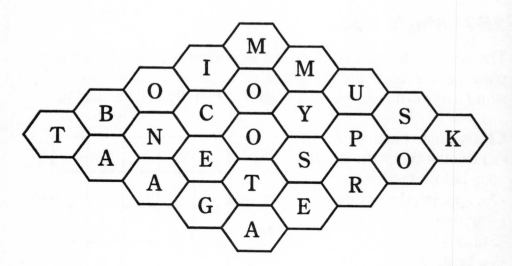

(Solution 137)

157 Missing Number

What is the missing number?

7	4	6	11
8	8	1	15
5	6	8	?

(Solution 132)

158 Pyramid Quotation

"Etiquette is the noise you don't make while having soup."

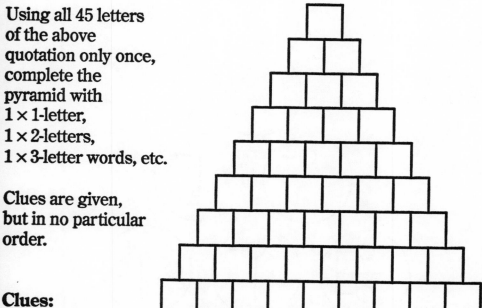

Using all 45 letters of the above quotation only once, complete the pyramid with
1 × 1-letter,
1 × 2-letters,
1 × 3-letter words, etc.

Clues are given, but in no particular order.

Clues:
- Loud cry
- Crib
- Ornamental discs on dresses
- Large spotted dog
- An exclamation of surprise
- Steal
- Formal written application to persons in authority
- Very big
- The first person plural pronoun

(Solution 128)

159 Circles

Which of these fit into the blank circle to carry on a logical sequence?

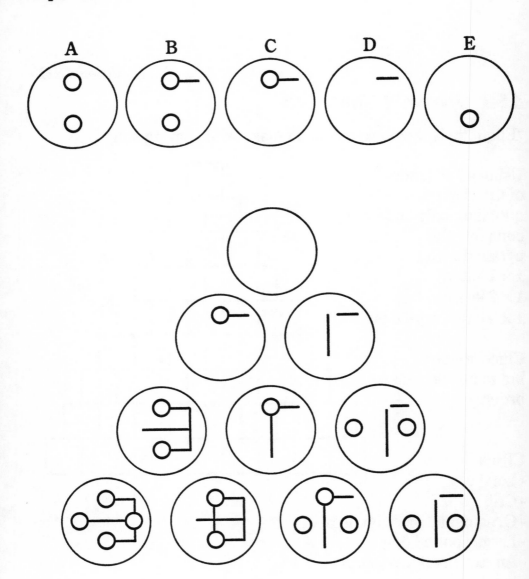

(Solution 125)

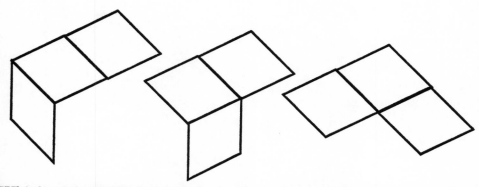

Which of the following options comes next in the above sequence?

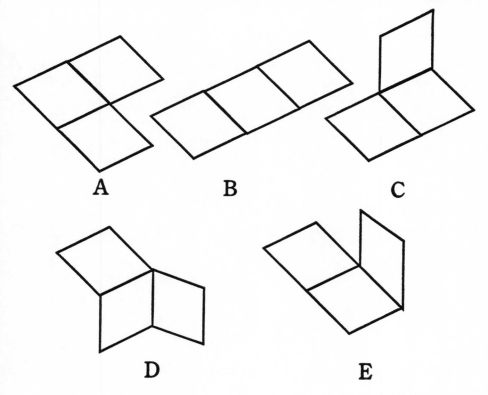

A   B   C

D   E

(Solution 119)

The
Solutions
1

(Solutions are presented out of numerical sequence
so that reading the answer to one puzzle will not inadvertently
reveal the answer to the next.)

1 Find a Word

Investigation

(Puzzle 41)

2 Magic "34"

7	2	9	16
13	12	3	6
4	5	14	11
10	15	8	1

(Puzzle 80)

3 Brain Strain

7	+	5	−	3	=	9
+	■	+	■	+	■	×
7	+	3	−	6	=	4
−	■	÷	■	−	■	÷
8	+	4	−	6	=	6
=	■	=	■	=	■	=
6	÷	2	+	3	=	6

(Puzzle 121)

4 "X" Puzzle

Xiphoid, Xylene, Xylem, Xyloid, Dexter, Lynx, Rex, Lax, Ax, Axe, Hex, Exact, Text, Tax, Taxes, Exam, Sex, Ox, Pix, Nix, Pyx, Tux.

(Puzzle 1)

5 Synonym Circles

Siblings
Children

(Puzzle 42)

6 Square Numbers

Across: 4489, 1681, 2916, 9604, 6241, 3025, 5776, 3136
Down: 4356, 1764, 9801, 2304, 5929, 1444, 3136, 2209

(Puzzle 81)

7 Circle

Less than 25%:

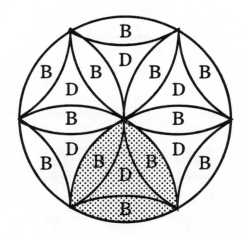

(Puzzle 122)

8 Warehouse

C:
| A | 8× | C | 7× |
| B | 4× | D | 6× |

Starting at A each mile move towards B increases mileage per week by 8, but decreases it by 17: 4 + 7 + 6 = 17.

From B to C we get + (8 + 4) − (7 + 6) − 1, so the number is still going down.

After C we get + (8 + 4 + 7) − 6, so it goes up. Therefore C is best.

(Puzzle 2)

9 Grid

2C.

(Puzzle 43)

10 Middle Letters

Fuss-budget
Miserly
Fuzzy-wuzzy
Frangipani
Flunkeydom
Dust-jacket
Farfetched
Eisteddfod
Daisy-chain
Dapple-gray

(Puzzle 82)

11 Alphabet Crossword

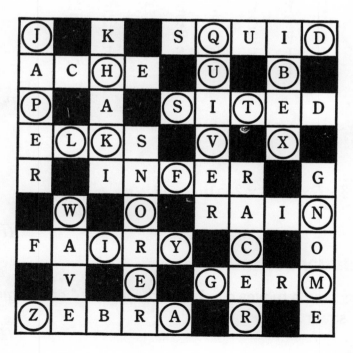

(Puzzle 3)

12 "E" Frame

DOWN

ACROSS	1	2	3	4	5	6	7	8	
1	**R**	L	**S**	P	T	L	**D**	**T**	DESERT
2	Y	**P**	L	**S**	**D**	**T**	L	**P**	STEPPED
3	**B**	B	**B**	P	**D**	H	**W**	L	WEBBED
4	K	**J**	R	**N**	S	**N**	N	**T**	JENNET
5	L	**D**	**N**	P	**L**	**S**	N	**S**	ENDLESS
6	**N**	R	**L**	**K**	R	T	**N**	B	KENNEL
7	W	**R**	C	R	**F**	B	**D**	M	DEFER
8	**N**	T	H	**T**	M	**R**	F	M	ENTER
	WEEKLY	TREBLE	LECHER	PEPPER	MEREST	BETHEL	FENNEL	EMBLEM	

(Puzzle 123)

13 Chairs

$2 \times 7!$
$= 2 \times 7 \times 6 \times 5 \times 4 \times 3 \times 2 \times 1$
$= 10080$

(Puzzle 44)

14 Sequence

B. The rectangle moves clockwise through 45° each time, as does the square.

(Puzzle 83)

15 Symbols

D.

(Puzzle 124)

16 Reverse Anagram

Tambourine

(Puzzle 4)

17 Double Bigrams

Hippopotamus, Philology, Sereneness, Convivial, Balalaika,
Entities, Imbibing, Stowaway, Prototype, Rhododendron,
Uninitiated, Training, Sordidity, Catatonic.

(Puzzle 45)

18 Baby

7.2 lbs:
$12.96 \div 1.8 = 7.2$

(Puzzle 84)

19 Add a Letter

A:
Cashew
Sumach
Orange
Orache
Sesame

(Puzzle 125)

20 Number

The first two numbers in each line or column are divided by
either 4 or 3, whichever is possible, and the quotients added
together to produce the third number, i.e., $(8 \div 4) + (12 \div 3) = 6$.
Thus the missing number is 4.

(Puzzle 46)

21 No Blanks

S	C	A	L	A	R	■	R	E	M	A	N	D
E	■	R	I	C	E	P	A	P	E	R	■	I
M	I	T	T	E	N	■	M	E	T	R	E	S
I	■	I	■	R	E	V	U	E	■	I	■	I
C	A	S	T	■	W	A	S	■	O	V	E	N
O	■	T	E	G	■	T	■	H	O	E	■	V
N	■	■	N	E	W	■	F	E	Z	■	■	E
D	■	C	O	T	■	M	■	N	E	T	■	S
U	P	O	N	■	L	A	C	■	S	O	F	T
C	■	V	■	D	O	N	O	R	■	I	■	M
T	R	E	P	A	N	■	M	E	A	L	I	E
O	■	R	E	M	E	D	I	A	T	E	■	N
R	O	T	T	E	R	■	C	R	E	D	I	T

(Puzzle 5)

22 Names

They all end the names of COUNTRIES:

       AfghaniSTAN — PakiSTAN
       ArgenTINA
       DenMARK
       JorDAN — SuDAN

(Puzzle 85)

23 Fair Play

13.5 minutes: $\dfrac{15 \times 36}{40}$

(Puzzle 6)

24 Directional Crossword

¹M	⁵E	V	A	W	E	D	I	⁴T
¹⁰E	I	D	¹³N	E	P	¹²O	N	⁷S
P	L	S	U	E	C	E	T	S
I	¹⁷E	B	G	C	L	E	¹⁵O	U
T	R	O	A	U	A	L	E	C
H	¹⁸R	B	B	M	I	T	¹⁴Y	S
E	O	R	E	¹⁶O	A	D	E	I
¹¹T	U	⁸R	O	B	O	⁹T	E	⁶D
³T	N	A	R	O	D	O	E	²D

1. Misguided
2. Deodorant
3. Turbulent
4. Tidewave
5. Educated
6. Discuss
7. Steamer
8. Robot
9. Tamable
10. Epithet
11. Tobacco
12. Open
13. Nelly
14. Yeo
15. Olio
16. Oboe
17. Err

(Puzzle 126)

25 Matrix

G. Looking both across and down, lines which are common in the first two squares are not carried forward to the third square.

(Puzzle 47)

26 Do-it-Yourself Crossword

I	L	L	U	S	T	R	A	T	E	D
N		A		O		O		O		U
T	U	T	O	R		B	A	T	O	N
E		H		T	H	E				E
R	U	E		S	I	S	T	E	R	S
		R		K			M			
D	E	S	I	R	E	D		B	A	R
O				A	R	E		A		I
L	I	K	E	N		B	U	R	N	T
T		E		E		U		G		E
S	U	G	G	E	S	T	I	O	N	S

(Puzzle 86)

27 Anagrammed Synonyms

1. TOO – BESIDES
2. WEAK – ENERVATED
3. HIND – POSTERIOR
4. KISS – OSCULATE
5. POST – PALISADE
6. EBB – RETREAT
7. WHET – STIMULATE
8. ACT – ORDINANCE
9. EAT – INGEST
10. VICE – WEAKNESS

(Puzzle 7)

28   Quartering a Square

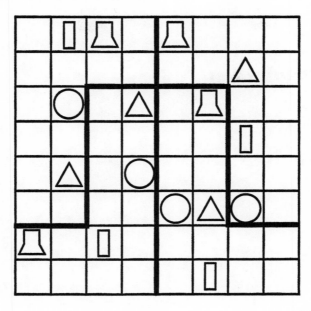

(Puzzle 127)

29   Anagrammed Magic Square

S	C	A	R	F
C	A	T	E	R
A	T	O	N	E
R	E	N	T	S
F	R	E	S	H

(Puzzle 48)

30 Comparison

C.

(Puzzle 87)

31 Concentration

F.

(Puzzle 128)

32 1984

5:

```
    780
    941
+   263
   1984
```

(Puzzle 8)

33 Stations

56:
8×7

(Puzzle 49)

34 The Puzzling Puzzle

Mystery, Conundrum, Enigma, Paradox, Problem, Bewilderment.

(Puzzle 88)

35 Polling Day

Add 23,968 + 1026 + 2822 + 6428 = 34,244.
Divide by four = 8561.
8561 is the number of votes received by the successful candidate. The second received 7535 (8561 – 1026), the third 5739 (8561 – 2822), and fourth 2133 (8561 – 6428).

(Puzzle 129)

36 Round the Hexagons

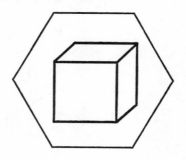

Working from top to bottom, every third hexagon contains the contents of the two previous hexagons.

(Puzzle 9)

37 Hexagram

Salmon, Grilse, Burbot, Groper, Blenny, Plaice.
Key = BARBEL

(Puzzle 50)

38 Bath

This is solved by reciprocals in the formula $(a^{-1} + b^{-1} - c^{-1})^{-1}$
$= (8^{-1} + 10^{-1} - 5^{-1})^{-1}$, i.e., $8^{-1} = \frac{1}{8}$
$= (0.125 + 0.1 - 0.2)^{-1} = 0.025^{-1}$
$= \frac{1}{0.025} = 40$ minutes

(Puzzle 89)

39 Alternatives

1.	(c)		5.	(a)
2.	(a)		6.	(a)
3.	(a)		7.	(a)
4.	(b)		8.	(a)

(Puzzle 130)

40 Hexagon

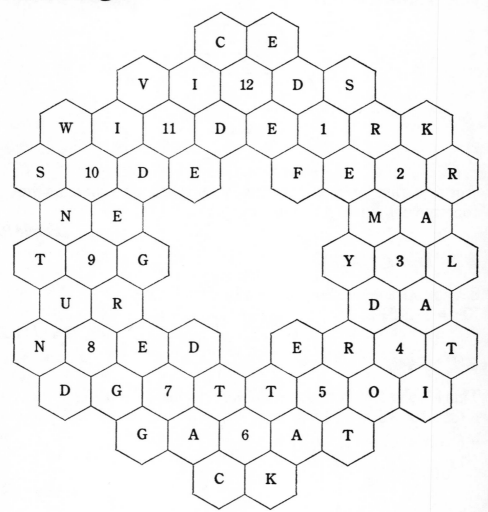

(Puzzle 10)

41 Homonym

You – Ewe

(Puzzle 51)

42 Ten-Digit Number

2100010006

(Puzzle 131)

43 Circles

The contents of the middle circle are determined by the contents of the four circles surrounding it. Only when the same circle appears in the same position in three (and only three) of the surrounding circles is it carried forward to the middle circle.

(Puzzle 90)

44 Circles

C

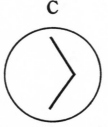

Each pair of circles produces the circle above by carrying forward only the similar elements.

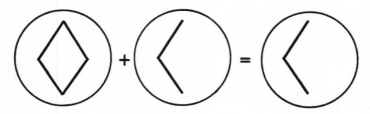

(Puzzle 11)

45 Comparison

C.

(Puzzle 132)

46 Circles

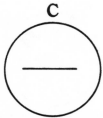

Each pair of circles produces the circle above by carrying forward only the similar elements.

(Puzzle 52)

47 Fish

1. Proper – Groper
2. Cattle – Cuttle
3. Gunner – Gunnel
4. Nipper – Kipper
5. Duffer – Puffer
6. Dudgeon – Gudgeon
7. Sapper – Wapper
8. Dream – Bream
9. Bullet – Mullet

(Puzzle 91)

48 Pentagram

Civet
Camel
Panda   Key = COATI
Stoat
Tapir

(Puzzle 53)

49 Work It Out

C. The final figure in each line is determined by the number of sides in each figure as follows:

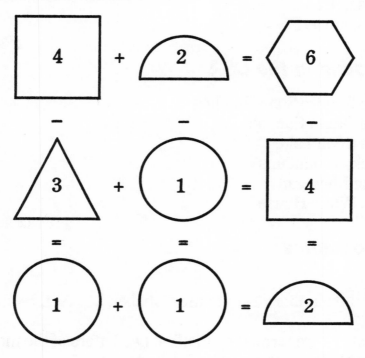

(Puzzle 133)

50 Target Crossword

- Noggin
- Possum
- Sexton
- Seesaw
- Eyelid
- Picnic
- Poseur
- Shandy
- Lineal
- Shaman
- Rouble
- Parody
- Sconce
- Rights
- Piazza
- Gingko

(Puzzle 12)

51 Something in Common

They are all names of SHIPS or BOATS:
Packet, Punt, Barge, Liner, Smack, Tramp, Tender, Trader

(Puzzle 54)

119

52 Odd One Out

G:
B is the same as E
A is the same as D
C is the same as F

(Puzzle 92)

53 Found in the USA

1. The Empire State Building
2. The Grand Canyon
3. Great Salt Lake
4. Rocky Mountains
5. Lake Michigan
6. The White House

(Puzzle 134)

54 Sequence

1021:
Allocate the numbers 1–26 to the alphabet, i.e., A=1, B=2, C=3, etc.
The numbers are formed by the first two letters of the months of the year starting with January: J(10), A(1) = 101.
The seventh month is, therefore July: J(10), U(21) = 1021.

(Puzzle 13)

55 Octagons

D. The shield twists around three sides of the octagon each time. The arrow moves from top to bottom of the shield in turn and points to the outside, then the inside, of the shield in turn.

(Puzzle 55)

56 Odd One Out

E:
A is the same as C
B is the same as G
D is the same as F

(Puzzle 135)

57 Nursery Rhyme Crossword

M	A	J	E	S	T	Y
E		E		C		I
R	E	S	T	O	R	E
I		T		O		L
T	R	E	A	T	E	D
E		R		E		E
D	E	S	I	R	E	D

58 No Repeat Letters

Speculator

(Puzzle 14)

59 Cards

$52p_4 = 52 \times 51 \times 50 \times 49$

$\quad = 6{,}497{,}400$

(Puzzle 56)

60 Network

Representative

(Puzzle 94)

61 Word Circle

Starch, Cheese, Senate, Tenure, Resume, Mettle, Legacy, Cypher, Ermine, Nebula, Lavish, Shelve, Vendor, Origin, Infest.

(Puzzle 15)

62 Anagram Theme

The theme is COUNTRIES:

Nigeria	Gain	Ire
Finland	Flan	Din
Austria	Aura	Sit
Sweden	Sew	End
Argentina	Grain	Neat
Algeria	Rail	Age
Hungary	Rung	Hay

(Puzzle 136)

63 Number Logic

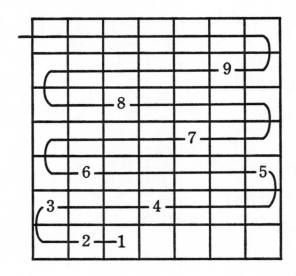

Start at the top left-hand corner and work in the direction indicated, counting the same number of squares as the next number each time.

(Puzzle 57)

64 Find Another Word

LONG. All words can be prefixed with FUR to form another word: Furbelow, Furore, Furrower, Furlong.

(Puzzle 95)

65 Nines

3	8	5	2
8	7	9	3
6	6	5	1
1	6	8	3

(Puzzle 137)

66 Missing Square

D. The number of sides in the figures in each horizontal, vertical and corner-to-corner line add up to 15.

(Puzzle 16)

67 Sequence

B. The figure alternates:

The lines are first introduced into the circles on the left, one at a time in rotation, and then transfer to the circle on the right at the next stage.

(Puzzle 58)

68 Missing Letters

1. Anatomist
2. Stuntman
3. Boatswain
4. Rivetter
5. Japanner
6. Dietician
7. Usherette
8. Violinist
9. Mercenary
10. Gasfitter

(Puzzle 138)

69 Connections

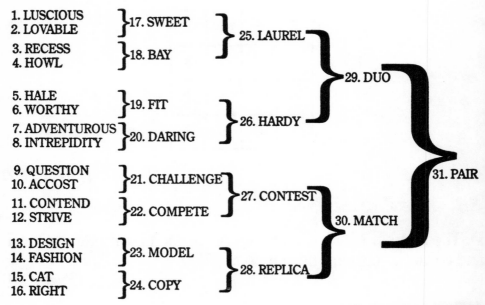

1. LUSCIOUS
2. LOVABLE
} 17. SWEET
3. RECESS
4. HOWL
} 18. BAY
} 25. LAUREL

5. HALE
6. WORTHY
} 19. FIT
7. ADVENTUROUS
8. INTREPIDITY
} 20. DARING
} 26. HARDY

29. DUO

9. QUESTION
10. ACCOST
} 21. CHALLENGE
11. CONTEND
12. STRIVE
} 22. COMPETE
} 27. CONTEST

13. DESIGN
14. FASHION
} 23. MODEL
15. CAT
16. RIGHT
} 24. COPY
} 28. REPLICA

30. MATCH

31. PAIR

(Puzzle 96)

70 Logic

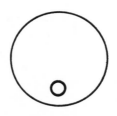

Carrying forward only similar symbols:

Row 1	A added to B = C
Row 2	A added to B = C
Row 3	A added to B = C
Column A	1 added to 2 = 3
Column B	1 added to 2 = 3
Column C	1 added to 2 = 3

(Puzzle 17)

71 Word Power

1. Pussyfoot
2. Musketeer
3. Cantaloup
4. Debaucher
5. Flagstone
6. Marijuana
7. Recumbent
8. Objection
9. Gallivant

(Puzzle 59)

72 Ending

PER:
Hamper
Pamper
Hopper
Whimper
Supper
Slipper

(Puzzle 97)

73 Sequence

E. The rectangle and diamond form alternate sequences. First the rectangle turns through 90°, then the diamond does the same.

(Puzzle 139)

74 Old Age

88:
$100 - (4 \times 10) = 60$
$60 + (4 \times 7) = 88$

(Puzzle 19)

75 Logic

Carrying forward only similar symbols:

Row 1	A added to B = C
Row 2	A added to B = C
Row 3	A added to B = C
Column A	1 added to 2 = 3
Column B	1 added to 2 = 3
Column C	1 added to 2 = 3

(Puzzle 60)

76 Arrows

F:

The arrow moves 45° clockwise each time.

The arrow head alternates black/striped.

The arrow body alternates striped/black.

The ellipse rotates 45° each time and moves from bottom to top, etc., of arrow.

The circle moves from top to bottom, etc., of arrow and black and white segments alternate.

(Puzzle 98)

77 Niners

Across	Down	Diagonal
1. Announcer	1. Anarchist	1. Accusable
4. Crossover	2. Unreserve	3. Renascent
5. Teakettle	3. Recursive	

(Puzzle 140)

78 Pyramid

Unsportsmanlike

(Puzzle 61)

79 Sequence

D:

D	E F G H	I	(4)
I	J K L M N	O	(5)
O	P Q R S T U	V	(6)
V	W X Y Z A B C	D	(7)

(Puzzle 18)

80 Sequence

Trudy: The names can all be made from the days of the week starting SuNDAY (ANDY). Trudy can be produced from SaTURDaY.

(Puzzle 62)

81 Safe

Lynx

(Puzzle 99)

82 Safe

3W.

(Puzzle 141)

83 Word Search

DRINKS:
Chartreuse, Grenadine, Cappuccino, Cointreau, Muscadine, Orangeade, Martini, Arrack, Alcohol, Lager, Grog, Gimlet, Nog, Ale, Rosé, Cha, Hock, Tea, Fizz, Rye.

(Puzzle 20)

84 Clueless Crossword

P	L	U	M	B	E	R
L	■	P	■	U	■	E
A	P	P	A	R	E	L
T	■	E	■	S	■	I
E	R	R	A	T	I	C

(Puzzle 63)

85 Complete the Calculation

$6^3 \div 36 = 6$

(Puzzle 100)

86 Song

All around the mulberry bush,
The monkey chased the weasel,
The monkey thought it was such fun –
Pop goes the weasel!

(Puzzle 142)

87 Letters Sequence

TH. They are the last two letters of each planet in reverse order from the Sun:
PluTO, NeptuNE, UranUS, SatuRN, JupitER, MaRS, EarTH.

(Puzzle 21)

88 Three Triangles

(Puzzle 64)

89 Grid

2A.

(Puzzle 101)

90 Pyramid Word

L, Pi, Gun, Deer, Drive.
15-letter word: UNDERPRIVILEGED

(Puzzle 143)

91 Bracket Word

Altogether

(Puzzle 22)

92 No Neighbors

Transmogrification

(Puzzle 103)

93 Alternative Crossword

F	R	O	M	■	A	I	R	S
L	■	R	U	M	P	S	■	P
I	T	■	D	I	E	■	M	E
P	I	T	■	N	■	R	O	D
■	D	E	C	I	D	E	D	■
H	E	N	■	M	■	D	E	W
U	S	■	N	U	B	■	S	O
N	■	T	I	M	E	D	■	R
T	O	O	L	■	G	O	O	D

(Puzzle 65)

94 Middle Word

1. Joss
2. Jib
3. Girandole
4. Glutton
5. Farce
6. Fawn
7. Ferret
8. Fitch
9. Poppet
10. Shard

(Puzzle 144)

95 Odd One Out

B:
A is the same as D with Black and White reversed.
C is the same as E with Black and White reversed.

(Puzzle 23)

96 Circles

E:

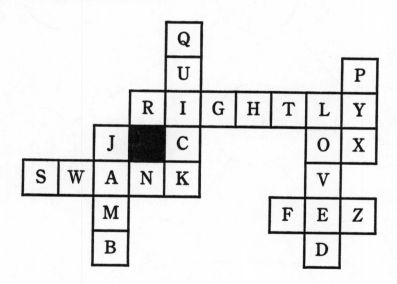

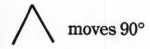 moves 135° clockwise

○ moves 180°

∧ moves 90°

—◉ moves 135°

(Puzzle 66)

97 Cross-Alphabet

(Puzzle 145)

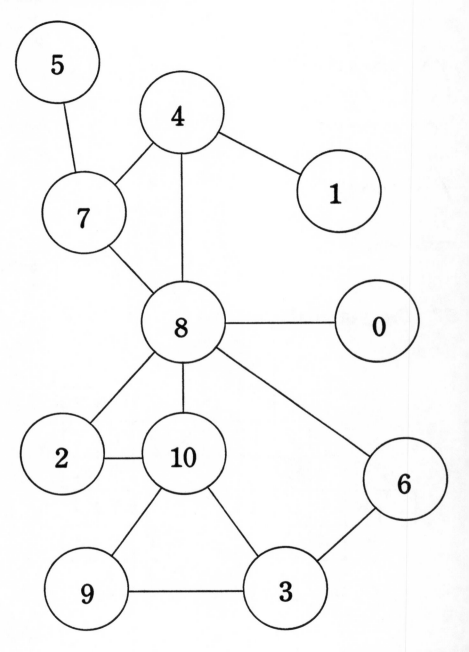

(Puzzle 102)

99   Word Power

Eldrich
Ukase
Refection
Extirpate
Kohl
Amain
Impecunious
Vicarious
Esculent
Gerund
Odalisk
Termagant
Inanition
Tolu
"Eureka! I've got it." – *Archimedes*

(Puzzle 24)

100   Square Roots

No.
Square these end digits and note last digit: 0 1 2 3 4 5 6 7 8 9
Last digit of squares: 0 1 4 9 6 5 6 9 4 1
No number ending in 2, 3, 7, or 8 can have a square root of
integers only.

(Puzzle 67)

101   Missing Links

2798 – 2646 – 1196
4389 – 3827 – 1026
4051 – 2040 – 800
$27 \times 98 = 2646, 26 \times 46 = 1196$

(Puzzle 104)

102 Number Sequence

$$50746$$
$$1 \times 9 - 1 = 8$$
$$8 \times 9 - 2 = 70$$
$$70 \times 9 - 3 = 627$$
$$627 \times 9 - 4 = 5639$$
$$5639 \times 9 - 5 = 50746$$

(Puzzle 146)

103 Greek Cross to Square Puzzle

The lines AB and CD are drawn from the center of their respective sides of the Greek cross.

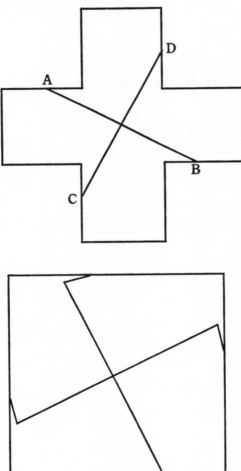

(Puzzle 25)

104 Wine

	hours	reciprocal	decimal
Man	2.5	$1/2.5$	.400
Wife	1.5	$1/1.5$	.667
		Add	1.067

Take reciprocal
$1/1.067 = .9375$ hrs.
$= .9375 \times 60$
$= 56.25$ minutes.

(Puzzle 68)

105 Multiple Magic

13	12	63	3	61	73	59	80	5
81	26	71	28	57	30	55	20	1
78	68	35	60	29	50	31	14	4
6	24	36	40	45	38	46	58	76
75	17	49	39	41	43	33	65	7
8	18	34	44	37	42	48	64	74
15	72	51	22	53	32	47	10	67
16	62	11	54	25	52	27	56	66
77	70	19	79	21	9	23	2	69

(Puzzle 147)

106 Occupations

Ploughman
Professor
Major-domo
Puppeteer
Harpooner
Geologist
Osteopath
Zookeeper
Ropemaker
Gondolier
Herbalist
Hypnotist

(Puzzle 105)

107 Appropriate Anagrams

Dead Respire Again
Is Lit For Seamen
Causes Sin
Is No Meal
Sit Not At Ale Bars
A Stew Sir
Apt Is The Cure
No Hat, A Smile
Noted Miscalculations
Faces One At The End

(Puzzle 26)

108 Alternative Crossword

S	W	A	G	E
H	A	R	E	M
O	V	O	L	O
R	E	M	I	T
T	R	A	D	E

(Puzzle 69)

109 Sea Level

8.7 miles:

The formula is $Height = \dfrac{2n^2}{3}$ feet

(where n = distance in miles)

$\therefore 50 = \dfrac{2n^2}{3}$

$150 = 2n^2$

$75 = n^2$

$n = \sqrt{75}$

$n = 8.7$ miles

(Puzzle 106)

110 Three squares

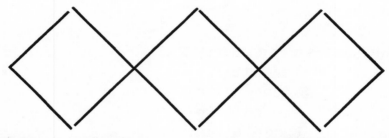

Sorry if this was a bit sneaky, but we didn't say that you couldn't break the matches.

(Puzzle 148)

111 Jumble

Vaccination
Ventilation
Venturesome
Viceroyship
Versatility
Vermiculate
Vicariously
Vexatiously

(Puzzle 27)

112 Anagrammed Phrases

1. Let sleeping dogs lie
2. To give up the ghost
3. To beg the question
4. A fly on the wall
5. Play fast and loose

(Puzzle 70)

113 Logic

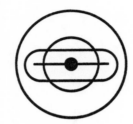

Carrying forward only similar symbols:

Row 1	A added to B = C
Row 2	A added to B = C
Row 3	A added to B = C
Column A	1 added to 2 = 3
Column B	1 added to 2 = 3
Column C	1 added to 2 = 3

(Puzzle 107)

114 Four Integers

A = 9
B = 6
C = 3
D = 1
CABA = 3969
DCBA = 1369
DACB = 1936

(Puzzle 28)

115 Plan in Works

1. To cut it fine
2. Win hands down
3. Look here
4. Dull as ditch water
5. Facts of life
6. Ball of fire
7. To lick the dust
8. See stars
9. Yum yum
10. Woe is me
11. Not to say
12. To try out

(Puzzle 149)

116 Symbols

A.

(Puzzle 29)

117 Work it Out

63: $\dfrac{15 \times 3 \times 7}{5}$

Likewise: $\dfrac{4 \times 3 \times 8}{6} = 16$

$\dfrac{9 \times 12 \times 2}{9} = 24$

(Puzzle 71)

118 Cheeses

63 moves ($2^6 - 1$)

(Puzzle 30)

119   Logical Movement

B. There are three components:

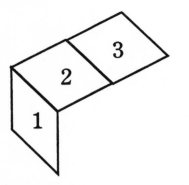

All pieces are laid flat.
Pieces 2 and 3 never move.
Piece 1 moves by rotating
counterclockwise and clamping
itself onto the next available
side.

Thus option 2:

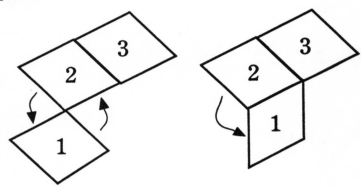

(Puzzle 160)

120   Quotation

"Anyone who thinks that there is a safety in numbers has not
looked at the stock market pages." – *Irene Peter*

(Puzzle 108)

121   Comparison

A.

(Puzzle 34)

122 Cryptogram

Write we know is written right, when we see it written write;
But when we see it written wright, we know 'tis not then written
    right;
For write to have it written right, must not be written right nor
    wright;
Nor yet should it be written rite, but write – for so 'tis written
    right.

(Puzzle 72)

123 Dominoes

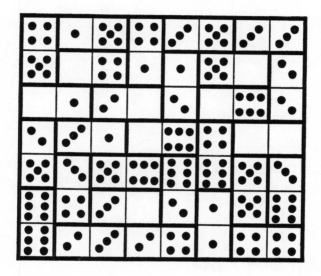

(Puzzle 109)

124 The Gallopers

ANNOYING (Exasperating), LAG (Delay)

LING (Heather), OBLONG (Rectangular)

PRIG (Puritan), EVERLASTING (Imperishable)

ROUSING (Stimulating), SPRING (Fountainhead)

(Puzzle 31)

125 Circles

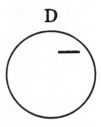

Each pair of circles produces the circle above by carrying forward only the similar elements.

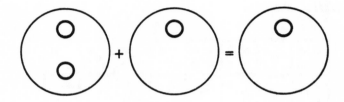

(Puzzle 159)

126 Sequence

C. Break them into groups of four. They tumble over one at a time from the right, and change from black to white one at a time from the left.

(Puzzle 73)

127 Letter Sequence

R. They are all alternate letters in:
    ThE uNiTeD sTaTeS oF aMeRica

(Puzzle 110)

128 Pyramid Quotation

O, we, key, huge, shout, thieve, sequins, petition, dalmation

(Puzzle 158)

129 Analogy

C. The figure is inverted and the inverted figure placed on top on the original figure touching the top and bottom of it. The external parts in the figure created are shaded.

(Puzzle 32)

130 Sequence

REEF:

RAY (ON E) PAULE (T WO) R (TH REE) F

(Puzzle 74)

131 Odd One Out

Open.

All other words are made up from the initials of the numbers 1–10 : OTTFFSSENT.

(Puzzle 111)

132 Missing Number

1. The link is in each horizontal line:

$$7 = \frac{4 + 6 + 11}{3}$$

$$8 = \frac{8 + 1 + 15}{3}$$

$$5 = \frac{6 + 8 + 1}{3}$$

(Puzzle 157)

133 Birds

Crested	Grebe
Carrier	Pigeon
Stormy	Petrel
Snow	Goose
Muscovy	Duck
Tawny	Owl
Night	Hawk
Water	Ousel
Turtle	Dove
House	Martin
Willow	Warbler
Black	Cockatoo

Odd word: PEACOCK

(Puzzle 33)

134 Missing Number

4:
The number inside the octagon is produced by doing the opposite calculation to that indicated immediately above.

i.e.

$7 + 3$ ∴ actual calculation $7 - 3 = 4$

3×3 ∴ actual calculation $3 \div 3 = 1$

$3 - 2$ ∴ actual calculation $3 + 2 = 5$

$2 - 7$ ∴ actual calculation $2 + 7 = 9$

(Puzzle 112)

135 Knight

We find it hard to believe that other people's thoughts are as silly as our own, but they probably are.

(Puzzle 35)

136 Threes

They are all names of groups:

Pack	{	Hyenas Wolves Cigarettes
Rookery	{	Penguins Rooks Seals
Drove	{	Pigs Swine Oxen
Nest	{	Machine Guns Wasps Mice
Pod	{	Peas Whales Hippopotamuses
Troop	{	Scouts Baboons Actors

(Puzzle 75)

137 Honeycomb

ANIMALS:

Moose	Coyote	Coypu
Pup	Puppy	Sore
Mice	Possum	Teg
Musk	Cob	Bat
Nag	Tat	Moco
Stag		

(Puzzle 156)

138 Series

To get from one term to the next term, multiply by 3,
e.g., $6 \times 3 = 18$.
We require the 10th term, i.e., 6×3^9:
$= 6 \times 19683$
$= 118098$

(Puzzle 36)

139 Common

They all begin with things associated with water but with letters
reversed.

1. Bib	5. Gar
2. Carp	6. Tide
3. Dab	7. Newt
4. Crab	8. Orca

(Puzzle 76)

140 Middle Words

1. By	5. Me	9. He
2. King	6. Ring	10. Cap
3. Fish	7. Ate	
4. Wood	8. Lock	

(Puzzle 113)

141 1-2-3

1113213211:
Each line describes the number above it.
For example, 1221 would be:
One 1, Two 2, One 1, etc.

(Puzzle 155)

142 Division

YOUNGSTER

N	T	G	E	O	O
N	U	Y	N	S	S
Y	U	R	R	Y	E
R	G	O	S	U	G
E	Y	S	O	T	U
T	G	E	T	R	N

(Puzzle 37)

143 Scales

13.5 grams:
$9 \times 6 = 4 \times 13.5$

(Puzzle 77)

144 Track Word

Instantaneously

(Puzzle 114)

145 Magic Square

G	R	A	N	T
R	I	G	O	R
A	G	O	N	Y
N	O	N	E	S
T	R	Y	S	T

(Puzzle 154)

146 Three Animals

Panther, Antelope, Llama

(Puzzle 38)

147 Symbols

A.

(Puzzle 78)

148 Quotation

"The minute you read something you can't understand, you can almost be sure it was drawn up by a lawyer." – *Will Rogers*

(Puzzle 115)

149 Brackets

1. Proof
2. Light
3. Play
4. Whip
5. Lock

6. Over
7. Fire
8. Fly
9. Land
10. Point

(Puzzle 153)

150 Number

14:

$(7 \times 2) + 7 - 7 = 14$

(Puzzle 152)

(Puzzle 39)

152 Eponyms

1. Leotard – after Jules Léotard
2. Draconian – after Draco
3. Maverick – after Samual Maverick
4. Cardigan – after the Earl of Cardigan
5. Platonic – after Plato
6. Lucullan – after Lucius Licinius Lucullus
7. Martinet – after Jean Martinet
8. Dunce – after John Duns Scotus
9. Mesmerize – after Franz Anton Mesmer
10. Machiavellian – after Nicolò Machiavelli

(Puzzle 79)

153 Circles

B:

moves 135°
clockwise

moves 90°
counterclockwise

moves 90°
clockwise

moves 180°

(Puzzle 116)

154 Trios

1. Adjustment	Variation	Alteration
2. Cessation	Conclusion	Resolution
3. Divine	Revered	Venerable
4. Graceful	Charming	Elegant
5. Deceitful	Imitation	Counterfeit
6. Swivel	Intertwine	Weave

(Puzzle 151)

155 Odd One Out

D:
A is the same as F
B is the same as E
C is the same as G

(Puzzle 150)

156 Quotation

"I have made it a rule never to smoke more than one cigar at a time." – *Mark Twain*

(Puzzle 117)

157 Directional Numbers

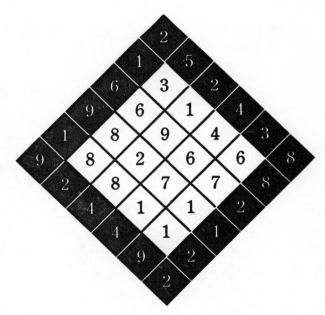

(Puzzle 40)

158 The Hexagonal Pyramid

The content of each hexagon is made up by merging the contents of the two hexagons directly below, with the exception that where two identical lines appear they are not carried forward.

(Puzzle 119)

159 Synchronized Synonyms

Towering, Gigantic
Dextrous, Polished
Director, Governor
Isolated, Solitary
Swindler, Deceiver
Calendar, Schedule
Disallow, Preclude
Latitude, Wideness

(Puzzle 120)

160 Spots

The formula is by Leo Moser: $n + \dbinom{n}{4} \; \dbinom{n-1}{2}$

Written in full: $\dfrac{n^4 - 6n^3 + 23n^2 - 18n + 24}{24}$

Amazingly the answer is not 32. It is as follows:

Spots	Regions	Spots	Regions
1	1	7	57
2	2	8	99
3	4	9	163
4	8	10	256
5	16	11	386
6	31		

Answers can be obtained by a cut from Pascal's triangle.

```
                    1
                  1   1
                1   2   1
              1   3   3   1
            1   4   6   4   1  /
          1   5  10  10   5 / 1
        1   6  15  20  15 / 6   1
      1   7  21  35  35 / 21  7   1
                       /
```

(Puzzle 118)

Power
Puzzles
2

1 Alternative Crossword

Select the correct letters to complete the crossword.

1	5	5	3	2	2	6	7
5	■	■	1	5	7	■	2
7	5	■	2	1	7	■	6
7	3	6	■	4	5	6	2
2	4	1	5	■	6	2	5
7	■	8	5	8	■	8	2
2	■	2	8	1	■	■	4
2	3	4	1	7	5	6	9

KEY

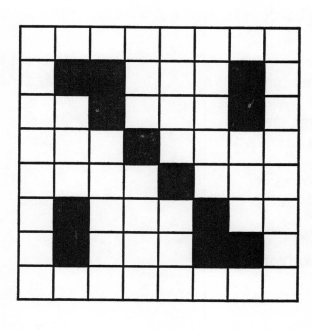

1	A	B	C
2	D	E	F
3	G	H	I
4	J	K	L
5	M	N	O
6	P	Q	R
7	S	T	U
8	V	W	X
9	Y	Z	–

(Solution 4)

1

2 Batteries

A day's production of batteries has 10% spoilage. If three batteries are selected at random, what are the chances that all three will be defective?

(Solution 8)

3 Link Word

Find a 5-letter word that when placed in front of these words produces new words.

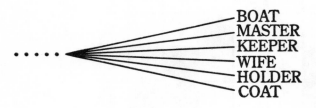

(Solution 10)

4 Common Clues

What does each pair of words have in common?

Vex
Summit

Implement
A fine silk net

Necessity
Pound

Strip
Forbidden

Reconsider
A light entertainment

Meter
A pledge

Encroach
Railed

(Solution 16)

5 Comparison

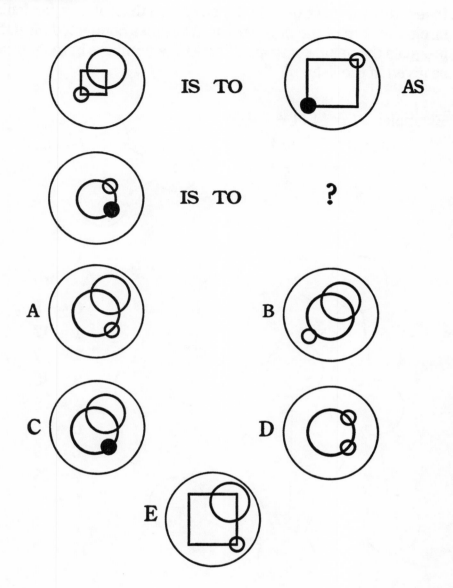

IS TO ... AS

IS TO ... ?

A

B

C

D

E

(Solution 20)

3

6 Connections

Insert the numbers 0–10 in the circles so that for any particular circle the sum of the numbers in the circles connected directly to it equals the value corresponding to the numbers in that circle, as given in the list.

Example: $1 = 14 \ (4 + 7 + 3)$
$4 = 8 \ (7 + 1)$
$7 = 5 \ (4 + 1)$
$3 = 1$

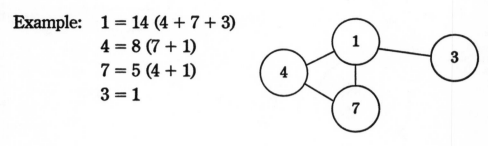

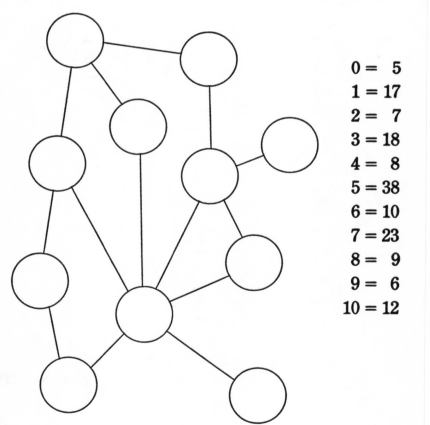

$0 = \ 5$
$1 = 17$
$2 = \ 7$
$3 = 18$
$4 = \ 8$
$5 = 38$
$6 = 10$
$7 = 23$
$8 = \ 9$
$9 = \ 6$
$10 = 12$

(Solution 24)

4

7 Pyramid Word

Solve the five clues, enter the correct words in the pyramid, and then rearrange all the letters to find a 15-letter word.

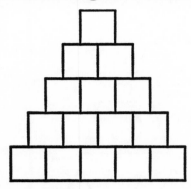

1. The first known quantity in an algebraic expression
2. Denoting direction to or towards
3. To droop
4. To plunge
5. Noise

(Solution 28)

8 Twelve Letters

Find the four 12-letter words. The first half is inside the star. The second half is outside the star and is joined to the first half by a hyphen.

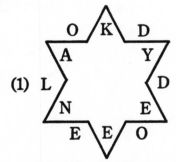

(1)

Clue: Bit of a dandy!

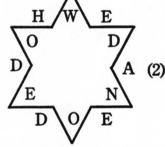

(2)

Clue: Don't scratch it!

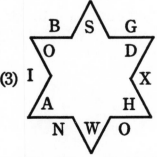

(3)

Clue: Win on points?

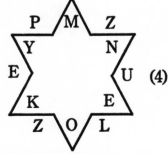

(4)

Clue: Kind of tree?

(Solution 29)

9 Pyramidal Logic

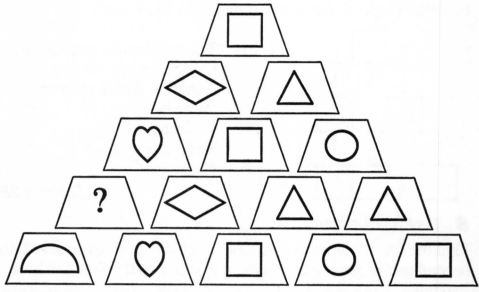

Which of the following symbols should logically replace the question mark?

(Solution 36)

10 Analogy

If 3694 is to 97, and 5382 is to 54, what number is to 83?

(Solution 40)

11 Racetrack

There is a circular racetrack twenty-seven miles long. On the track are six racing cars that have broken down. The distances between any two cars or any combination of cars can add up to every whole number between one and twenty-six.

What are the six distances between the cars?

(Diagram below does not necessarily depict the actual ratio of distances between the cars accurately.)

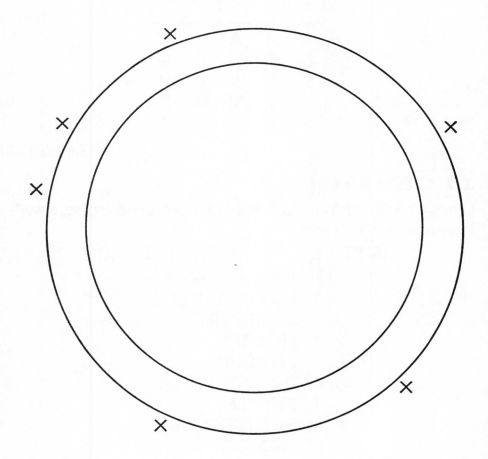

(Solution 44)

12 Magic Word Square

Place the letters in the grid. Words are the same across and down. (One of the words is a proper noun.)

				S
			M	
		D		
	M			
S				

A	A	A	A	A
A	D̸	E	E	E
E	L	L	L	M
M	M	M̸	M̸	P
S̸	S̸	U	U	Z

(Solution 48)

13 Letter Change

Change one letter from each word to make, in each case, a well-known phrase, for example:

PET RICE QUACK = GET RICH QUICK

1. PROD ANY SONS
2. GO FILL ANY COT
3. DO BET FRY
4. I BEG US
5. GO GONG
6. DRY SUITS
7. READ LET
8. SO PUT IN LINE
9. TALL GUN
10. SO NIP US

(Solution 52)

8

14 Grid

Each of the nine squares marked 1A to 3C should incorporate all the lines and symbols that are shown in the outer squares A, B, or C and 1, 2, or 3. Thus 2B should incorporate all the lines and symbols in 2 and B.

One of the squares, 1A to 3C, is incorrect. Which one is it?

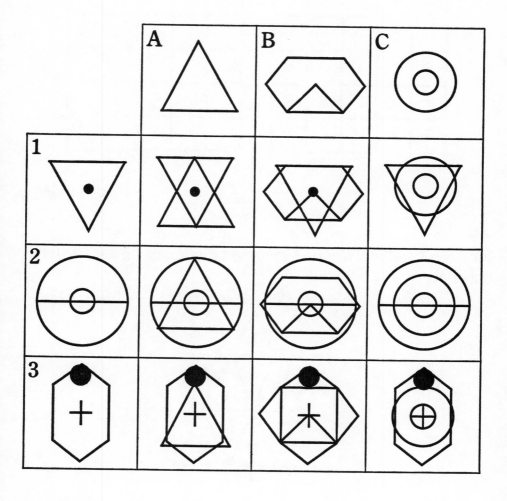

(Solution 56)

9

15 Magic Square

Rearrange the twenty-five letters to form five new words so that when placed in the correct order in the blank grid a magic word square will be formed, where the same five words can be read both across and down.

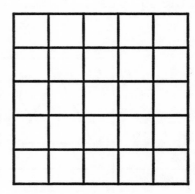

(Solution 61)

16 Star

Find the 12-letter word that uses every letter, using each letter only once.

(Solution 64)

17 Analogy

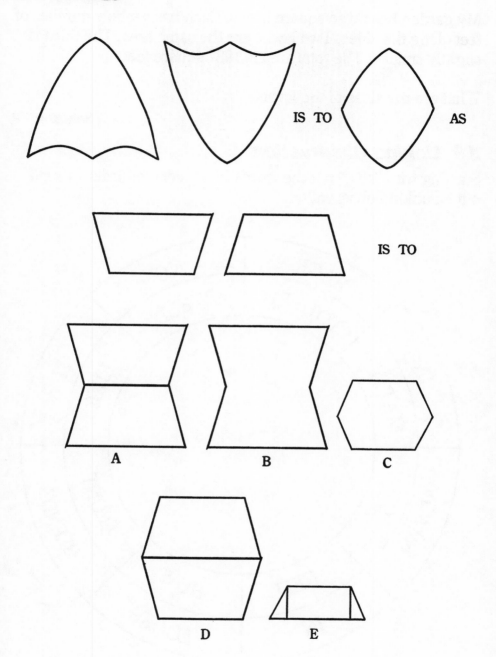

IS TO ... AS

IS TO

A   B   C

D   E

(Solution 68)

11

18 Lawns

My garden has three square lawns. Each has a whole number of feet along the sides. Two lawns are the same area. The third is slightly smaller. The total area is 1987 square feet.

What are the sizes of the lawns?

(Solution 72)

19 Unkind Observation

Starting with "NO," put the words in the correct order to spell out an unkind observation.

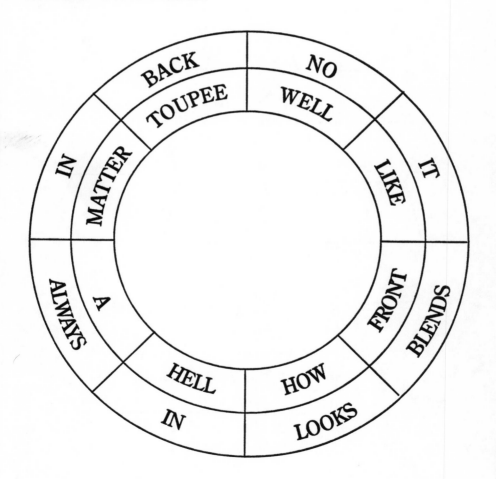

(Solution 76)

20 Links Jigsaw Puzzle

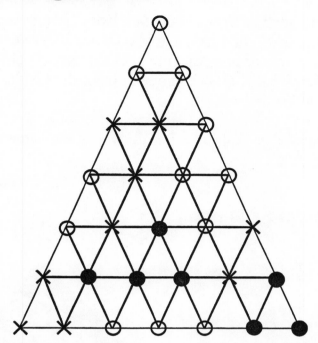

Place the twelve segments below over the triangular grid, above, in such a way that each link symbol is covered by exactly the same symbol. The connecting segments must not be rotated. Note that not all the connecting lines will be covered.

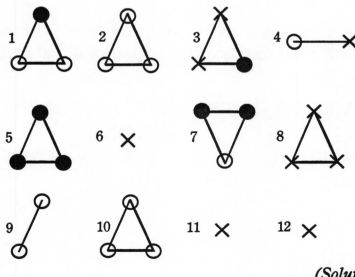

(Solution 80)

13

21 Bertrand's Paradox

Three identical chests of drawers contain two drawers each. Each drawer of chest A contains a gold coin, each drawer of chest B contains a silver coin, and chest C has a gold coin in one drawer and silver in the other. You open one of the six drawers at random and find inside a silver coin.

What is the probability that the other drawer of the same chest contains a gold coin?

(Solution 84)

22 The Enigma Diamond

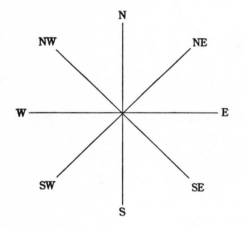

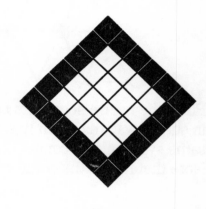

Fit all the words below into the grid. Each word must travel in a straight line in the direction of a compass point and start and finish in a shaded square.

GROUND	NOTED	ITEM	MY
DOUBLE		OMEN	
GAGGLE		GURU	
ACTING		GONG	

(Solution 89)

23 Find Another Word

Consider the following words:
                MARE, CAP, LIGHT

Now choose one of the following words that has something in common with all the words above.
                IN, OUT, CLIMB, FALL

(Solution 92)

24 Circles Matrix

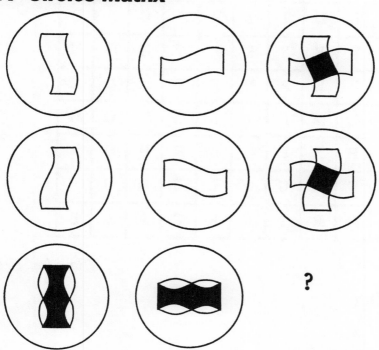

Which circle is missing from the arrangement above?

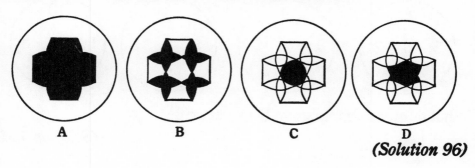

A   B   C   D

(Solution 96)

15

25 Word Search

Find the names of twenty-two birds in this puzzle. Words can be found in any direction but only in a straight line.

R	E	D	S	H	A	N	K	U	H
T	A	M	E	W	T	E	O	C	R
O	R	G	A	O	S	B	N	U	E
M	E	D	I	T	A	I	C	R	D
E	V	R	R	R	F	R	E	O	N
L	O	E	A	N	E	T	M	C	A
L	L	M	E	T	S	G	U	O	G
I	P	E	R	O	K	R	D	B	R
U	R	A	O	W	L	U	O	U	E
G	D	R	I	B	K	C	A	L	B

(Solution 101)

26 Number

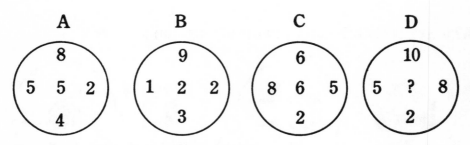

What number should go in D to a set rule?

(Solution 104)

27 Diamond

Find the names of twelve fish moving in any direction, not
necessarily in a straight line. Letters may be used more than
once in each word. Corners count as connected.

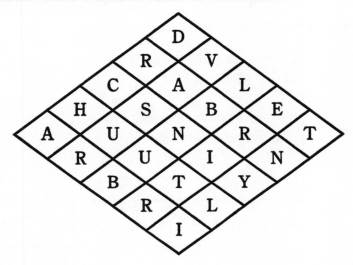

(Solution 108)

28 Circles

What number should replace the question mark?

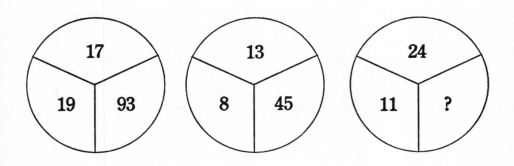

(Solution 112)

29 Treasure

The treasure is on square C6. You have to find the starting square that will lead to the treasure.

Instructions are read as follows:

2S ⎫ means 2 squares south
1E ⎭ and 1 square east

6N ⎫ means 6 squares north
6W ⎭ and 6 squares west

N

	A	B	C	D	E	F	G
1	3S 3E	6S 4E	6S 1W	2S 2W	3S 2E	4S 4W	2S 3W
2	2S 4E	5S 1E	1N 1E	4S 1E	1N 2W	1N 1E	4S 3W
3	2S 3E	1N 1W	3S 2W	2N 2W	2N 1E	2S 1W	1S 5W
4	2S 6E	1N 1W	2N 3E	3S 3E	1N 1E	2N 3W	2S 1W
5	3N 1E	2S 1W	3N 1E	4N 1E	1S 2W	2N 1E	2N 2W
6	1N 2E	1S 2E	T	2N 3W	2N 1E	1S 1W	4N 2W
7	1N 1E	4N 1E	2N 4E	2N 2E	5N 2E	2N 5W	3N 4W

W ← → E

S

(Solution 114)

30 The Enigmasig Wheel

This puzzle is named after "Enigmasig" the special interest group (SIG) within MENSA devoted to the setting and solving of puzzles that is run jointly by the two authors.

Complete the words in each column, all of which end in E. The scrambled letters in the section to the right of each column are an anagram of a word that will give you a clue to the word you are trying to find, to put in the column.

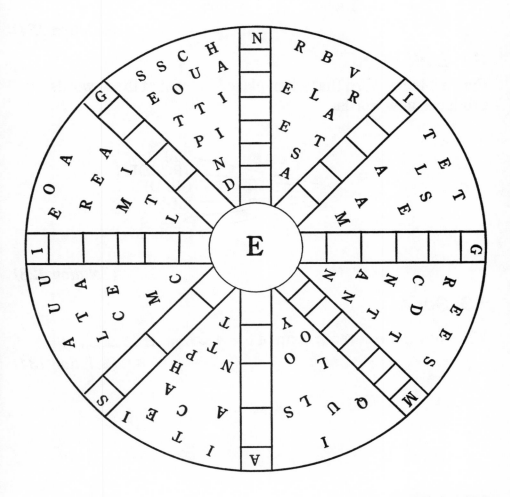

(Solution 120)

19

31 Categories

Arrange the twelve words below into four groups of three.

Copper	Knot
Fawn	Lemon
Foot	Palm
Gold	Perch
Gum	Plane
Hazel	Stone

(Solution 124)

32 Link Word

Find a 4-letter word that when placed in front of these words produces new words.

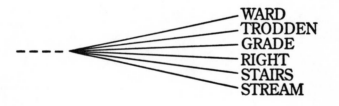

(Solution 128)

33 Series

Write down the seventh term of 6, −4, 2 ⅔, __ __ __ __.

(Solution 134)

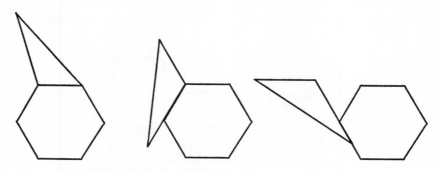

Which option below continues the above sequence?

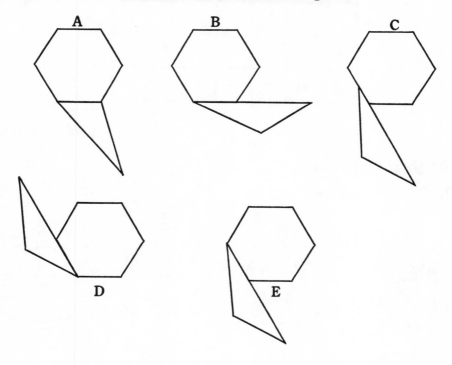

(Solution 136)

35 "Z" Puzzle

Find fourteen words in the grid. Each must have at least one "Z" in it. Words may be in any direction but always in a straight line.

M	Z	H	Z	F	W	V
U	Z	A	U	Z	H	I
Z	Y	Z	O	D	I	Z
Z	Z	Y	U	I	Z	F
Y	A	Z	L	Z	I	A
Z	M	P	U	Z	P	Z
Z	Z	B	Z	Y	Z	E

(Solution 140)

36 Odd One Out

Which is the odd one?

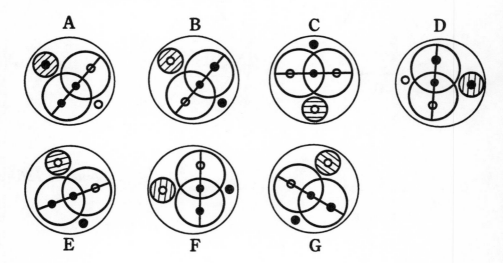

A   B   C   D

E   F   G

(Solution 144)

22

37 Anagrammed Synonyms

In each of the following, study the list of three words. Your task is to discover which two of the three words can be paired to form an anagram of a word that is a synonym of the word remaining. For example:

LEG – MEEK – NET

The words LEG and NET are an anagram of GENTLE, which is a synonym of the word remaining, MEEK.

1. SHIM – SHAM – HASH
2. SNIP – THEM – LOAD
3. FEN – OLD – PET
4. GALE – MET – STEP
5. TIN – SEQUENCES – PITH
6. MUSE – SPUR – PIT
7. RED – VERSE – COY
8. RULE – BLUE – CANE
9. TROUP – DUN – MINE
10. VANE – TITLE – AIR

(Solution 148)

38 Two in One

Two quotations by Charles Caleb Colton (1780–1832) have been fused together. All letters remain in the correct order. Can you find the two quotations?

Cross out the letters to one and the other will automatically appear.

WIHEMNIYTAOTIUHONAIVSENTOTHEHISNIGNTCEOSR AEYSSTAFYORNMOTOHFIFNLATTEGRY.

(Solution 152)

39 Brain Strain

Insert the missing numbers so that the calculations are correct, both across and down. All numbers to be inserted are less than 10 (there is no zero).

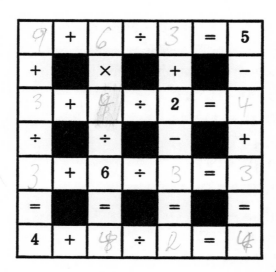

(Solution 157)

40 Hexagons

Which hexagon below continues the sequence above?

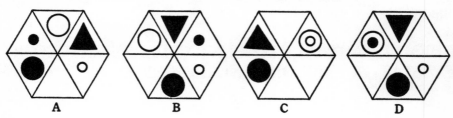

(Solution 2)

41 WOT! No Vowels?

Find sixteen words of three or more letters contained in the **grid**. Words run in any direction, backward and forward, horizontal, vertical, and diagonal, but only in a straight line.

C	W	H	Y	R	D
R	F	R	P	Y	X
Y	L	R	L	H	Y
P	Y	Y	Y	T	R
T	R	M	C	P	P
W	N	Y	Y	H	S

(Solution 6)

42 Three Too Many

Delete three of the letters in each 4-letter square in order to complete the crossword.

ST LR	E	DR TN	U	CR DP	E	DL BC
E	■	E	■	A		E
VR TD	I	SL MN	I	RL VT	O	RS DL
I	■	I	■	E	■	I
SL TV	U	TG PN	A	RG NL	E	DM PR
E	■	N	■	E	■	E
DT SR	E	SL BC	I	RG TL	E	DF NL

(Solution 11)

25

43 Committee

A committee of six is to be formed from a group of seven men and four women. How many different committees can be formed if at least two women are always included in each committee?

(Solution 14)

44 Odd One Out

Which is the odd one?

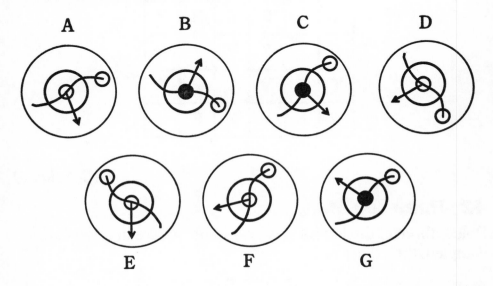

(Solution 18)

45 Subtraction

100, 90, 84, 74, 63, 53, 43, 33, ?

What number comes next?

(Solution 22)

46 Sequence

ACE, LANDING, SNIPE, REFLATE, TEMPO, ?

Which word below continues the sequence that is occurring above?

PRIDE, CHART, TRAMP, NEVER, REGAL

(Solution 26)

47 Segments

What is the smallest number of segments of equal area that the rectangle can be divided up into so that each segment contains the same number of triangles, bells, and circles?

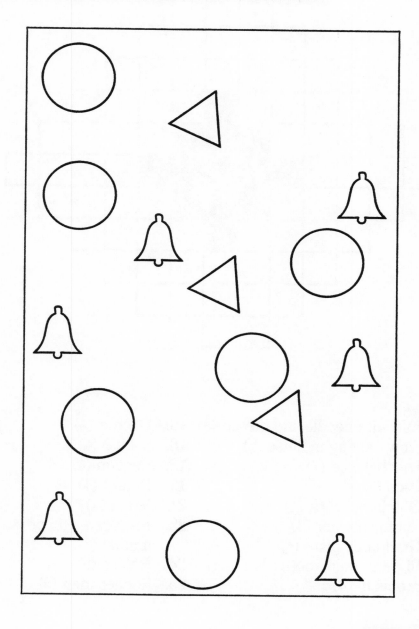

(Solution 30)

48 Word-Cross Puzzle

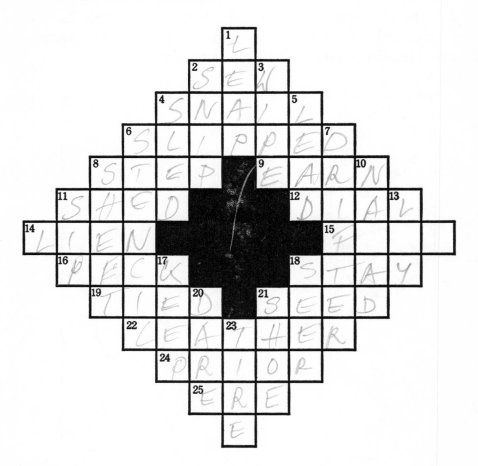

Across

2. Join with needle and thread (3)
4. Slow moving mollusc (5)
6. Lost balance (7)
8. Pace (4)
9. Obtain by work (4)
11. Roofed shelter (4)
12. Graduated plate (4)
14. Right to hold another's property (4)
15. Decree (4)
16. Nibble (4)
18. Remain (4)
19 Bound (4)
21. Grain (4)
22. Prepared skin of animal (7)
24. Before (5)
25. Sooner than (3)

Down

1. Jump (4)
2. Cut (4)
3. Rub so as to clean (4)
4. Toboggan (4)
5. Guide (4)
6. Thin sheet pierced with pattern (7)
7. Aimless person (7)
8. Broad piece of material (5)

10. Water nymph (5)
11. Drink in small portions (3)
13. Minstrel's song (3)
17. Retain (4)
18. Prophet (4)
20. Venture (4)
21. Covering for foot (4)
23. Exhaust (4)

(Solution 33)

49 Square

How many 3-letter words can you find in any direction if you arrange the following letters as the example? (Maximum possible = 12.)

A A B D G O O O T

Example:

RID   TIP
BID   DIB
AIR   BAD
PIT   DAB

```
  ↘ ↓
→ B A D ←
→ P I T ←
↗ R R D ↖
```

(Solution 38)

29

50 Missing Number

Find the missing number.

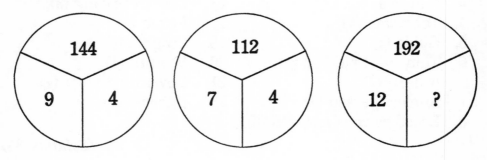

(Solution 42)

51 Bracket Word

Place two letters in each bracket so that these finish the word on the left and start the word on the right. The letters in the brackets, read downwards in pairs, will spell out a 12-letter word.

$$
\begin{array}{ccc}
\text{SA} & (\_\_) & \text{AR} \\
\text{CL} & (\_\_) & \text{LE} \\
\text{E} & (\_\_) & \text{TE} \\
\text{GRA} & (\_\_) & \text{IAL} \\
\text{T} & (\_\_) & \text{E} \\
\text{RE} & (\_\_) & \text{L}
\end{array}
$$

(Solution 46)

52 Nursery Rhyme Crossword

The clues are hidden in the narrative, in parentheses.

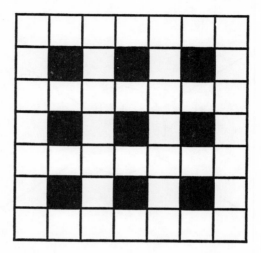

Solve the clues and determine where to place the answers in the grid.

Clues

1. Little boy blue who was one of the (Spanish ladies) brothers,
2. And (was one of those who cut fleece),
3. And who's (kidney was troubled), come blow your horn.
4. (The llamas) are in the meadow
5. (The deer) are in the corn.
   Where is the boy that looks after the sheep?
6. The lady (observes) that he has been
7. Knocked down like a (bottle-shaped pin)
8. And the (notion) is that he is asleep.

(Solution 50)

53 Symbols

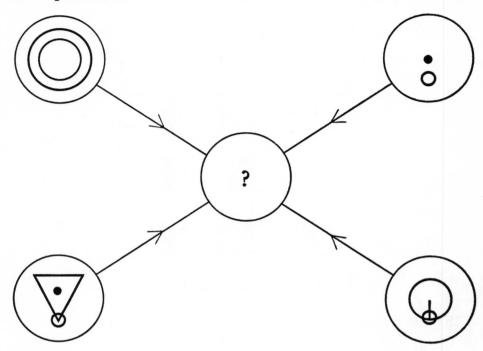

Each line and symbol that appears in the four outer circles is transferred to the middle circle according to these rules:

If a line or symbol occurs in the outer circle:

once	it is transferred
twice	it is possibly transferred
three times	it is transferred
four times	it is not transferred

Which of the circles A, B, C, D, or E, shown on the next page should appear in the middle of the diagram?

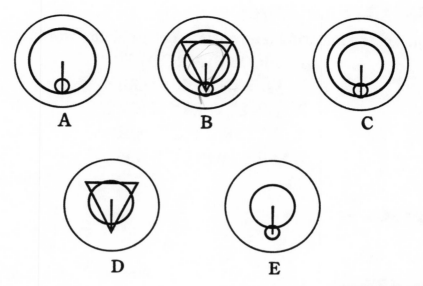

A   B   C

D   E

(Solution 54)

54 Round Table

Five people are seated at a round table. In how many different ways can the people be seated, where two arrangements in which everyone has the same neighbors are considered the same? For example, consider these arrangements of just four people:

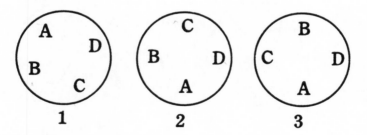

Figures 1 and 2 would be considered the same because everyone has the same neighbors, but 1 and 3 and 2 and 3 are different.

(Solution 58)

55 15-Letter Words

Each of the following is an anagram of a 15-letter word:

1. PRIDE STAIR GOT IT
2. QUEEN LAST IN COIN
3. MY LOVER IN SPEECH
4. UTTERLY PIOUS SIR
5. FIRE LION CITE CAT

(Solution 62)

56 Curve

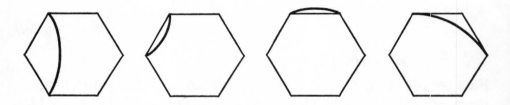

Which option below continues the above sequence?

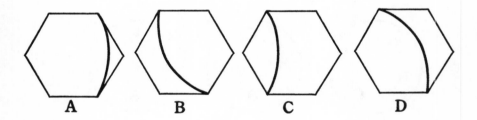

(Solution 66)

57 Common

What do all of these words have in common?

1.	HUNGER	6.	TACTIC
2.	GANNET	7.	FLOWER
3.	MARKER	8.	TABBED
4.	GETTING	9.	REPAIR
5.	GODLY	10.	UPSALA

(Solution 70)

58 Alphabet Clueless-Cross

Insert the twenty-six letters of the alphabet to complete the crossword.

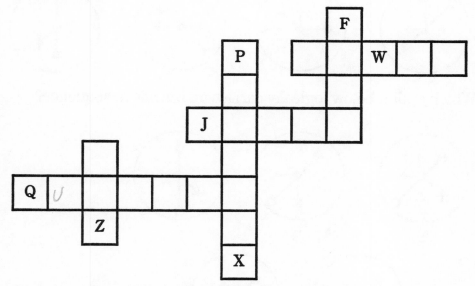

Seven of the letters have already been inserted.

A B C D E F̶ G H I J̶ K L M

N O P̶ Q̶ R S T U V W̶ X Y Z̶

(Solution 74)

59 Alphametics

Replace the letters with numbers:

$$\begin{array}{r} \text{LABEL} \\ \text{ALL} \\ +\ \text{SEAL} \\ \hline \text{BALES} \end{array}$$

(Solution 78)

60 Sequence

 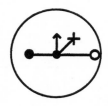  

Which option below logically carries on the above sequence?

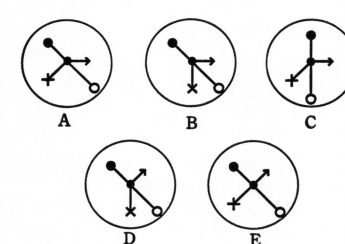

A   B   C

D   E

(Solution 82)

61 Network

Find the starting point and travel along the connecting lines in a continuous path to adjacent circles to spell out a 14-letter word. Every circle must be visited only once.

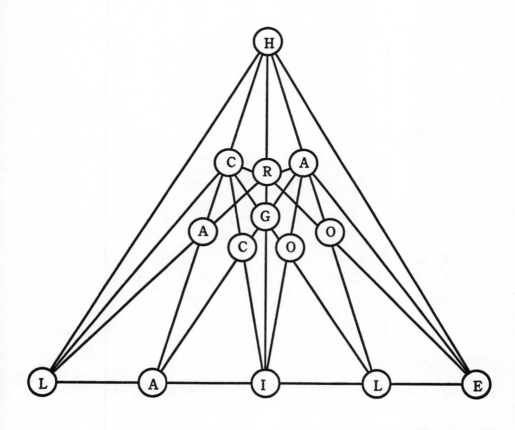

(Solution 86)

62 Array

Study the array of numbers below. What numbers should replace the question mark?

8	15	17
18	80	82
27	36	45
42	56	?

(Solution 90)

63 A Common Thread

What do these words have in common?

> HOUNDS
> PLEAT
> LINE
> TRIBE
> ROBE

(Solution 94)

64 Sequence

Which of the following options comes next in the above sequence?

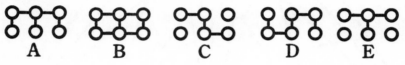

(Solution 97)

65 Countries

The thirty-two 4-letter bits can be combined to form sixteen 8-letter names of countries, past and present.

INIA	IDAD	CAMB	ZANZ
PAKI	OLIA	MALA	TANZ
RHOD	IBAR	STAN	BULG
ARIA	ZIMB	ADOS	HOND
PARA	URAS	MONG	TRIN
LAND	BARB	UGAL	ABWE
PORT	GUAY	SCOT	YSIA
ANIA	ESIA	ODIA	SARD

(Solution 102)

66 Soccer Ball

A soccer ball is to be made up of leather squares and triangles that are to be sewn together. The squares are all of the same size and triangles are also identical. How many squares and triangles are needed?

(Solution 106)

67 Niners

Solve the eight clues.

(Solution 110)

Across
1. Act of going away
4. Imparting secrets
5. To bargain

Down
1. A careful likeness
2. Unvarying person
3. Coming out

Diagonal
1. Interchange
   of embraces
5. Blackness

68 Logic

Logically, which arrangement should be placed in the final circle?

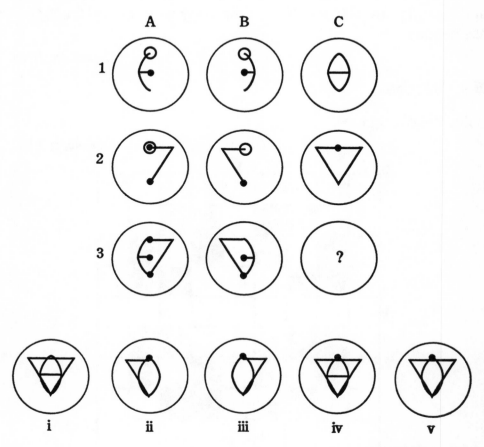

(Solution 115)

69 Percussion

Use all the letters of the sentence below once each to spell out three percussion instruments.

STAB MAN, I ACT, ARREST A MOB

(Solution 117)

70 Double Digits

In the following multiplication sum, each letter stands for a different digit; in other words, each of the digits 0–9 occurs twice.

Can you complete the sum?

```
    GHA
    FFB
   ─────
    HGD
   PJC
  PJC
 ──────
  BKKAD
```

(Solution 122)

71 Diamonds

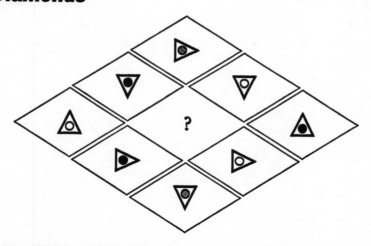

Which diamond below belongs in the middle of the above pattern?

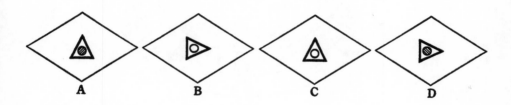

(Solution 126)

72 Anagram Theme

Arrange the fourteen words in pairs so that each pair is an anagram of a name. The seven names produced will have a linking theme. For example, if the words DIAL and THAN were in the list, they could be paired to form an anagram of THAILAND and the theme would be countries.

ANY	CAR	CLIP
HALT	HELL	JUT
LIE	LIT	ME
NOT	TOO	SEA
SEER	SOUR	

(Solution 131)

73 Zoetrope

Find a 3-letter word on the inner scale that, when transposed on to the outer scale, will produce another 3-letter word. Then try 4- and 5-letter words.

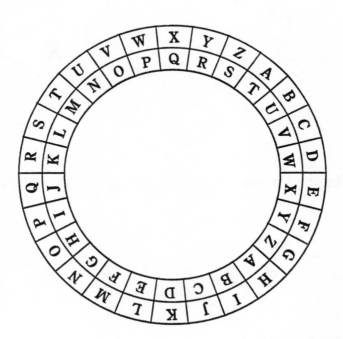

(Solution 133)

74 Darts

At the fairground one had to score 100 exactly with just six darts to win a prize. Three players scored 120, 110, 100. If every dart was a scoring dart, how did each player score?

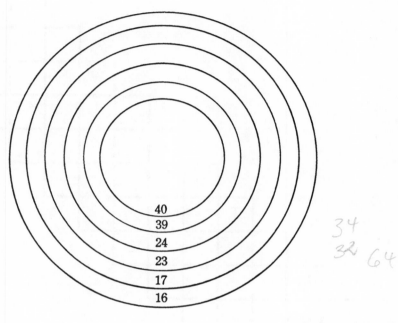

(Solution 138)

75 Dice

With a standard 6-sided die, how many throws on average are required before each of the six numbers has landed face upwards?

(Solution 142)

76 No Blanks

Place the twenty words in the crossword (some vertically, some horizontally) so that each horizontal and vertical line forms a word.

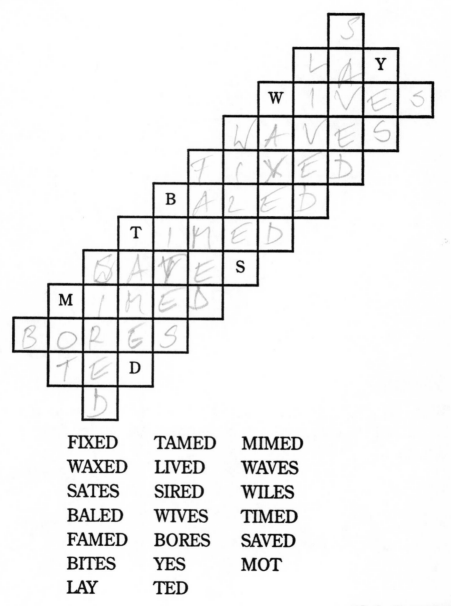

FIXED	TAMED	MIMED
WAXED	LIVED	WAVES
SATES	SIRED	WILES
BALED	WIVES	TIMED
FAMED	BORES	SAVED
BITES	YES	MOT
LAY	TED	

(Solution 147)

44

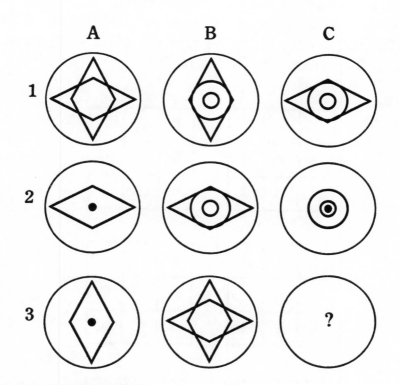

Logically, which circle fits the pattern?

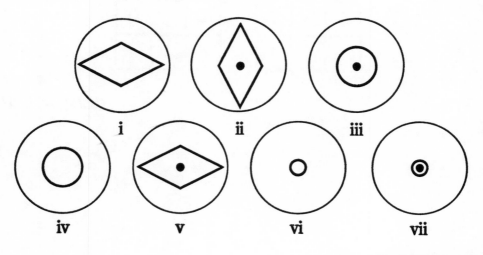

(Solution 151)

78 Square Words

In each of the following, start at a corner square and spiral clockwise around the perimeter to spell out a 9-letter word. You have to find the starting point and fill in the missing letters. You are looking for three pairs of synonyms.

	T	
A	E	R
	E	D

R		I
E	T	M
		E

I		A
	E	
R	E	S

E	N	
D		O
I		N

	I	A
E	N	T
		I

I	T	
L		O
A	I	

(Solution 154)

46

79 Clueless Crossword

In each square there are four letters. Your task is to cross out three of each four, leaving one letter in each square so that the crossword is made up in the usual way with interlocking words.

P J / A D	C Y / R D	A N / E I	V P / A E	T A / M E	E I / T L	E R / C D
I O / R N	■	I E / U X	■	O E / X R	■	E I / R A
I G / M O	R E / A N	U V / R G	O B / M E	B N / I A	G N / E L	G E / D B
I D / E N	■	E D / H S	■	N A / E P	■	H A / E L
S T / E R	T H / R I	E N / T R	E K / R A	L T / E Y	I E / R L	T E / D R

(Solution 160)

80 Saying

This saying has had all of its vowels removed. The consonants are in the correct order but have been broken up into groups of four. Replace the vowels and reconstitute the saying.

THMN	WHKN	WSHW	WLLL	WYSH
VJBT	HMNW	HKNW	SWHY	WLLL
WYSB	HSBS	S.		

(Solution 1)

81 Squares

Which option below continues the above sequence?

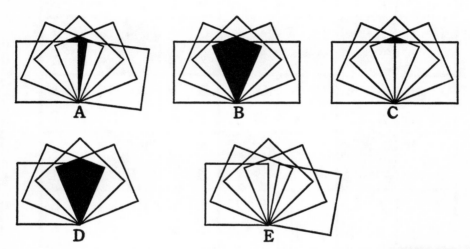

(Solution 5)

82 Horse Race

In a 7-horse race, a bookmaker has laid the following odds on six of the horses.

No. 1	4 to 1 against
No. 2	4 to 1 against
No. 3	4 to 1 against
No. 4	5 to 1 against
No. 5	6 to 1 against
No. 6	7 to 1 against
No. 7	?

What odds should he give on the seventh horse in order to give himself approximately 20% margin of profit?

(Solution 9)

83 Triple Choice

Select the correct meaning from the three choices.

1. FRANGIPANI:
   - (a) Red-flowered tree
   - (b) Mincemeat
   - (c) Bird of the partridge family

2. GLOTTIS:
   - (a) A veil
   - (b) Musical instrument
   - (c) Entrance to the windpipe

3. PERSIMMON:
   - (a) Date-plum
   - (b) Flippancy
   - (c) Cambric

4. HYPERBOLE:
   - (a) Exaggerated speech
   - (b) Part of a tree
   - (c) Living in the north

5. KINKAJOU:
   - (a) Relative of the raccoon
   - (b) Type of kingfisher
   - (c) Type of squid

6. VALGUS:
   - (a) Bow-legged
   - (b) Brave and foolish
   - (c) Smaller intestine

7. BRASSARD:
   - (a) Arm band
   - (b) Vegetable
   - (c) Braggart

8. CASSATA:
   - (a) Root yielding starch
   - (b) Kind of cinnamon
   - (c) Italian ice cream

(Solution 13)

84 Circles

Which of these fit into the blank circle to create a logical sequence?

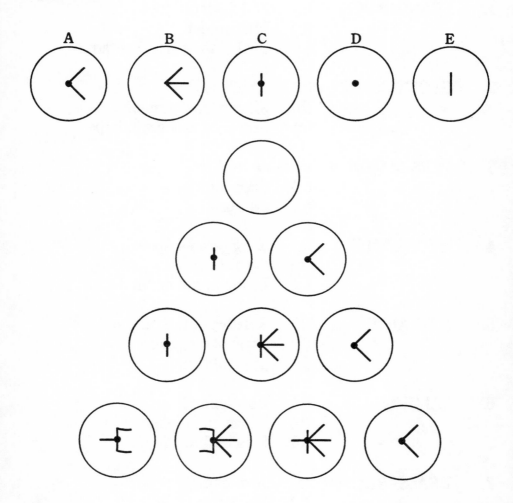

(Solution 17)

85 Two Letters

Can you think of two common English 2-letter words that double their length when pluralized and end in different suffixes?

(Solution 21)

86 Anagram Phrases

Each of the following is an anagram of a well-known phrase or saying. For example: SO NOTE HOLE = ON THE LOOSE.

1. TRAINED STONES HOW TO WHIP

2. KESTREL SHOT DOWN I BOIL TIT NOW

3. FLAT LIE WOKE POOPER

4. RAW SEVENTY TO COME LOOSE

5. TAG I OWN SHOCK

(Solution 25)

87 Missing Links

Fill in the missing numbers. The link between each of the three numbers is the same in each row, and just enough information has been provided to enable you to carry out your task.

528		16

957	485	

	161	

(Solution 31)

88 Decadice

With a pair of 10-sided dice, what are the odds of scoring at least eleven in one throw of the pair?

(Solution 34)

89 Elliptical Illusion

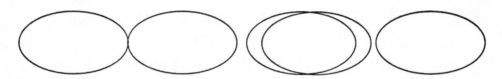

Which option below continues the above sequence?

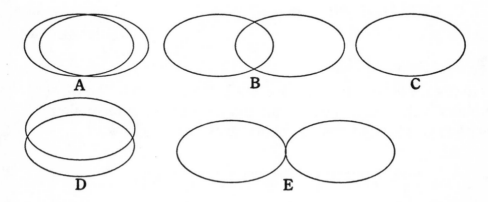

(Solution 37)

90 No Repeat Letters

The grid contains twenty-five different letters. What is the longest word that can be found by starting anywhere and working from square to square, horizontally, vertically, or diagonally, and not repeating a letter?

B	G	W	L	R
P	X	J	O	Y
K	A	T	U	F
C	V	D	Q	E
N	I	S	H	M

(Solution 41)

91 Rebuses

A rebus is an arrangement of letters or symbols to represent a familiar word or phrase. For example:

ONE   ONE
ST   ST   = NO STONE UNTURNED

Now try these.

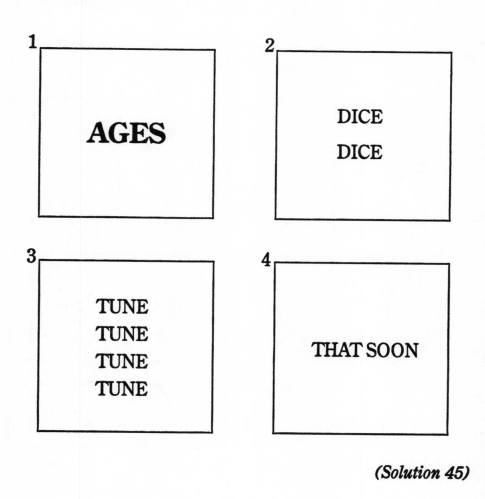

1 **AGES**

2 DICE
DICE

3 TUNE
TUNE
TUNE
TUNE

4 THAT SOON

(Solution 45)

92 Grid

Each of the nine squares marked 1A to 3C should incorporate all the lines and symbols that are shown in the outer squares A, B, or C and 1, 2, or 3. Thus 2B should incorporate all the lines and symbols in 2 and B.

One of the squares, 1A to 3C, is incorrect. Which one is it?

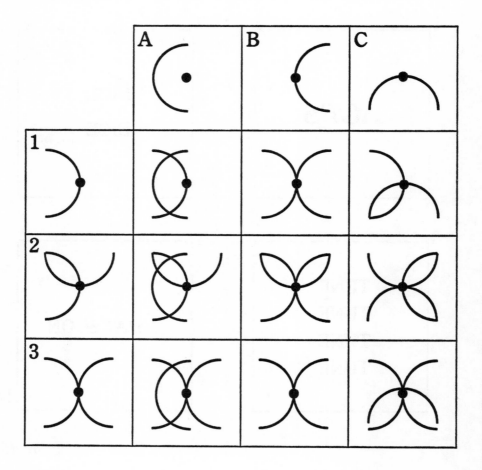

(Solution 49)

54

93 Cryptogram

The following is a straightforward substitution cryptogram in which each letter of the alphabet has been substituted for another.

QU M AQFFAL HSCPALBVL QY BMSVLICKY,
PJLIL QY FJL DMS PJC JMY YC
DXRJ MY FC GL CXF CU BMSVLI?

F.J. JXZALO

(Solution 53)

94 Magic Square

Insert the remaining numbers from 1 to 25 to form a magic square where each horizontal, vertical, and corner-to-corner line adds up to 65.

5	2	11	22	25
16	8	14	12	10
23	17	13	19	3
20	18	7	13	6
1	24	15	4	21

(Solution 57)

5 10 15 20 25

5 10 15 20 25

55

95 Pyramid Quotation

"All I know is that I am not a Marxist." – *Karl Marx*

Using all 28 letters of the above quotation only once, complete the pyramid with one 1-letter, one 2-letter, one 3-letter word, and so on.

Clues are given, but in no particular order.

Clues
- Gland in throat
- Which thing
- The Roman numeral for 1000
- Request
- Pertaining to a line around which a body revolves
- Type of cocktail
- In the direction of

(Solution 60)

96 Words

What have the following words all got in common?

TRY	VIABLE
ABLE	VISION
DURING	GRAVE
SHRINE	SIGN

(Solution 65)

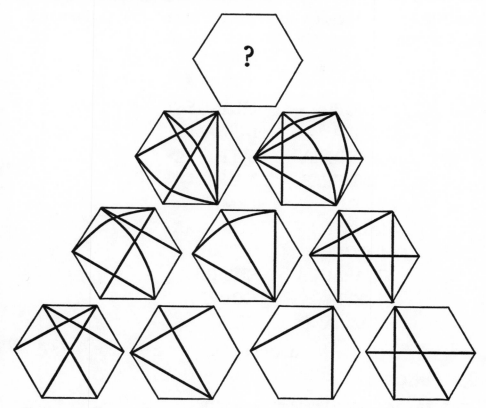

Which of the options below belongs at the top of the pyramid?

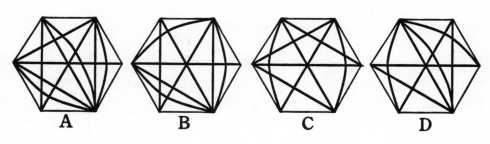

A   B   C   D

(Solution 69)

98 Mixed Currency

Match the name of each country in the left column to the name
of its currency in the right column.

ECUADOR	RUPIAH
HAITI	KWACHA
ETHIOPIA	LILANGENI
GUINEA	DIRHAM
INDONESIA	SYLI
HONDURAS	NAIRA
ISRAEL	LEMPIRA
MALAWI	CORDOBA
MOROCCO	SUCRE
NICARAGUA	SHEKEL
NIGERIA	GOURDE
SWAZILAND	BIRR

(Solution 73)

99 Fence

One man can paint a fence in six hours.
One man can paint a fence in three hours.
One man can paint a fence in two hours.
One man can paint a fence in four hours.

If they all worked together on the same fence at their respective
speeds, and assuming that they did not obstruct each other, how
long would it take them to paint it?

(Solution 77)

60

100 Nine Letters

Find the eight 9-letter words. The first three letters of each word have been given. The other two sets of three letters can be found somewhere in the letter groupings below.

1.	TAU		
2.	PIT		
3.	NIT		
4.	LAI		
5.	HAR		
6.	DIA		
7.	CHA		
8.	BLO		

KER	TOL
SIS	ANG
ILY	PIC
HIP	NTE
OGY	TCH
UER	CHF
ORK	RDS
USE	GNO

(Solution 81)

101 Grid

Each of the nine squares marked 1A to 3C should incorporate all the lines and symbols that are shown in the outer squares A, B, or C and 1, 2, or 3. Thus 2B should incorporate all the lines and symbols in 2 and B.

One of the squares, 1A to 3C, is incorrect. Which one is it?

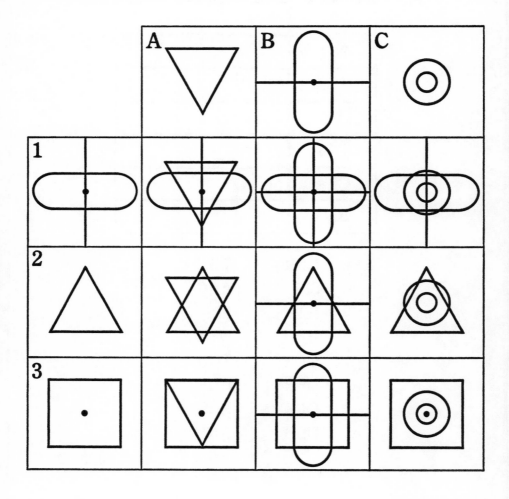

(Solution 85)

60

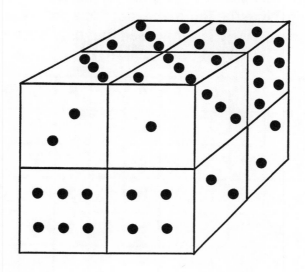

Eight dice are stacked together to form a cube. One example of how this is possible is shown above. In how many different ways is it possible to stack the cubes together in this way?

Note that simply changing two dice and retaining the same position of the spots is not considered a different assembly since the spots that appear on the outside of the cube will be identical and thus it will, in appearance, be the same cube.

If, however, a die is rotated in any way, this is considered different. For example:

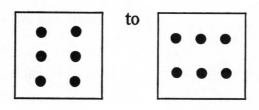

(Solution 88)

103 Lads and Lasses

Each horizontal line contains the jumbled letters of a boy's name and each vertical line the jumbled letters of a girl's name. Find the twenty names. Every letter is used, but only once each.

A	I	A	O	L	B	I	S	L	E
A	Y	L	R	A	L	P	R	H	I
T	E	O	S	C	S	Z	H	T	A
R	E	U	L	N	W	T	S	I	C
H	I	N	D	T	S	E	A	E	K
Y	W	H	R	I	R	M	N	A	E
L	E	A	D	K	A	E	S	C	R
A	D	S	V	A	L	G	N	I	L
U	S	A	I	T	J	I	N	I	O
A	N	S	R	I	Y	N	A	A	B

(Solution 93)

104 Group Puzzle

Arrange the following words into groups of three.

- Porbeagle
- Hyacinth
- Corncrake
- Tumbrel
- Cassowary
- Barkentine
- Pinnace
- Snapper
- Popinjay
- Argosy
- Carbuncle
- Cachalot
- Grayling
- Tonneau
- Pichiciago
- Capybara
- Hackney
- Iridium

(Solution 98)

105 Arcs Matrix

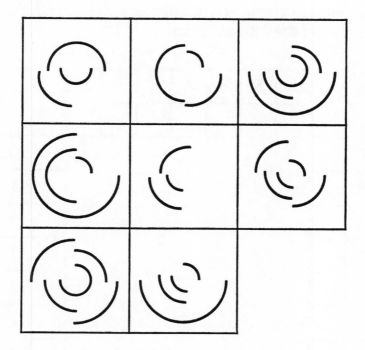

Choose the missing tile from the options below.

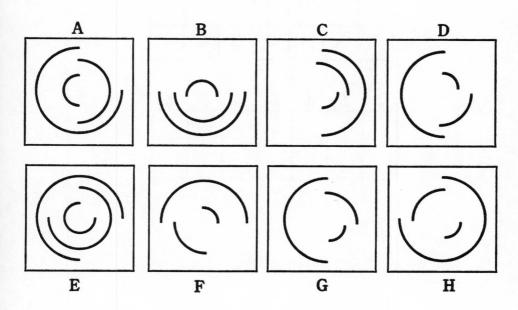

(Solution 100)

106 Enigmagram

Solve the four anagrams of types of boats. Transfer the arrowed letters and solve the fifth anagram.

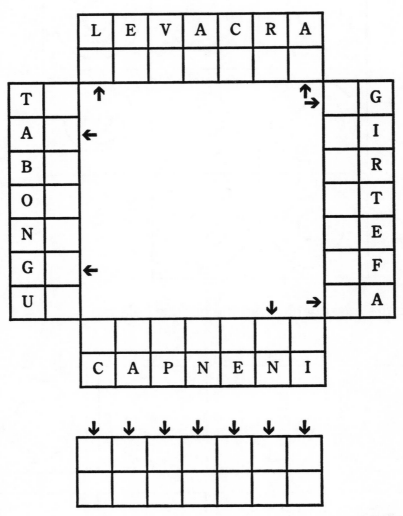

(Solution 105)

64

107 Tennis

At the local tennis club the following members entered the championships for singles and doubles.

	Men	Women
Men's Singles	41	
Women's Singles		29
Men's Doubles	20 pairs	
Women's Doubles		14 pairs
Mixed Doubles	26 pairs	26 pairs

They were knockout competitions, so by using byes the numbers first had to be reduced to 32 – 16 – 8 – 4 – 2 – winner.

How many matches had been played by the end of Championship Day?

(Solution 109)

108 No Repeat Letters

The grid below contains twenty-five different letters of the alphabet. What is the longest word that can be found by starting anywhere and working from square to square horizontally, vertically, and diagonally, and not repeating a letter?

B	V	R	U	Q
M	Y	I	E	J
L	N	P	W	F
G	T	O	K	S
H	X	D	C	A

(Solution 113)

109 Links Jigsaw Puzzle

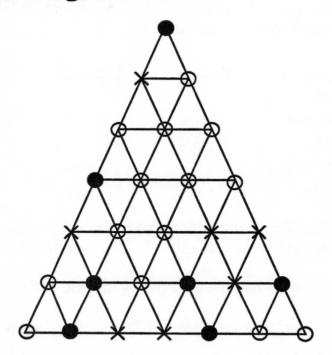

Place the twelve segment links below over the triangular grid, above, in such a way that each link symbol is covered by exactly the same symbol. The connecting segments must not be rotated. Note that not all the connecting lines will be covered.

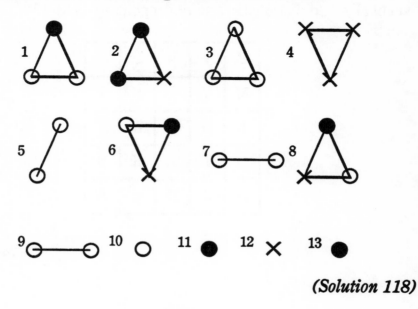

(Solution 118)

110 Cubes

Each horizontal and vertical line contains the digits of a 5-figure cube number. The digits are always in the correct order, but not necessarily adjacent. Each digit is used once only, and they are all used. Find the twenty 5-figure cube numbers.

6	4	1	6	6	8	5	6	1	5
8	3	3	5	7	9	1	7	3	7
9	1	3	2	1	5	2	9	7	5
1	9	2	1	4	1	6	7	5	4
9	2	4	1	3	8	8	5	9	8
9	3	8	7	0	3	9	3	6	7
2	3	2	9	8	2	6	7	6	8
5	0	4	5	9	3	1	0	7	9
1	4	5	6	8	4	8	2	5	2
1	1	0	2	6	4	3	7	6	8

(Solution 121)

111 Sequence

What number comes next in this sequence?

149, 162, 536, 496, 481, ?

(Solution 125)

112 Sequence

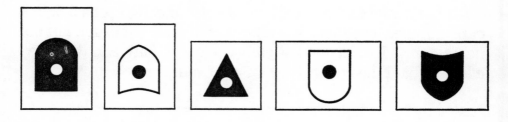

Which option below continues the above sequence?

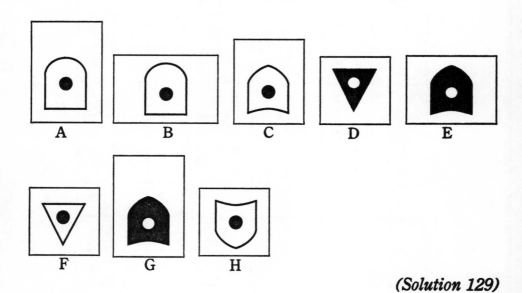

(Solution 129)

113 Cliff

The height of a cliff can be measured by dropping a stone from the top and timing its descent. How is this calculated?

(Solution 130)

114 Tampa

Place the letters in the grid to spell five 5-letter words.
Five letters have been placed. Clues are not necessarily in the correct order.

1.	T					A A A A E
2.		A				G G H K L
3.			M			L M M M M
4.				P		N O P P T
5.					A	T U U V Y

Clues
Fleshy body in throat
A pasty or doughy mass
A dance
Pure water
Tidy

(Solution 137)

115 Hidden Lands

Can you find the words that include the names of these countries?

```
 • W A • • L E S
 • • • • • T U N I S •
 • • T • • • O G • • • O •
C • • U • B A • • • •
 • • C H A • D
N A T • • • A L • • •
 • • I T • A L • Y
 • • • O M • • • • A • • • N
 • • P E R • • • U •
C O N G • • • • • • • • O • •
```

(Solution 141)

69

116 Links Jigsaw Puzzle

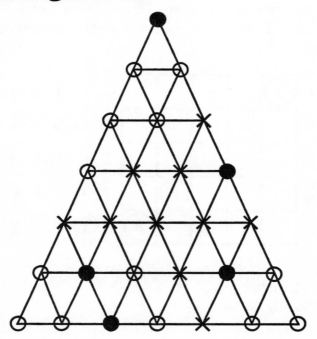

Place the twelve segment links below over the triangular grid, above, in such a way that each link symbol is covered by exactly the same symbol. The connecting segments must not be rotated. Note that not all the connecting lines will be covered.

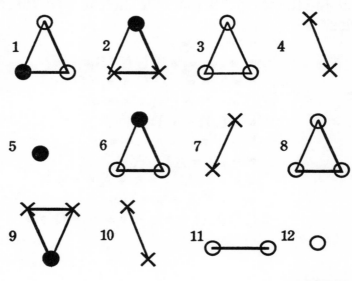

(Solution 145)

117 Margana

If we presented you with the words MAR, AM, and FAR and asked you to find the shortest English word that contained all the letters from which these words could be produced, we would expect you to come up with the word FARM.

Here is another list of words:

STAIN, YES, COUNT, CLEAN

What is the shortest English word from which all these words can be produced?

(Solution 149)

118 Unscramble a Sequence

Start at the starred square and work from square to square horizontally, vertically, and diagonally to unscramble a meaningful sequence. Every square must be visited once only. Finish at the top left-hand square.

	3	0	1	6	2	8
	5	1	5	3	1	3
	1	6	1	2	6	5
	3	2	★	4	5	5
	1	1	0	1	7	6
	5	0	1	8	9	6

(Solution 153)

STAIYECUNL

119 Track Word

Work around the track to find a 14-letter word. You have to provide the missing letters and find the starting point. The word might appear reading clockwise or counterclockwise, and the overlapping letter appears twice.

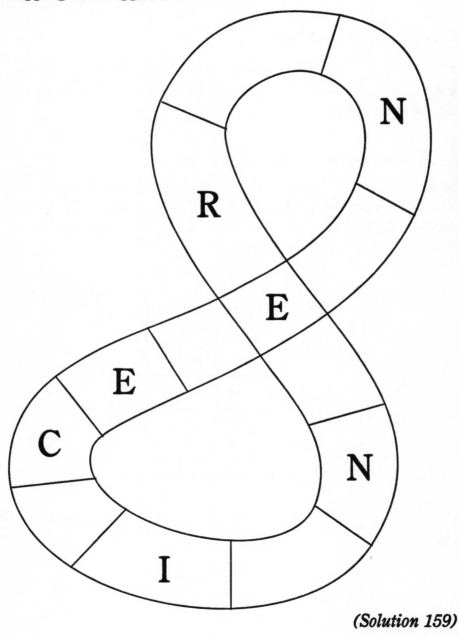

(Solution 159)

120 Octagons

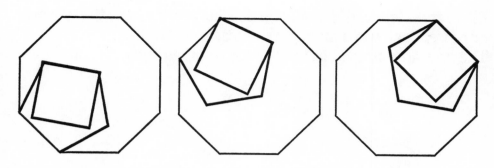

Which octagon below continues the above sequence?

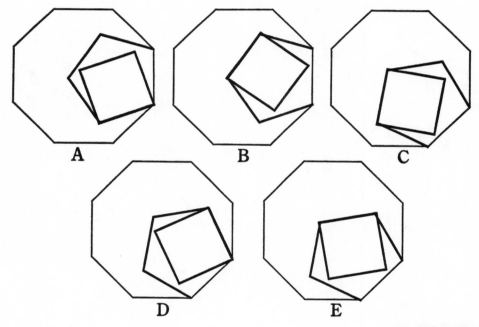

A   B   C

D   E

(Solution 3)

121 1984

The ten digits 0, 1, 2, 3, 4, 5, 6, 7, 8, 9 can be arranged into numbers and added to equal many totals but nobody has ever made them equal 1984. However, nine digits can equal 1984. Which digit has to be omitted?

(Solution 7)

122 "X" Puzzle

Move from letter to letter along the lines to spell out thirty words or more. Each word must have at least one "X" in it.
The arcs around the circumference count as lines.

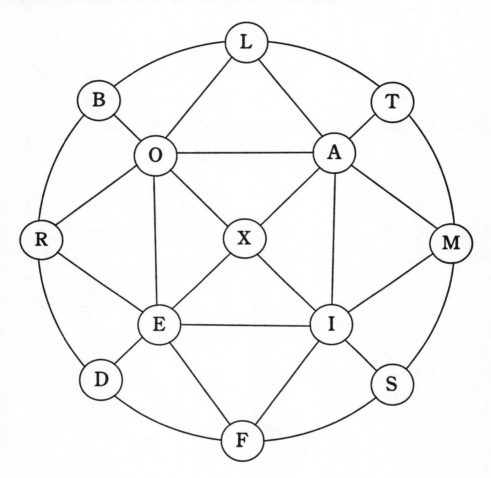

(Solution 12)

123 Playing Cards

Here is a pack of fifty-two playing cards. Each card has been designated a letter. Select no more than twelve cards and arrange into a word to make the highest score that you can. The maximum score possible is 160.

		(11)	(12)	(13)	(15)

POINTS	2	3	4	5	6	7	8	9	10	J	Q	K	A
♡	L	R	S	Z	H	X	Q	J	C	U	P	I	T
◇	B	M	A	Z	Y	G	V	E	Q	J	A	N	I
♤	S	D	N	F	Y	X	K	W	D	K	T	R	E
♣	G	W	L	O	C	P	H	B	M	F	U	O	V
POINTS	2	3	4	5	6	7	8	9	10	J	Q	K	A

(SUITS shown at left)

		(11)	(12)	(13)	(15)

(Solution 15)

124 Biblical Characters

Complete the names of the biblical characters below. Only alternate letters are shown. Then rearrange the first letters of each name to find a tenth biblical character.

• I • A •
• P • R • I •
• A • N • B • S
• A • O •
• I • O • H •
• E • J • M • N
• H • D • A • H
• B • A • A •
• E • O •

(Solution 19)

75

125 Treasure

The treasure is on square D7. You have to find the starting square that will lead to the treasure.

Instructions are read as follows:

2S ⎫ means 2 squares South
1E ⎭ and 1 square East

6N ⎫ means 6 squares North
6W ⎭ and 6 squares West

N

	A	B	C	D	E	F	G
1	2S 2E	2S 4E	3S 4E	3S 1W	6S 3W	5S 1W	6S 6W
2	1N 1E	2S 1W	4S 4E	1N 1E	5S 2W	4S 4W	1N 1W
3	1N 3E	3S 1W	3S 3E	2N 3W	2S 2W	2N 2W	1S 2W
4	2N 2E	3N 1E	1N 1W	3S 3E	1S 1W	1N 2W	2N 6W
5	3N 4E	2S 2E	1N 1E	1S 1W	2S 1E	2N 1E	2N 6W
6	1N 4E	3N 3E	2N 1W	1S 1E	1N 3W	1N 1E	2N 1W
7	5N 5E	2N 1W	1N 1E	Ⓣ	2N 1E	5N 1E	5N 5W

W ⟶ E

S

(Solution 23)

76

126   The Palindromic Biennium

A palindrome is a word, phrase, or number that reads the same both backwards and forwards. For example,

MADAM I'M ADAM, CIVIC, or 1881.

When is the next time that two consecutive palindromic years will occur?

(Solution 27)

127   Word Compasses

Place the letters in the correct sectors in each quadrant to obtain two 8-letter words, one reading clockwise and the other counterclockwise. The two words are antonyms.

NE : EIFA
SE : NLUG
NW : LANC
SW : RUGY

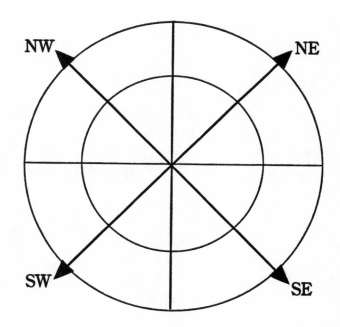

(Solution 32)

128 Triangles

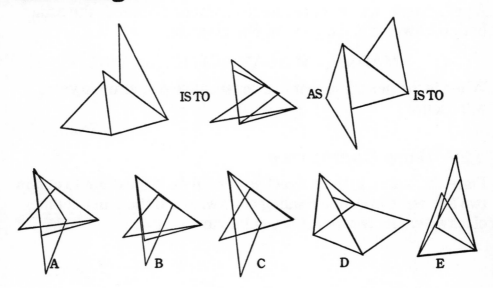

IS TO ... AS ... IS TO

A   B   C   D   E

(Solution 35)

129 Fish

Add the same letter to each side. Rearrange the letters to form
the 2-word name of a fish.

Example: WINBOA   (R)   TOTU
Answer: RAINBOW TROUT

ADDED LETTER

BINGKA	RAHK
DIPERS	SACHIF
DETNIP	TONGRED
DUCETS	FUNLODE
FRYTUTLE	MARE
CARTES	RANGE
SHOE	LACEMEK
DRABE	FAGHIS
NOBW	PEGOR
NIPY	HOSEARE

(Solution 39)

130 Aliens

One hundred aliens attended the intergalactic meeting on earth.

73 had two heads
28 had three eyes
21 had four arms
12 had two heads and three eyes
9 had three eyes and four arms
8 had two heads and four arms
3 had all three unusual features

How many had none of these unusual features?

(Solution 43)

131 Saying

Letters have been omitted from the saying. See if you can fill them in the grid.

A		W	A		S	
O	R		I		E	
O	U	R			E	
I	E		N	O		H
I	N		A	N	N	
	S		H	E		S
O	M		C			

E	M	T
F	M	U
G	N	V
G	O	Y
H	S	Y
L	T	Y

(Solution 47)

79

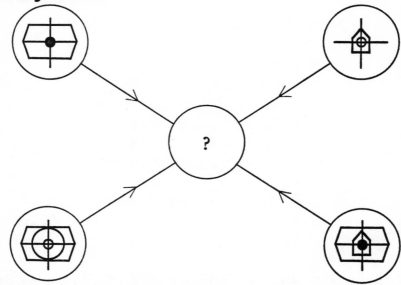

Each line and symbol that appears in the four outer circles is transferred to the middle circle according to these rules:

If a line or symbol occurs in the outer circle:

once	it is transferred
twice	it is possibly transferred
three times	it is transferred
four times	it is not transferred

Which of the circles A, B, C, D, or E, shown below, should appear in the middle of the diagram?

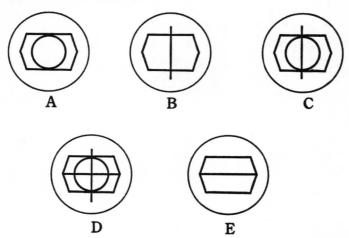

(Solution 51)

133 Found in America

All the following are anagrams of things that can be found in the United States of America.

1. ACHED NOT A BAY
2. TALES AND TINS
3. A FEISTY HOTEL BUTTER
4. WASTE SHEER ROT
5. SLUM ABOUT NINE
6. AVERSE A DRAIN
7. HELL YET VADA
8. DID GET COY
9. POUR LAD A COOL TEA
10. BARE ON GOUT

(Solution 55)

134 Work it Out

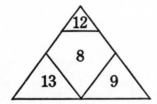 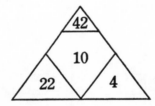 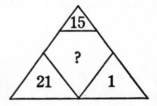

Work out the number that should replace the question mark in the third triangle.

(Solution 59)

135 Three Birds and a Fish

Rearrange all of the letters below into three birds and a fish.

HARD   BEHIND   SIT   SAFER

(Solution 63)

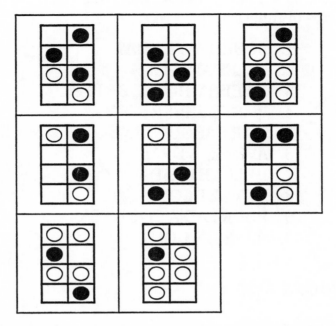

Choose the correct missing tile from the options below.

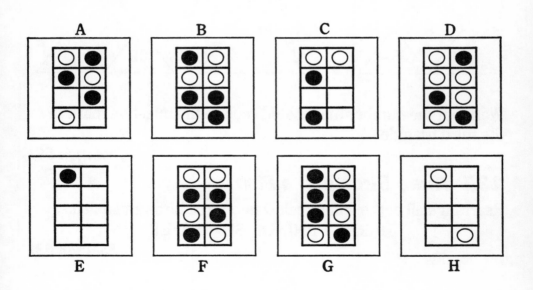

(Solution 67)

137 Bull's Eye

Find the answer to the sixteen questions.

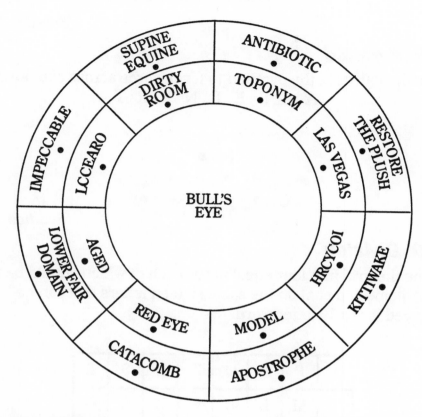

1. Vegetable (anag.)
2. One familiar word (anag.)
3. Person named after a place
4. Salvages (anag.)
5. West to East overnight
6. Dormitory (anag.)
7. A direct address to a dead person
8. Opposite of peccable
9. Sleeping donkey
10. Kidnapped (4 consecutive letters of the alphabet missing)
11. Tomb
12. Boat (anag.)
13. The upholsterers (anag.)
14. Species of gull
15. Cheesecake
16. Opposite to biotic (relating to life)

(Solution 71)

138 Cycle

How many revolutions are made by a 28" bicycle wheel over one mile?

(Solution 75)

139 Pyramid

Place the letters in the pyramid to form words across and down.

A A B E E N R R T

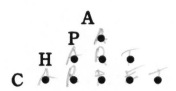

(Solution 79)

140 Division

Divide the grid into four equal parts, each of which should be the same shape and contain the same sixteen letters that can be arranged into a 16-letter word.

S	P	P	O	T	S	S	R
T	M	E	U	S	U	S	O
U	E	U	U	P	U	R	T
S	P	S	E	P	U	O	U
S	O	R	S	E	E	N	P
R	M	S	N	M	N	S	U
N	S	E	U	M	S	E	E
T	S	P	U	S	P	S	U

(Solution 83)

141 Symbols

Which of the circles A, B, C, D, or E should appear in the middle circle?

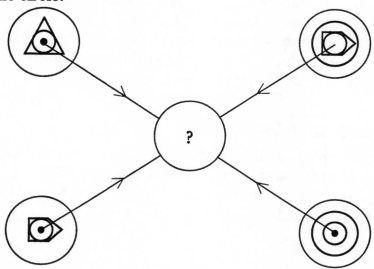

Each line and symbol that appears in the four outer circles is transferred to the middle circle according to these rules:

If a line or symbol occurs in the outer circle:

once	it is transferred
twice	it is possibly transferred
three times	it is transferred
four times	it is not transferred

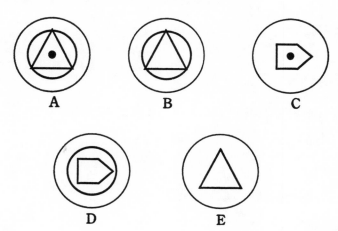

(Solution 87)

142 Sweepstakes

A bag contains nine balls numbered 1–9. To decide the winner of a sweepstakes, six balls are drawn out successively and their numbers written down to form a 6-digit number. Each person is allowed one ticket only, which contains a 6-digit number that must correspond with the 6-digit number drawn to win the first prize. What are the odds against winning?

(Solution 91)

143 Piecemeal Quotation

The quotation below, by J. M. Keynes, has been broken down into 2-letter bits that have been arranged in the alphabetical order of the bits. Restore the letters to their correct place to reconstruct the quotation. For example:

$$- - - - / - - - / - - - - -$$

Bits: EQ, FI, ND, TE, TH, UO
Answer: Find the Quote.

$$- - - - - - - - - / - - - / - - - - / - - - - /$$
$$- - - - - - - - - - / - - - / - - - / - / - - - /$$
$$- - - / - - / - - - - / - - - / - / - - - .$$

AD, AM, AN, AV, AY, EF, EN, ER, ES, EV, FW,
GS, HI, IN, IV, KF, LL, OR, OR, OU, TO, UP,
US, UT, WH, YO, YO .

(Solution 95)

144 Series

Which of the alternatives below should replace the "?" ?

S – SC – SSS – SS – SSSS – SSS – C – ?

Choose from:

SC	SS	SSS	C	C	SSS
P	T	H	O	U	Z

(Solution 99)

145 Circles

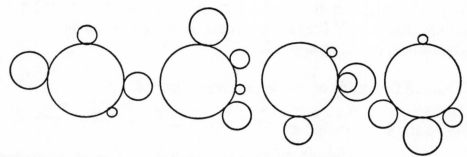

Which option below continues the above sequence?

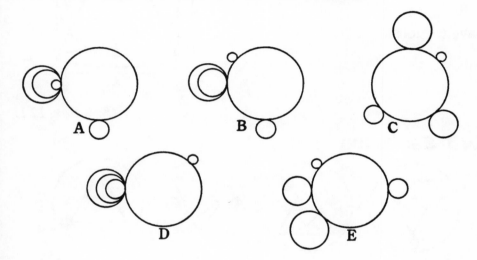

(Solution 103)

146 Ten Letters

Strike out ten letters to leave a word that can be found in the dictionary.

C O T N E G N R L A E T T U L T A T E I O R N S S

(Solution 107)

147 Cylinder

A cylinder whose height is the same as its diameter contains a sphere that exactly fits inside. A cone also exactly fits inside when the sphere is removed.

What are the ratios of the respective volumes?

For example: cylinder 2.75
                      sphere 1.75
                      cone 1

Have a guess!

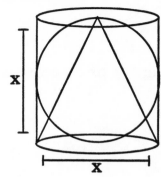

(Solution 111)

148 Sequence

  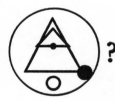

Which option continues the above sequence?

    A   B   C

    D   E

(Solution 116)

149 Letter Search

K	D	G	A	N
R	O	U	L	E
P	J	C	T	Q
Y	S	F	B	I
H	V	M	X	W

1. What letter is two above the letter immediately to the right of the letter three below the letter two to the right of the letter immediately above the letter "J"?

2. What letter is immediately to the left of the letter immediately below the letter two to the left of the letter two below the letter three to the right of the letter three letters above the letter "S"?

3. What letter is two to the right of the letter immediately above the letter two to the left of the letter two letters above the letter immediately to the right of the letter immediately below the letter which is midway between the letters "T" and "V"?

4. What letter is two to the left of the letter immediately above the letter two to the left of the letter immediately to the right of the letter immediately below the letter that is midway between the letter two to the right of the letter "D" and the letter immediately to the left of the letter "W"?

(Solution 119)

150 Plurals

Can you find a word that is a plural of a word that is also a plural?

(Solution 123)

151 Nines

When the sum of the digits of a number will divide exactly by nine, then the number itself will also divide by nine. For example, 2673; 2 + 6 + 7 + 3 = 18. With this in mind, place the digits into the grid so that each horizontal and vertical line, when read both forwards and backwards, will divide exactly by nine.

```
1  1  1
2  2  2
3  3
4  4
5  5  5
6  6  6  6
7  7  7
8  8
9  9  9
```

(Solution 127)

152 Analogy

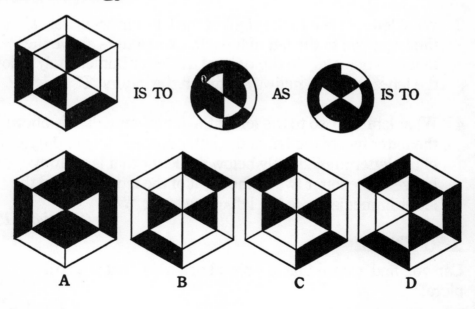

IS TO ⬤ AS ⬤ IS TO

A   B   C   D

(Solution 132)

153 Nine Letters

The twenty-five words can be grouped into twelve pairs of words that belong together, which will leave one odd word. Find the odd word.

GUINEVERE   CATAMOUNT
FOMALHAUT   FARANDOLE
SHILLALAH   HIPPODROME
SHELDRAKE   FRICASSEE
AUBERGINE   NICOTIANA
MERCENARY   DROMEDARY
BODYGUARD   ALDEBARAN
ARGONAUTS   WHITEBEAM
MARSUPIAL   MONOTREME
JACARANDA   MANGETOUT
PYRACANTHA   MERGANSER
SUCCOTASH   DERRINGER
POUSSETTE

(Solution 135)

154 Twelve Letters

Thirty 4-letter bits can be formed into ten 12-letter words. (Four of the answers are hyphenated.)

OGRA   HIGH   RDEN
OARD   MENT   NDED
GENE   PHIC   FLEB
AWED   MARK   SHUF
ERNJ   WISH   PHON
SHRE   ICAL   ENCE
NESS   PING   STEP
SING   ELOC   LEHA
NIST   LANT   COMM
UTIO   ETGA   ALOG

(Solution 139)

155 Boat

A boat is to be rowed straight across a river, which has a constant current that flows downstream at six meters a minute. The rower makes a constant effort, which through still water is at the rate of ten meters a minute.

In which direction must the rower head and how far will he travel across the river in one minute?

(Solution 143)

156 Circles

Which of these fits into the blank circle to carry on a logical sequence?

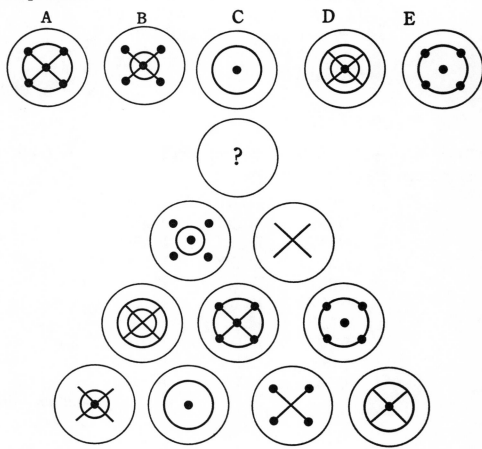

(Solution 146)

157 Synonyms

In each of the following a number of synonyms of the keyword are shown. Take one letter from each of the synonyms to find a further synonym of the keyword. The letters appear in the correct order.

1. Keyword : FAST
   Synonyms : HASTY, MERCURIAL, RAPID, BRISK, SWIFT, FLEET, WINGED

2. Keyword : EVIDENT
   Synonyms : PATENT, MANIFEST, BLATANT, CONSPICUOUS, PLAIN, OBVIOUS, VISIBLE, CLEAR

3. Keyword : ECCENTRIC
   Synonyms : ERRATIC, BIZARRE, PECULIAR, ABERRANT, FREAKISH, IDIOSYNCRATIC, IRREGULAR, ODD, ANOMALOUS, OUTLANDISH

4. Keyword : HAZY
   Synonyms : OVERCAST, NEBULOUS, DIM, BLURRY, OBSCURE, DULL

5. Keyword : SCURRILOUS
   Synonyms : OBSCENE, SCANDALOUS, RIBALD, INFAMOUS, INDECENT, VITUPERATIVE, COARSE, INSULTING, OFFENSIVE

(Solution 150)

158 Twist and Turn

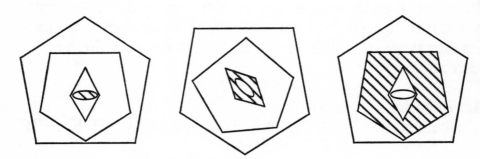

Which option below continues the above sequence?

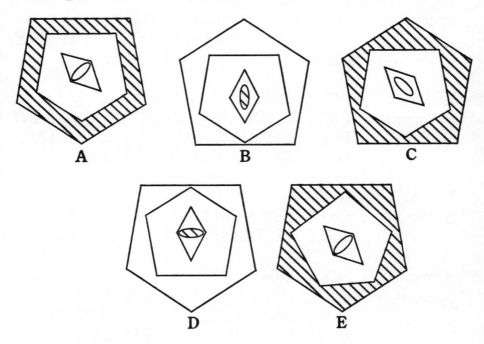

A   B   C

D   E

(Solution 158)

159 Synonym Circles

Work clockwise to find a pair of synonyms. You must provide the missing letters.

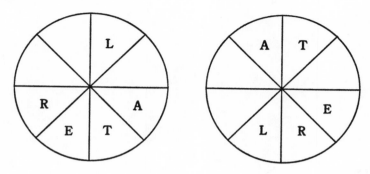

(Solution 155)

160 Sensible

Start at the middle square and move from square to square horizontally, vertically, or diagonally to spell out seven synonyms of SENSIBLE. Visit every square once and only once. Finish at the top right-hand square.

U	D	P	O	I	A	E	→
E	R	L	N	T	N	S	
N	C	A	A	T	I	C	
T	Y	A	★	R	S	L	
S	R	N	N	I	I	A	
H	W	E	D	C	U	E	
D	J	U	I	O	R	S	

(Solution 156)

The
Solutions
2

(Solutions are presented out of numerical sequence
so that reading the answer to one puzzle will not inadvertently
reveal the answer to the next.)

1 Saying

"The man who knows how will always have a job. The man who knows why will always be his boss." *(Anon.)*

(Puzzle 80)

2 Hexagons

D. Each symbol moves in its own sequence:

 moves one clockwise, then two clockwise, then three clockwise, etc.

 moves one counterclockwise, then two counterclockwise, then three counterclockwise, etc.

 moves one counterclockwise, then two clockwise, then one counterclockwise, etc.

○ moves one counterclockwise each time.

● moves one clockwise each time (in the fourth hexagon this symbol is hidden by the triangle).

(Puzzle 40)

3 Octagons

D. The pentagon moves two sides of the octagon clockwise each time. The square moves one side of the pentagon counterclockwise each time.

(Puzzle 120)

4 Alternative Crossword

C	O	N	I	F	E	R	S
O	■	■	C	O	S	■	E
S	O	■	E	A	T	■	R
S	I	R	■	L	O	P	E
E	L	A	N	■	P	E	N
T	■	V	O	W	■	W	E
E	■	E	V	A	■	■	L
D	I	L	A	T	O	R	Y

(Puzzle 1)

5 Squares

E. Another square is added at each stage and this rotates by half the length of the side of a square clockwise at each stage, and all squares are attached to the same pivot. Only the section common to all squares at a particular stage is shaded.

(Puzzle 81)

6 WOT! No Vowels?

Wry	Wryly	Hymn
Thy	Fly	Pry
Fry	Shy	Spy
Pyx	Crypt	Why
Cry	Dry	
Spry	Myrrh	

(Puzzle 41)

7 1984

5:

```
  869
  702
  413
─────
 1984
```

(Puzzle 121)

8 Batteries

$$\frac{1}{10} \times \frac{1}{10} \times \frac{1}{10} = \frac{1}{1000}$$

1 in one thousand chance.

(Puzzle 2)

9 Horse Race

No.	Odds	Stake to win 100, including stake returned
1	4 – 1	20
2	4 – 1	20
3	4 – 1	20
4	5 – 1	16.67
5	6 – 1	14.28
6	7 – 1	12.5
7	5 – 1	16.67

```
120.12  total stake
100.00  less payout
─────
 20.12  profit
```

$$\frac{20}{100} = 20\%$$

(Puzzle 82)

10 Link Word

House

(Puzzle 3)

11 Three Too Many

R	E	D	U	C	E	D
E	■	E	■	A	■	E
V	I	S	I	T	O	R
I	■	I	■	E	■	I
S	U	G	A	R	E	D
E	■	N	■	E	■	E
D	E	S	I	R	E	D

(Puzzle 42)

12 "X" Puzzle

Tax	Taxi	Axis	Taxis
Taxed	Axe	Axed	Six
Fix	Fixed	Fixer	Rex
Exam	Maxim	Maxims	Maxi
Maxis	Ax	Ox	Box
Boxed	Boxer	Lax	Lox
Laxed	Exalt	Exams	Mix
Mixed	Mixer	Laxer	Taxied

(Puzzle 122)

13 Triple Choice

1. (a) Red-flowered tree
2. (c) Entrance to the windpipe
3. (a) Date-plum
4. (a) Exaggerated speech
5. (a) Relative of the raccoon
6. (a) Bow-legged
7. (a) Arm band
8. (c) Italian ice cream

(Puzzle 83)

14 Committee

Assume two women and four men.

Then

$$\frac{4 \times 3}{2 \times 1} \times \frac{7 \times 6 \times 5 \times 4}{4 \times 3 \times 2 \times 1} = 6 \times 35 = 210$$

Assume three women and three men.

Then

$$\frac{4 \times 3 \times 2}{3 \times 2 \times 1} \times \frac{7 \times 6 \times 5}{3 \times 2 \times 1} = 4 \times 35 = 140$$

Assume four women and two men.

Then

$$\frac{4 \times 3 \times 2 \times 1}{4 \times 3 \times 2 \times 1} \times \frac{7 \times 6}{2 \times 1} = 1 \times 21 = 21$$

$$\overline{371}$$

Can be written as

$$\frac{4! - 2!}{2!} \times \frac{7! - 3!}{4!}$$

$$+ \quad \frac{4! - 1!}{3!} \times \frac{7! - 4!}{3!}$$

$$+ \quad \frac{4!}{4!} \times \frac{7! - 5!}{2!}$$

(Puzzle 43)

15 Playing Cards

Score	VITUPERATION
AC	15 - V
AD	15 - I
AH	15 - T
QC	12 - U
QH	12 - P
AS	15 - E
KS	13 - R
QD	12 - A
QS	12 - T
KH	13 - I
KC	13 - O
KD	13 - N
	160

(Puzzle 123)

16 Common Clues

They are pairs of homonyms: Pique, Peak; Tool, Tulle; Need, Knead; Band, Banned; Review, Revue; Gauge, Gage; Invade, Inveighed.

(Puzzle 4)

17 Circles

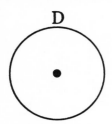

Starting at the base, each pair of circles determines the one above. Only similar symbols are carried forward.

(Puzzle 84)

18 Odd One Out

C:
A is the same as D
B is the same as G
E is the same as F

(Puzzle 44)

19 Biblical Characters

Hiram, Ephraim, Barnabas, Aaron, Timothy, Benjamin, Shadrach, Abraham, Herod.
Anagram: BATHSHEBA

(Puzzle 124)

20 Comparison

A.

(Puzzle 5)

21 Two Letters

OX – OXEN
NO – NOES
(As in, for example, "the ayes to the right, the noes to the left.")

(Puzzle 85)

22 Subtraction

22:
Subtract the number of letters in the previous number each time.
For example, one hundred (10 letters), therefore $100 - 10 = 90$.
Ninety (6 letters), therefore $90 - 6 = 84$.

(Puzzle 45)

23 Treasure

G1.

(Puzzle 125)

24 Connections

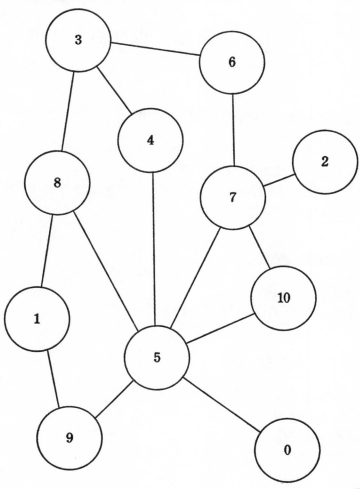

Puzzle 6)

25 Anagram Phrases

1. Hoist with one's own petard
2. To kill two birds with one stone
3. To keep a low profile
4. To overstay one's welcome
5. What's cooking

(Puzzle 86)

26 Sequence

Never:
The middle letter of each word is a roman numeral in alphabetical order.
ACE, LANDING, SNIPE, REFLATE, TEMPO, NEVER

(Puzzle 46)

27 The Palindromic Biennium

1999 – 2000:
MIM – MM in Roman numerals!
This will be the last time that palindromic years roman or arabic will occur consecutively.

(Puzzle 126)

28 Pyramid Word

A, At, Sag, Dive, Sound
15-letter word: DISADVANTAGEOUS

(Puzzle 7)

29 Twelve Letters

(1) Yankee-doodle
(2) Wooden-headed
(3) Shadow-boxing
(4) Monkey-puzzle

(Puzzle 8)

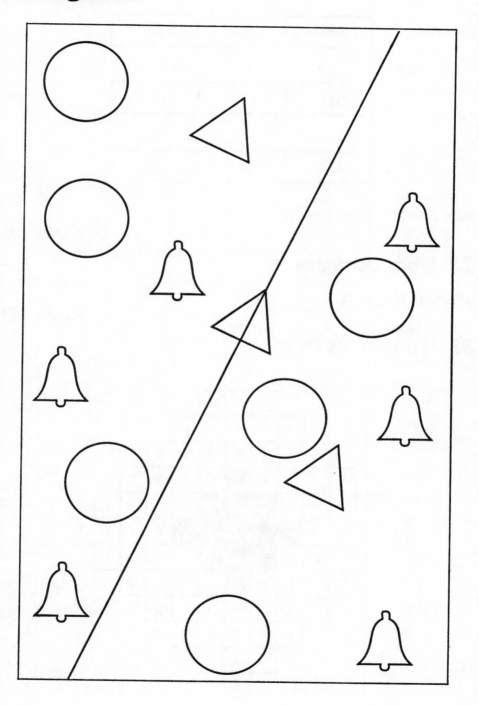

(Puzzle 47)

31 Missing Links

528	116	16

957	485	360

273	161	66

$58 \times 2 = 116, 16 \times 1 = 16$

(Puzzle 87)

32 Word Compasses

Graceful, Ungainly

(Puzzle 127)

33 Word-Cross Puzzle

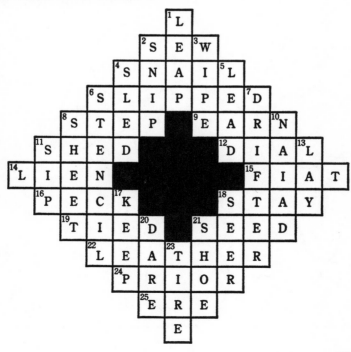

(Puzzle 48)

34 Decadice

Lose

1-1	2-1	3-1	4-1	5-1	6-1	7-1	8-1	9-1	10-1
1-2	2-2	3-2	4-2	5-2	6-2	7-2	8-2	9-2	10-2
1-3	2-3	3-3	4-3	5-3	6-3	7-3	8-3	9-3	10-3
1-4	2-4	3-4	4-4	5-4	6-4	7-4	8-4	9-4	10-4
1-5	2-5	3-5	4-5	5-5	6-5	7-5	8-5	9-5	10-5
1-6	2-6	3-4	4-6	5-6	6-6	7-6	8-6	9-6	10-6
1-7	2-7	3-7	4-7	5-7	6-7	7-7	8-7	9-7	10-7
1-8	2-8	3-8	4-8	5-8	6-8	7-8	8-8	9-8	10-8
1-9	2-9	3-9	4-9	5-9	6-9	7-9	8-9	9-9	10-9
1-10	2-10	3-10	4-10	5-10	6-10	7-10	8-10	9-10	10-10

Win

Lose	Win
9	1
8	2
7	3
6	4
5	5
4	6
3	7
2	8
1	9
–	10
45	55

Win 55–45 Lose or 55–45 Odds on

(Puzzle 88)

35 Triangles

A. There are three triangles. The middle triangle remains stationary and the two outer triangles are folded inwards along their adjoining edges of the middle triangle.

(Puzzle 128)

109

36 Pyramidal Logic

D

By logical process of elimination this is the only possible answer. Each symbol is linked to the two symbols below it. The same symbol never appears above the two symbols below it.
The symbols are produced as follows:

$$\heartsuit + \square = \diamond$$

$$\square + \bigcirc = \triangle$$

$$\triangle + \triangle = \bigcirc$$

$$\diamond + \triangle = \square$$

So that ⌓ + ♡ must equal something completely different to anything above. Of the other options shown this can only be ⬭.

(Puzzle 9)

37 Elliptical Illusion

A. The right-hand ellipse is moving across the left-hand ellipse. In the second stage it has moved across so that it touches the left-hand ellipse halfway across top and bottom. In the third stage it completely covers the left-hand ellipse.

In the answer, option A, it has reappeared having moved the same distance again and, in fact, now becomes the left-hand ellipse.

(Puzzle 89)

110

38 Square

Dog	Dab
Bat	Bad
God	Gob
Tab	Bog
Got	Dot
Tog	Tod

(Puzzle 49)

39 Fish

		Added letter
Basking	Shark	S
Striped	Catfish	T
Painted	Dragonet	A
Crusted	Flounder	R
Butterfly	Bream	B
Scarlet	Angler	L
Horse	Mackerel	R
Barred	Garfish	R
Brown	Groper	R
Spiny	Seahorse	S

(Puzzle 129)

40 Analogy

6512:

$3694 : \quad \dfrac{63}{7} \quad \dfrac{49}{7} = 97$

$5382 : \quad \dfrac{35}{7} \quad \dfrac{28}{7} = 54$

$6512 : \quad \dfrac{56}{7} \quad \dfrac{21}{7} = 83$

(Puzzle 10)

41 No Repeat Letters

Judicatory

(Puzzle 90)

42 Missing Number

$144 \div 9 = 16, \sqrt{16} = 4$
$112 \div 7 = 16, \sqrt{16} = 4$
$192 \div 12 = 16, \sqrt{16} = \boxed{4}$

(Puzzle 50)

43 Aliens

To solve this problem use a Venn diagram.

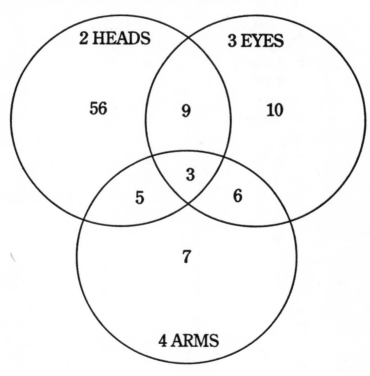

$$10 + 56 + 9 + 3 + 5 + 6 + 7 = \frac{\begin{array}{r} 100 \\ 96 \end{array}}{4}$$

Answer

(Puzzle 130)

44 Racetrack

1 – 1 – 4 – 4 – 3 – 14:

$$1$$
$$1+1=2$$
$$3$$
$$4$$
$$1+4=5$$
$$1+1+4=6$$
etc.

Other answers are possible.

(Puzzle 11)

45 Rebuses

1. Dark Ages
2. Paradise
3. Fortunes
4. Soon after that

(Puzzle 91)

46 Bracket Word

GEOGRAPHICAL

(Puzzle 51)

47 Saying

"Always forgive your enemies, nothing annoys them so much."

– Oscar Wilde

A	L	W	A	Y	S	F
O	R	G	I	V	E	Y
O	U	R	E	N	E	M
I	E	S	N	O	T	H
I	N	G	A	N	N	O
Y	S	T	H	E	M	S
O	M	U	C	H	■	

(Puzzle 131)

48 Magic Word Square

P	U	M	A	S
U	L	E	M	A
M	E	D	A	L
A	M	A	Z	E
S	A	L	E	M

(Puzzle 12)

49 Grid

2C.

(Puzzle 92)

50 Nursery Rhyme Crossword

V	E	N	I	S	O	N
I	■	I	■	H	■	O
C	O	N	C	E	P	T
U	■	E	■	A	■	I
N	E	P	H	R	I	C
A	■	I	■	E	■	E
S	E	N	O	R	A	S

(Puzzle 52)

51 Symbols

A.

(Puzzle 132)

52 Letter Change

1. Pros and cons
2. To bill and coo
3. To let fly
4. A leg up
5. So long
6. Cry quits
7. Dead set
8. To cut it fine
9. Fall guy
10. To zip up

(Puzzle 13)

53 Cryptogram

"If a little knowledge is dangerous, where is the man who has so much as to be out of danger?" – *T. H. Huxley*

(Puzzle 93)

54 Symbols

B.

(Puzzle 53)

55 Found in America

1. Daytona Beach
2. Staten Island
3. The Statue of Liberty
4. The Sears Tower
5. Blue Mountains
6. Sierra Nevada
7. Death Valley
8. Dodge City
9. Colorado Plateau
10. Baton Rouge

(Puzzle 133)

56 Grid

1C.

(Puzzle 14)

57 Magic Square

5	2	11	22	25
16	18	9	12	10
23	7	13	19	3
20	14	17	8	6
1	24	15	4	21

(Puzzle 94)

58 Round Table

Twelve different ways:
Calling the people 1, 2, 3, 4, 5, it is irrelevant where 1 is seated.
The remaining four people can be seated in 4! or
$4 \times 3 \times 2 \times 1 = 24$ ways. However, as left and right are
considered the same, the answer is $24 \div 2 = 12$ different ways.

(Puzzle 54)

59 Work it Out

7:
$15 + 21 = 36$ $\sqrt{36} + \sqrt{1} = 7$

Similarly in the first two triangles:
$12 + 13 = 25$ $\sqrt{25} + \sqrt{9} = 8$
$42 + 22 = 64$ $\sqrt{64} + \sqrt{4} = 10$

(Puzzle 134)

60 Pyramid Quotation

M, To, Ask, What, Axial, Tonsil, Martini

(Puzzle 95)

61 Magic Square

L	A	R	G	O
A	L	E	R	T
R	E	M	I	T
G	R	I	P	E
O	T	T	E	R

(Puzzle 15)

62 15-Letter Words

1. Prestidigitator
2. Inconsequential
3. Comprehensively
4. Surreptitiously
5. Electrification

(Puzzle 55)

63 Three Birds and a Fish

Three birds and a fish

(Puzzle 135)

64 Star

Harlequinade

(Puzzle 16)

65 Words

All words can be prefixed with EN-:
Entry, Enable, Enduring, Enshrine, Enviable, Envision, Engrave, Ensign.

(Puzzle 96)

66 Curve

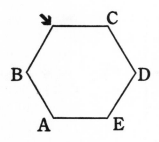

D. The curve has its pivot on the corner of the hexagon at all times. The curve moves clockwise around this pivot and adjusts its length to join corners A, B, C, D, and E in turn.

(Puzzle 56)

67 Dots Matrix

B. The end square in each horizontal and vertical line is determined by the contents of the previous two squares. The two previous squares are combined to form the third square. However, where two black spots appear in the same position in the previous two squares they appear as a white spot in the third square, and where two white spots coincide they appear as a black spot in the third square.

(Puzzle 136)

68 Analogy

C. One figure is superimposed on the other but only the internal lines are produced (i.e., only lines common to both figures appear).

(Puzzle 17)

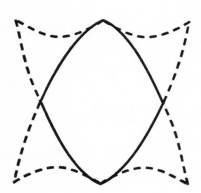

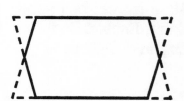

69 The Hexagonal Pyramid

B. The contents of each pyramid from the second row up are
determined by the contents of the two pyramids below it. All
lines are carried forward with the complication that if two
straight lines coincide in the same position they become a curved
line in the pyramid above, and if two curved lines coincide they
become straight.

(Puzzle 97)

70 Common

They all contain the names of creatures spelled backward.

1. Gnu	6. Cat
2. Nag	7. Wolf
3. Ram	8. Bat
4. Nit	9. Ape
5. Dog	10. Asp

(Puzzle 57)

71 Bull's Eye

1. Chicory (anag. HRCYCOI)
2. Lower fair domain
3. Toponym
4. Las Vegas (anag.)
5. Red eye
6. Dirty room
7. Apostrophe
8. Impeccable
9. Supine equine
10. Aced (hijacked)
11. Catacomb
12. Coracle (anag. LCCEARO)
13. Restore the plush (anag.)
14. Kittiwake
15. Model
16. Antibiotic

(Puzzle 137)

72 Lawns

$1987 = 27^2 + 27^2 + 23^2$
$1987 = 33^2 + 27^2 + 13^2$
$1987 = 39^2 + 21^2 + 5^2$
$1987 = 41^2 + 15^2 + 9^2$
Only $27^2 + 27^2 + 23^2$ fits the question.

(Puzzle 18)

73 Mixed Currency

Ecuador	–	Sucre
Haiti	–	Gourde
Ethiopia	–	Birr
Guinea	–	Syli
Indonesia	–	Rupiah
Honduras	–	Lempira
Israel	–	Shekel
Malawi	–	Kwacha
Morocco	–	Dirham
Nicaragua	–	Cordoba
Nigeria	–	Naira
Swaziland	–	Lilangeni

(Puzzle 98)

74 Alphabet Clueless-Cross

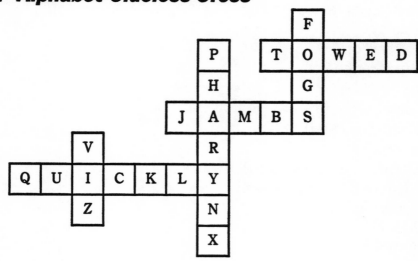

(Puzzle 58)

75 Cycle

(Take π as $\frac{22}{7}$)

Then C = $\frac{22}{7} \times 28 = 88$ inches

Number of revolutions $= \dfrac{1760 \times 3 \times 12}{88}$

$\qquad = 720$

(Puzzle 138)

76 Unkind Observation

"No matter how well a toupee blends in back, it always looks like hell in front." – *Sam Levenson*

(Puzzle 19)

77 Fence

	Hours	Reciprocal	Decimal
1 man	6	$\frac{1}{6}$	.166
1 man	3	$\frac{1}{3}$	.333
1 man	2	$\frac{1}{2}$	.500
1 man	4	$\frac{1}{4}$	.250
	Add		1.250

Now again take the reciprocal

$\therefore \quad \dfrac{1}{1.250} = .8$ hrs

$\therefore \quad .8 \times 60 = 48$ minutes

(Puzzle 99)

78 Alphametics

```
37413
  733
 9173
------
47319
```

(Puzzle 59)

79 Pyramid

```
      A
     P A
   H E R B
 C A N T E R
```

(Puzzle 139)

80 Links Jigsaw Puzzle

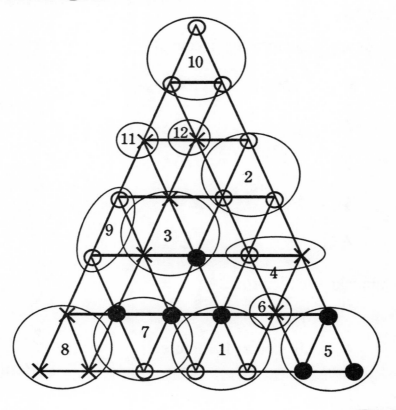

(Puzzle 20)

81 Nine Letters

1. Tautology
2. Pitchfork
3. Nitpicker
4. Lairdship
5. Haranguer
6. Diagnosis
7. Chanteuse
8. Blotchily

(Puzzle 100)

82 Sequence

B:
In each successive circle

●—→   moves 45° counterclockwise

●——○   moves 135° clockwise

●—×   moves 45° clockwise

●—●   moves 135° clockwise

(Puzzle 60)

83 Division

S	P	P	O	T	S	S	R
T	M	E	U	S	U	S	O
U	E	U	U	P	U	R	T
S	P	S	E	P	U	O	U
S	O	R	S	E	E	N	P
R	M	S	N	M	N	S	U
N	S	E	U	M	S	E	E
T	S	P	U	S	P	S	U

Presumptuousness

(Puzzle 140)

84 Bertrand's Paradox

Knowing that a drawer of either chest B or C has been opened would lead most people to believe that the probability is 1/2. However we are dealing here with drawers and not chests. The answer is actually 1/3.

The three drawers containing silver coins represent equally likely cases, and only one of these is favorable. That is the drawer with the silver coin in chest C. The probability that chest C has been opened is initially 1/3 and remains 1/3 when a drawer has been opened and found to have a silver coin, because gold and silver are distributed identically over drawers and chests. Someone having gambled on chest C would not regard his chances as better or worse after a silver coin has been found in the first drawer to be opened.

(Puzzle 21)

85 Grid

1C.

(Puzzle 101)

86 Network

Archaeological

(Puzzle 61)

87 Symbols

A.

(Puzzle 141)

88 Stacking Cubes

Taking just one die any one of six faces can be chosen as a base. These six faces can each be rotated 90° so that any one of four faces is at the front. This gives $6 \times 4 = 24$ different ways of positioning one cube. The same applies for each of the eight dice that are stacked to form the cube. The number of different ways in which they can be stacked, therefore, is 24^8, or 110,075,314,176.

(Puzzle 102)

89 The Enigma Diamond

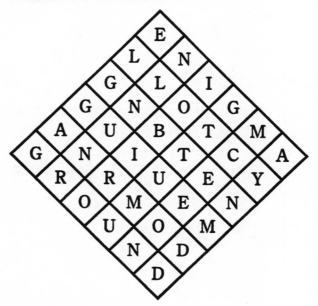

Or rotations of the same grid.

(Puzzle 22)

90 Array

70:
Reading across they are groups of Pythagorean numbers.

$17^2 = 15^2 + 8^2$

$82^2 = 18^2 + 80^2$

$45^2 = 27^2 + 36^2$

$70^2 = 42^2 + 56^2$

(Puzzle 62)

91 Sweepstakes

60479 to 1:
The number of ways in which the drawing of the six balls is
possible is $9 \times 8 \times 7 \times 6 \times 5 \times 4 = 60480$.

or $\quad \dfrac{9!}{3!} = \dfrac{9 \times 8 \times 7 \times 6 \times 5 \times 4 \times 3 \times 2 \times 1}{3 \times 2 \times 1}$

(Puzzle 142)

92 Find Another Word

FALL. All words can be prefixed with NIGHT.

(Puzzle 23)

93 Lads and Lasses

Across: Basil, Ralph, Scott, Lewis, Keith, Henry, Derek, Gavin, Jason, Brian

Down: Laura, Wendy, Susan, Doris, Anita, Sally, Mitzi, Sarah, Celia, Alice.

(Puzzle 103)

94 A Common Thread

They are all anagrams of RIVERS:
Hudson, Plate, Nile, Tiber, Ebro.

(Puzzle 63)

95 Piecemeal Quotation

"Whenever you save five shillings you put a man out of work for a day."

(Puzzle 143)

96 Circles Matrix

C. Looking both across and down, the figures in the first two circles are merged to produce the figure in the final circle, and the sections common to all components are shaded.

(Puzzle 24)

97 Sequence

D. It is the numbers 1, 2, 3, 4, 5 laid on their side. If in doubt look at the page sideways.

(Puzzle 64)

98 Group Puzzle

Hyacinth
Iridium } Minerals
Carbuncle

Popinjay
Cassowary } Birds
Corncrake

Barkentine
Pinnace } Boats
Argosy

Cachalot
Capybara } Animals
Pichiciago

Hackney
Tonneau } Vehicles
Tumbrel

Snapper
Grayling } Fish
Porbeagle

(Puzzle 104)

99 Series

The series describes the shape of letters of the alphabet.
i.e., A = Straight, Straight, Straight = SSS

The series is the run of letters
I – J – K – L – M – N – O – ?

Answer is P = SC (Straight line/Curved line).

(Puzzle 144)

100 Arcs Matrix

G. Looking both across and down, the final square is arrived at by combining the contents of the previous two squares, with the exception that lines that are common to the first two squares are not carried forward.

(Puzzle 105)

101 Word Search

Budgerigar
Greenfinch
Bergander (old name for Sheldrake)
Gander
Guillemot
Redshank
Blackbird
Darter
Marabou
Rooster
Kestrel
Loriot (Golden oriole)
Auk
Cob
Emu
Owl
Ruc (old form of Roc)
Roc
Plover
Daw
Mew
Finch

(Puzzle 25)

102 Countries

Paraguay	Mongolia
Tanzania	Sardinia
Cambodia	Honduras
Pakistan	Portugal
Zanzibar	Zimbabwe
Malaysia	Barbados
Rhodesia	Bulgaria
Scotland	Trinidad

(Puzzle 65)

103 Circles

B. There are five circles, in order of size A, B, C, D, E. The largest circle A remains stationary. The remaining circles move around the circumference of A as follows:

Circle B moves clockwise 90°
Circle C moves clockwise 45°
Circle D moves clockwise 45°
Circle E moves counterclockwise 45°

(Puzzle 145)

104 Number

2:
$(10 \div 2) + 5 - 8 = 2$

(Puzzle 26)

105 Enigmagram

Caravel
Frigate
Gunboat
Pinnace

Key: FELUCCA

(Puzzle 106)

106 Soccer Ball

18 squares
8 triangles

(Puzzle 66)

107 Ten Letters

C O A N E G X R L A E T T U L X A T E I O R N S S

(Puzzle 146)

108 Diamond

Anabas	Bass
Bret (Turbot)	Blenny
Brill	Bib (Whiting Pout)
Brit	Dab
Eel	Tuna
Char	Chub

(Puzzle 27)

109 Tennis

If there were 41 men in the singles there must have been 1 winner and 40 losers. So there must have been 40 matches. Therefore:

Matches

Men's singles	40
Women's singles	28
Men's doubles	19
Women's doubles	13
Mixed doubles	25
	125

(Puzzle 107)

110 Niners

Across
1. Departure
4. Confiding
5. Negotiate

Down
1. Depiction
2. Routinist
3. Emergence

Diagonal
1. Dalliance
5. Nigritude

(Puzzle 67)

111 Cylinder

Volume:

Cylinder: $\dfrac{\pi d^2 h}{4} = \dfrac{\pi d^3}{4}$ (since d = h)

Sphere: $\dfrac{4}{3}\pi r^3 = \dfrac{\pi d^3}{6}$

Cone: $\dfrac{1}{3}\dfrac{\pi d^2 h}{4} = \dfrac{\pi d^3}{12}$

Ratio is therefore   3 : 2 : 1
Cylinder : sphere : cone

(Puzzle 147)

112 Circles

68:
93 − 17 (÷ 4) = 19
45 − 13 (÷ 4) = 8
68 − 24 (÷ 4) = 11

(Puzzle 28)

113 No Repeat Letters

Toweringly

(Puzzle 108)

114 Treasure

1A.

(Puzzle 29)

115 Logic

Row 1   A is added to B = C
Row 2   A is added to B = C
Row 3   A is added to B = C
Column A   1 is added to 2 = 3
Column B   1 is added to 2 = 3
Column C   1 is added to 2 = 3
Similar symbols disappear.

(Puzzle 68)

116 Sequence

B:
In each circle

      moves 90° clockwise

      moves 180° clockwise

O   moves 90° clockwise

●   moves 225° clockwise

(Puzzle 148)

117 Percussion

Marimba, Castanets, Tabor

(Puzzle 69)

118 Links Jigsaw Puzzle

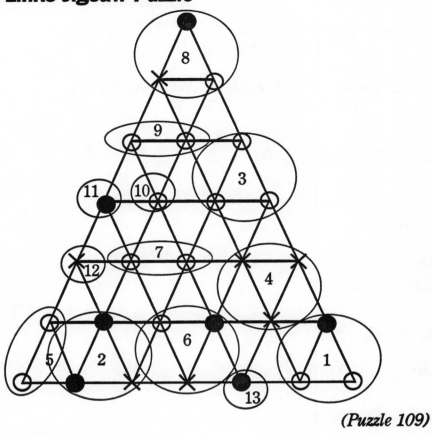

(Puzzle 109)

119 Letter Search

1. Q   2. S   3. L   4. P

(Puzzle 149)

120 The Enigmasig Wheel

NAVIGABLE (Traversable)
IMPASSE (Stalemate)
GODLIKE (Transcendent)
MONOLOGUE (Soliloquy)
AVERSE (Antipathetic)
STORE (Accumulate)
IMPROVE (Ameliorate)
GAUCHE (Unsophisticated)

(Puzzle 30)

121 Cubes

Across: 46656, 35937, 91125, 12167, 24389, 97336, 32768, 59319, 15625, 10648

Down: 68921, 39304, 13824, 21952, 74088, 85184, 19683, 79507, 17576, 54872

(Puzzle 110)

122 Double Digits

```
  179
  224
 ‾‾‾‾‾
  716
  358
 358
‾‾‾‾‾‾
40096
```

(Puzzle 70)

123 Plurals

Operas, the plural of Opera, which is, in turn, the plural of Opus.

(Puzzle 150)

124 Categories

Lemon, Hazel, Plane   – all trees
Palm, Gum, Foot   – parts of the body
Gold, Fawn, Copper   – all colors
Knot, Perch, Stone   – all measurements

(Puzzle 31)

125 Sequence

100. They are consecutive square numbers, starting with 1 and divided into groups of three numbers.
149, 162, 536, 496, 481, 100
1, 4, 9, 16, 25, 36, 49, 64, 81, 100

(Puzzle 111)

126 Diamonds

A. So that in each line of three, pointing SW/NE and NW/SE there is a black/white/striped circle and a triangle pointing North, South, and East.

(Puzzle 71)

127 Nines

4	8	7	6	2
2	7	3	1	5
7	1	6	9	4
5	8	6	2	6
9	3	5	9	1

(Puzzle 151)

128 Link Word

Down

(Puzzle 32)

129 Sequence

F. Each of the rectangles, after the first three stages, is repeated but rotates 90°. Each of the three internal figures, after the first three stages, is repeated but rotates 180°. The circle appears white/black alternately and the internal figures appear black/white alternately.

(Puzzle 112)

130 Cliff

Say seven seconds.
Then distance = $16x^2$ feet
$\therefore 16 \times 7 \times 7 = 784$ feet

(Puzzle 113)

131 Anagram Theme

They are all Shakespearean characters whose names have appeared in titles of Shakespeare plays:

>OTHELLO (Hell too)
>JULIET (Jut lie)
>ANTONY (Any not)
>CAESAR (Sea car)
>TROILUS (Sour lit)
>PERICLES (Clip seer)
>HAMLET (Halt me)

(Puzzle 72)

132 Analogy

C. This is **almost** a mirror-image puzzle. The shaded sections in the hexagon are **a mirror image** of the shaded sections in the circle and vice versa, with the added complication that shaded and white sections are reversed in the image.

For example, in a simple version the following would occur:

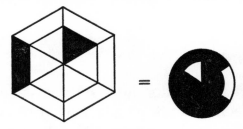

In effect the hexagon has flipped over, turned into a circle, and black has turned to white, white to black.

(Puzzle 152)

133 Zoetrope

Tee – All   Ate – Hal
Ling – Spun   Ibex – Pile
Later – Shaly   Cheer – Jolly

(Puzzle 73)

136

134 Series

To move from term to term multiply by $-\frac{2}{3}$, for example:

$$6 \times (-\frac{2}{3}) = -4$$

We require the seventh term, i.e., $6 \times (-\frac{2}{3})^6$

$$= 6 \times .0878$$
$$= .5268$$

(Puzzle 33)

135 Nine Letters

HIPPODROME

Marsupial
Monotreme } Orders of mammals

Whitebeam
Jacaranda } Trees

Aubergine
Mangetout } Vegetables

Guinevere
Argonauts } Mythology

Nicotiana
Pyracantha } Plants

Fomalhaut
Aldebaran } Stars

Sheldrake
Merganser } Birds

Catamount
Dromedary } Animals

Fricassee
Succotash } Food

Farandole
Poussette } Dances

Shillalah
Derringer } Weapons

Mercenary
Bodyguard } Professionals

(Puzzle 153)

136 The Triangle and Hexagon

C. The hexagon remains stationary and the triangle flips round the sides using as its pivot its southernmost touching point on the hexagon each time and clamping itself on the next available side in a counterclockwise direction.

(Puzzle 34)

137 Tampa

1. Tango
2. Magma
3. Lymph
4. Kempt
5. Uvula

(Puzzle 114)

138 Darts

Player	A	B	C
	40	23	17
	16	23	17
	16	16	17
	16	16	17
	16	16	16
	16	16	16
	120	110	100

(Puzzle 74)

139 Twelve Letters

High-stepping
Commencement
Elocutionist
Genealogical
Lantern-jawed
Market-garden
Phonographic
Shrewishness
Shuffleboard
Single-handed

(Puzzle 154)

140 "Z" Puzzle

Buzz	Whiz
Zulu	Fizz
Zip	Dizzy
Fuzzy	Hazy
Muzzy	Dozy
Mazy	Zap
Faze	Viz

(Puzzle 35)

141 Hidden Lands

Swaddles
Opportunist
Interrogation
Conurbation
Pochard
Nationality
Initially
Recommendation
Impervious
Congratulations

(Puzzle 115)

142 Dice

14.7 throws:
Say 2 appears face upwards on the first throw. Then continue
until another number appears. The probability of this occuring on
the next throw is 5/6, the average number of throws needed to
obtain a different number being 6/5. Say the number 6 is next to
appear, then it is necessary to continue until a number differing
from 2 or 6 appears. The probability of this occuring on the next
throw (irrespective of how many throws have occurred up to
now) is 4/6. The calculation for all six numbers is therefore:

$$1 + \frac{6}{5} + \frac{6}{4} + \frac{6}{3} + \frac{6}{2} + \frac{6}{1} = 14.7$$

(Puzzle 75)

143 Boat

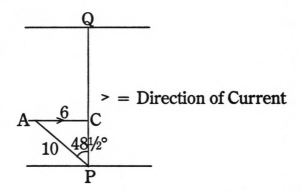

To get from P to Q the rower must head in the direction
$48\frac{1}{2}° = x$

His speed across will be CP

PA = 10

AC = 6

∴ $(AP)^2 = (AC)^2 + (CP)^2$

∴ $10^2 = 6^2 + (CP)^2$

∴ $(CP)^2 = 10^2 - 6^2$

∴ $(CP)^2 = 64$

∴ $CP = \sqrt{64}$

∴ CP = 8 meters per minute

(Puzzle 155)

144 Odd One Out

C:
A is the same as D
E is the same as F
B is the same as G

(Puzzle 36)

145 Links Jigsaw Puzzle

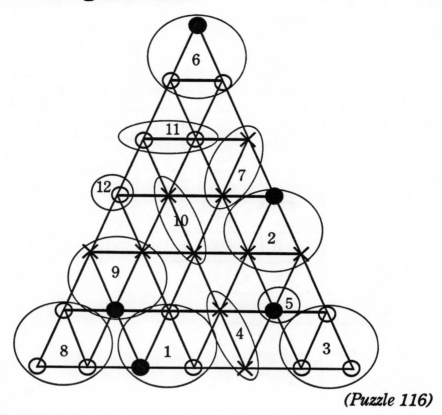

(Puzzle 116)

146 Circles

Each pair of circles produces the circle above by carrying forward the elements, but similar elements are canceled out, for example:

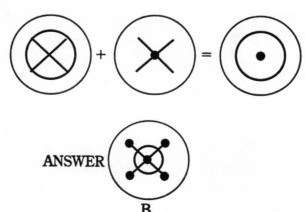

(Puzzle 156)

147 No Blanks

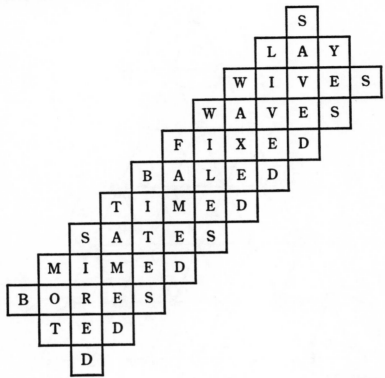

(Puzzle 76)

148 Anagrammed Synonyms

1. Hash – Mishmash
2. Load – Shipment
3. Pet – Fondle
4. Gale – Tempest
5. Pith – Quintessence
6. Spur – Impetus
7. Coy – Reserved
8. Blue – Cerulean
9. Dun – Importune
10. Air – Ventilate

(Puzzle 37)

149 Margana

Tenaciously

(Puzzle 117)

150 Synonyms

1. Hurried
2. Palpable
3. Capricious
4. Veiled
5. Salacious

(Puzzle 157)

151 Logic

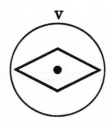

Row 1   A is added to B = C
Row 2   A is added to B = C
Row 3   A is added to B = C
Column A   1 is added to 2 = 3
Column B   1 is added to 2 = 3
Column C   1 is added to 2 = 3
Similar symbols disappear.

(Puzzle 77)

152 Two In One

1. "Imitation is the sincerest form of flattery."
2. "When you have nothing to say, say nothing."

(Puzzle 38)

153 Unscramble a Sequence

Proceed via triangular numbers: 1, 3, 6, 10, 15, 21, 28, 36, 45, 55, 66, 78, 91, 105, 120, 136, 153. Triangular numbers are numbers arranged in triangular form in one layer.

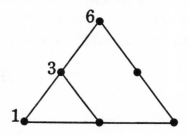

(Puzzle 118)

154 Square Words

Departure, Assertive, Deviation, Merriment, Confident, Joviality.
The three pairs of synonyms are: Departure – Deviation,
Assertive – Confident, Merriment – Joviality.

(Puzzle 78)

155 Synonym Circles

Paternal, Fatherly

(Puzzle 159)

156 Sensible

Rational, Prudent, Canny, Shrewd, Judicious, Realistic, Sane

(Puzzle 160)

157 Brain Strain

7	+	8	÷	3	=	5
+	■	×	■	+	■	−
5	+	3	÷	2	=	4
÷	■	÷	■	−	■	+
3	+	6	÷	3	=	3
=	■	=	■	=	■	=
4	+	4	÷	2	=	4

(Puzzle 39)

158 Twist and Turn

E. The shaded segment moves outwards to each portion in turn. The pentagon moves through 180° each time. The diamond moves with the inner pentagon and the ellipse turns 90° within the diamond.

(Puzzle 158)

159 Track Word

Electioneering

(Puzzle 119)

D	Y	N	A	M	I	C
I	■	U	■	E	■	R
G	A	R	B	A	G	E
I	■	S	■	N	■	E
T	R	E	A	T	E	D

(Puzzle 79)

145

Power
Puzzles
3

1 Knight's Saying

Using the knight's move as in chess, spell out the message and the name of its author. You have to find the starting point.

FINISH

TO	IS	WORK	BRAINS	•
BY	THE	OTHERS	GREAT	HIS
MAN	CARRY	CAN	PIATT	OF
USE	DON	THAT	OUT	WHO

	×		×	
×				×
		KN		
×				×
	×		×	

(Solution 3)

2 Center Word

Find a 3-letter word that completes all three words on the left-hand side and prefixes all three words on the right-hand side.

(Solution 7)

3 Pulleys

The inner wheel is 50 percent of the outer wheel's diameter.
A revolves at a speed of 10.

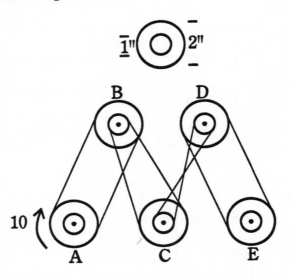

How fast does **E** revolve and in which direction?

(Solution 11)

4 Poser

Arrange the letters P - O - S - E - R into the grid so that the same
letter does not appear twice in the same horizontal, vertical, or
diagonal line.

P	O	S	E	R
O	S	E	R	P
S	E	R	P	O
E	R	P	O	S
R	P	O	S	E

(Solution 15)

5 Grid

Each of the nine squares 1A to 3C should incorporate all the lines and symbols shown in the outer squares A, B, or C and 1, 2, or 3. Thus 2B should incorporate all the lines and symbols in 2 and B.

One of the squares, 1A to 3C, is incorrect. Which one is it?

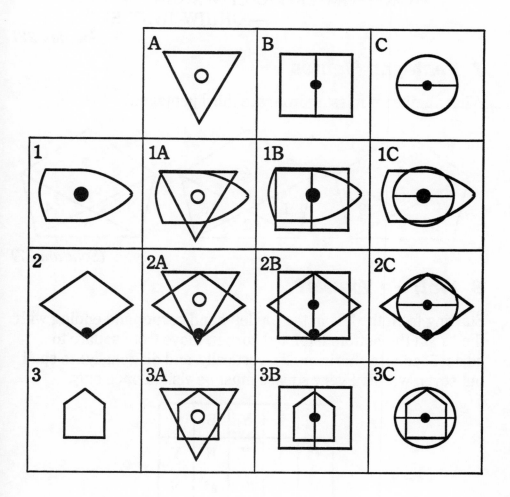

(Solution 19)

3

6 Cryptogram I

This is a straightforward cryptogram in which each letter of the quotation has been replaced by another.

XW XKHM. JL RKV 'UW ZKJTZ CK ONSW
NT WUUKU, ONSW N MKKER, NTM MKT'C
XW NLUNJM CK PJC CPW XNHH.
　　　　　　　　　　—XJHHJW IWNT SJTZ

(Solution 22)

7 Pentagon Figures

What number is missing from the third pentagon?

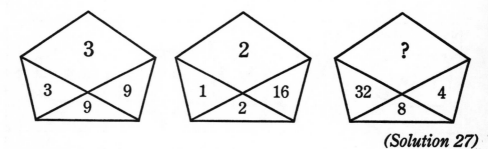

(Solution 27)

8 Wot! No Vowels?

Starting from the "B" in the top left-hand corner and ending with the "Y" in the bottom left-hand corner, move from square to adjacent square (horizontally, vertically, and diagonally) to spell out seven words. Every square must be visited once only.

B	L	Y	S	P
P	Y	Y	H	Y
Y	Y	S	M	N
L	L	W	T	R
Y	R	T	S	Y

(Solution 31)

9 Sequence

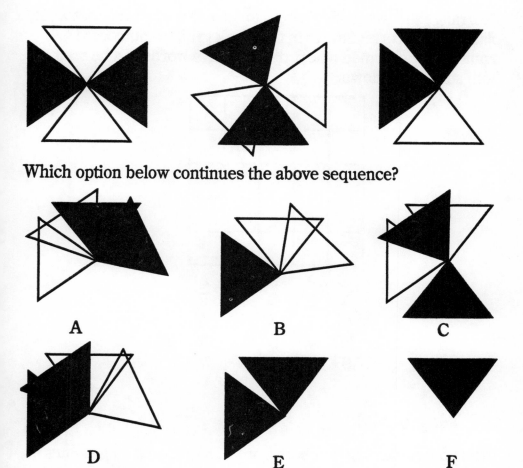

Which option below continues the above sequence?

A   B   C

D   E   F

(Solution 35)

10 Children

In a class of thirty children, fifteen can play table tennis and nineteen can play soccer. Six cannot play either table tennis or soccer.

How many children can play both table tennis and soccer?

(Solution 40)

11 Magic Word Square

Rearrange the twenty-five letters to form five words so that when placed in the correct order in the blank grid, a magic word square will be formed where the same five words can be read both across and down.

				T
			M	
		C		
	M			
T				

A	A	A	A	A
A	C̶	D	E	E
G	I	I	L	L
M̶	M̶	O	O	R
S	T̶	T̶	V	V

(Solution 43)

12 Magic "65"

Insert the remaining numbers from 1-25 to form a magic square whereby each horizontal, vertical, and corner-to-corner line totals 65.

20				
				5
				10
		25		
15				

(Solution 47)

6

13 Twelve Letters

Find the four 12-letter words (each word consists of two 6-letter parts). The first half is inside the star, the second half is outside the star.

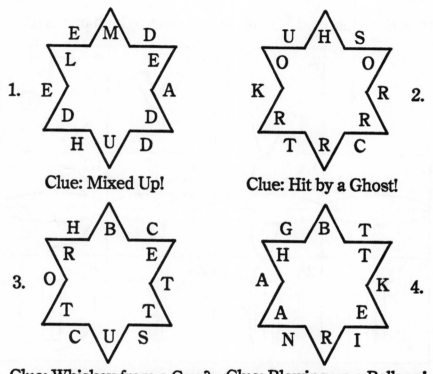

1. Clue: Mixed Up!

2. Clue: Hit by a Ghost!

3. Clue: Whiskey from a Cow?

4. Clue: Blowing up a Balloon!

(Solution 51)

14 Odd One Out

Who is the odd one out?

Ethel Noble
Cyril Lord
Stella Strong
Clive Cliff
Lloyd Gray

(Solution 55)

15 Grid

Each of the nine squares 1A to 3C should incorporate all the lines and symbols shown in the outer squares A, B, or C and 1, 2, or 3. Thus 2B should incorporate all the lines and symbols in 2 and B.

One of the squares, 1A to 3C, is incorrect. Which one is it?

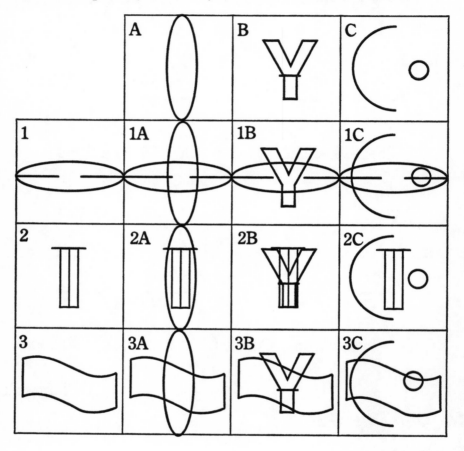

(Solution 59)

16 Do-It-Yourself Diamond Crossword

Insert into the grid all the words listed so that each word travels in a straight line in the direction of one of the compass points indicated.

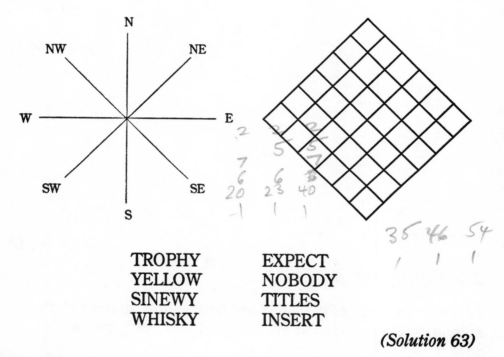

TROPHY	EXPECT
YELLOW	NOBODY
SINEWY	TITLES
WHISKY	INSERT

(Solution 63)

17 Survey

A survey was carried out on one hundred people concerning their eating habits:

20	had breakfast
23	had lunch
40	had dinner
6	had breakfast and lunch
7	had breakfast and dinner
5	had lunch and dinner
2	had breakfast, lunch, and dinner

How many had only one meal?

(Solution 68)

18 Pyramid

What symbol should replace the question mark?

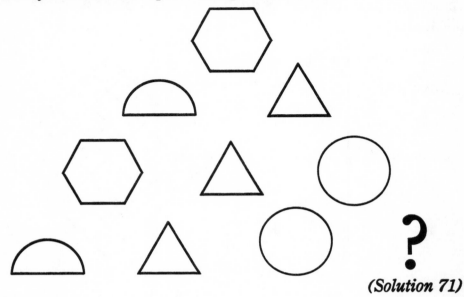

(Solution 71)

19 Honeycomb

Find eighteen names of food. A word may move in any direction as long as letters are adjacent, but a letter can only be visited once in each word.

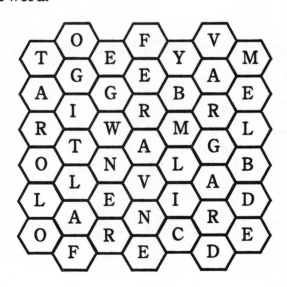

(Solution 74)

10

20 Find a Word

Trace out a 13-letter word by traveling along the lines. You need to find the starting letter—it cannot be crossed twice.

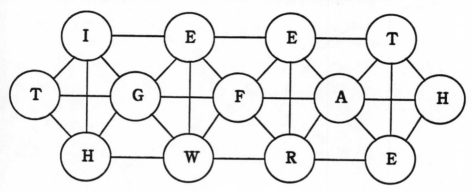

(Solution 79)

21 No Repeat Letters

The grid contains twenty-five different letters of the alphabet. What is the longest word that can be found by starting anywhere and working from square to square horizontally, vertically, or diagonally, without repeating a letter?

P	L	A	H	W
D	Q	N	T	V
X	E	U	G	O
J	S	I	R	F
Y	M	K	C	B

(Solution 83)

22 Symbols

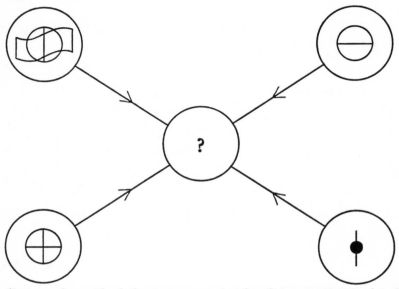

Each line and symbol that appears in the four outer circles is transferred to the center circle according to these rules:

If a line or symbol occurs in the outer circles:

once	it is transferred
twice	it is possibly transferred
three times	it is transferred
four times	it is not transferred

Which of the circles A, B, C, D, or E, shown below, should appear at the center of the diagram?

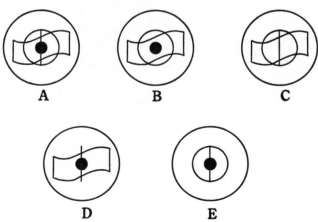

(Solution 87)

12

23 The Five Pennies

Someone tosses five coins in the air at the same time and you are betting on the outcome. What are the chances that at least four of the coins will finish up either all heads or all tails?

(Solution 91)

24 Hexagon Logic

What symbols should go inside the hexagons marked **A** and **B**?

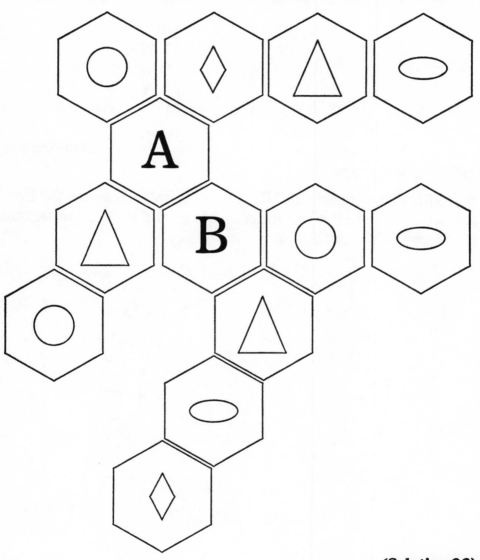

(Solution 96)

25 Links

Find the words that, when placed in the brackets, will complete the first word and start the second. One word is hyphenated. The number of dots equals the number of letters in the missing word.

1.	MAR	(...)	BOAT
2.	ROUND	(..)	PITY
3.	RIB	(...)	IRON
4.	BACK	(.....)	ROOM
5.	OUT	(...)	TROT
6.	TRY	(....)	CLOTH
7.	WELL	(....)	LONG
8.	PAS	(.....)	PLAY
9.	PALL	(..)	BIT
10.	SEAS	(....)	BENT

(Solution 99)

26 Pentagram

Solve the five anagrams of MILITARY TERMS. Transfer the five arrowed letters to the key anagram boxes and solve this anagram to discover a key sixth term.

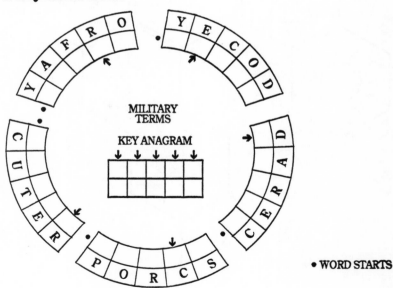

• WORD STARTS

(Solution 103)

14

27 Three to Choose

Select the correct meaning from the three alternatives.

1. Tarn
   - (a) Sick cow
   - (b) Hobgoblin
   - (c) Highland lake

2. Furlough
   - (a) Legal possession
   - (b) Leave of absence
   - (c) Free transport

3. Gharry
   - (a) Horse-drawn carriage
   - (b) Ale house
   - (c) Pension

4. Izzard
   - (a) The letter "Z"
   - (b) Bird's throat
   - (c) Mythical sea

5. Mountebank
   - (a) Jasmine
   - (b) Rogue
   - (c) Marshy area

6. Machete
   - (a) Sharp cutting knife
   - (b) Farm machinery
   - (c) Platform for tiger shooting

7. Marchpane
   - (a) Wild flower
   - (b) Marzipan
   - (c) Heat haze

8. Nuncio
   - (a) Papal envoy
   - (b) Idiot
   - (c) Novice nun

9. Ounce
   - (a) Lynx
   - (b) Trivial object
   - (c) Bone in the ear

10. Rutabaga
   - (a) Turnip
   - (b) Hungarian dance
   - (c) Melée

(Solution 107)

28 Cricket Ground

One man can mow a cricket ground in two hours.
One man can mow a cricket ground in three hours.
One man can mow a cricket ground in four hours.
One man can mow a cricket ground in five hours.
One man can mow a cricket ground in six hours.

If they all worked together over the same area at their respective speeds, and assuming that they did not obstruct each other, how long would they take collectively to finish the job?

(Solution 110)

29 Word Circles

Reading clockwise, provide the missing letters to spell an 8-letter word in each circle. You are looking for a pair of synonyms and a pair of antonyms.

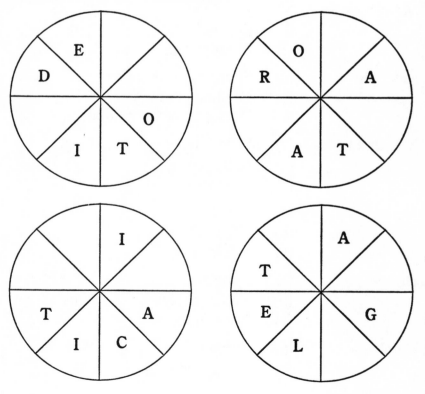

(Solution 115)

30 Circles

Which of these fits into the blank circle to carry out the pattern?

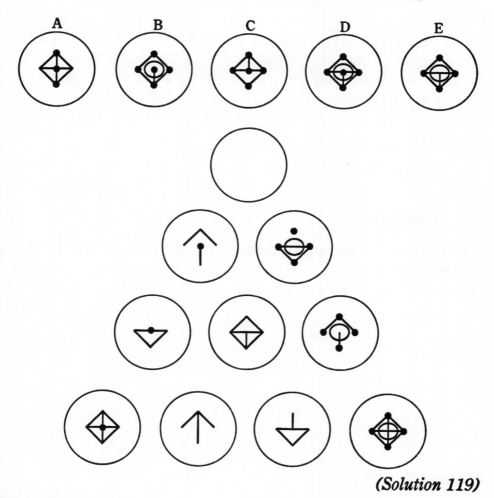

(Solution 119)

31 Eggs

In a crate of eggs six out of one hundred are bad. What are the chances of drawing out two and finding them both bad?

(Solution 123)

32 Number-Crunching Series

48, ? , 57120, 1940448

The four numbers in this series are the only numbers below two million with a certain property. The property is that if you add 1 to the number you produce a square number (for example, 1 + 48 = 49), and if you add 1 to half of the number you produce another square number (1 + 24 = 25). Similarly, 57120 + 1 = 239^2 and (57120 ÷ 2) + 1 = 169^2. 1940448 + 1 = 1393^2 and (1940448 ÷ 2) + 1 = 985^2.

Now find the missing number.

(Solution 127)

33 Pyramid

Spell out the 15-letter word by going into the pyramid one room at a time. Go into each room once only. You may go into the outer passage as many times as you wish.

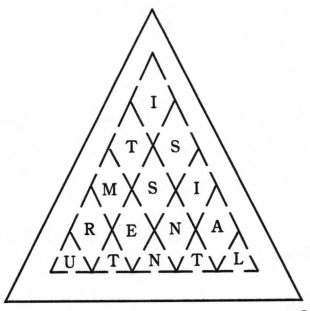

(Solution 131)

34 Track Word

Work around the track and provide the missing letters to find a 15-letter word. The word might appear clockwise or counter-clockwise, and the overlapping letter appears twice.

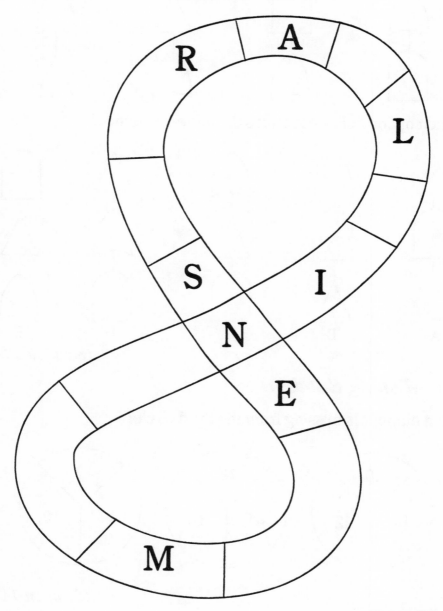

(Solution 135)

35 Sequence

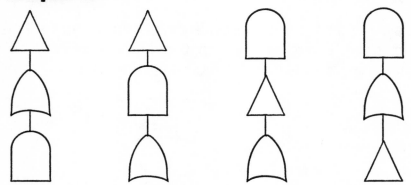

Which option below continues the above sequence?

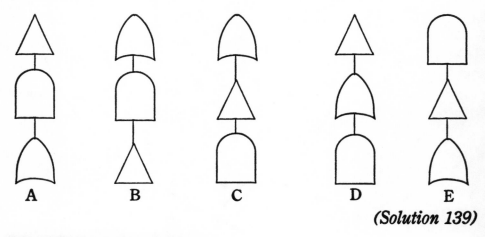

A   B   C   D   E

(Solution 139)

36 Missing Number

What number is missing from the third circle?

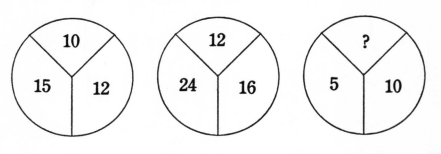

(Solution 143)

37 Wot! No Vowels?

Find seventeen words of three or more letters contained in the grid. Words run in any direction (backward and forward, horizontally, vertically, and diagonally), but only in a straight line.

C	D	S	Y	L	P
N	R	L	L	R	Y
Y	Y	Y	Y	R	F
S	C	L	P	Y	Y
H	F	Y	R	T	R
Y	X	W	Y	N	D

(Solution 147)

38 Consonants

Restore consonants to the words below to create groups of four synonyms.

1. • A • • • • I • •
   • E • • • • A • •
   • • A • • A • •
   • • I • E • I O •

2. • E • A • • I • • A • •
   O • • • I • A • E
   • A • • A • •
   I • • • A • • A • • E

3. E • • • A • •
   • E • I • • •
   • E • I • • •
   • E • • E • I

4. • O • U • I O •
   A • • I • U • A • I O •
   I • • O • A • I O •
   A • • E • •

5. A • • E • O • •
   • A • A • • E
   A • O • O • U E
   • A • • E

6. • U I • E • U •
   • U • • I • •
   U • • E • • A • •
   • E • E I • • U •

(Solution 151)

21

39 Grid

Each of the nine squares 1A to 3C should incorporate all the lines and symbols shown in the outer squares A, B, or C and 1, 2, or 3. Thus 2B should incorporate all the lines and symbols in 2 and B.

One of the squares, 1A to 3C, is incorrect. Which one is it?

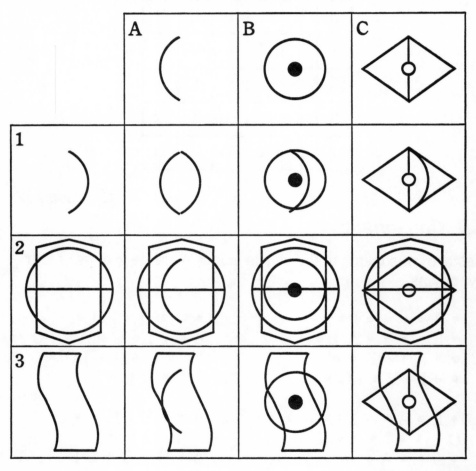

(Solution 155)

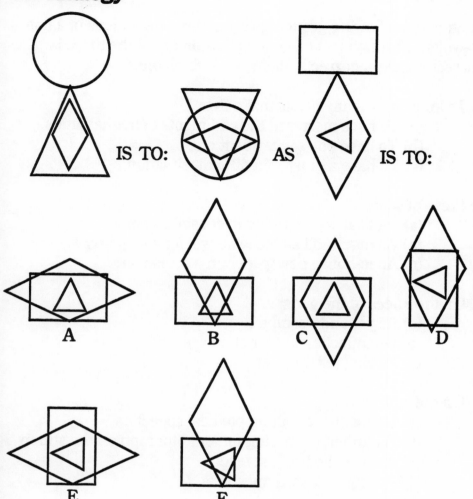

IS TO: ... AS ... IS TO:

A   B   C   D

E   F

(Solution 159)

41 Triple Choice

Each of the following groupings gives three definitions of a not-so-well-known saying. Only one definition out of the three is correct. Can you correctly determine which one?

1. To know how many beans make five:
    (a) To have mastered the rudiments of mathematics
    (b) To have one's wits about one
    (c) To have a grasp of a difficult situation

2. Press of sail:
    (a) Journalists operating in coastal regions
    (b) As much sail as the wind will let a ship carry
    (c) An in-house newspaper on a cruise liner

3. On the knees of the gods:
    (a) As yet undetermined
    (b) Genuflecting at church in prayer
    (c) Hoping for the best

4. On the stump:
    (a) Going about making political speeches
    (b) A lumberjack posing for a photograph on the stump
        of a tree he has just felled
    (c) Asking awkward questions

5. To kick against the pricks:
    (a) To disobey the rules of authority in the armed forces
    (b) To campaign against someone in high authority
    (c) To hurt oneself in an unavailing struggle against
        something

6. Lop and top:
    (a) Trimming of trees
    (b) A quick haircut
    (c) Execution by guillotine

7. To take to the heather:
   - (a) To take a walking tour
   - (b) To adopt a nomadic lifestyle
   - (c) To become an outlaw

8. In the pouts:
   - (a) Sullen
   - (b) Sexy
   - (c) Carefree

9. To row down:
   - (a) To collide with another boat
   - (b) To win a heated argument
   - (c) To overtake by rowing

10. To heap coals of fire:
    - (a) To return good for evil
    - (b) To fuel an argument
    - (c) To earn great riches

(Solution 4)

42 Link Words

Find a 3-letter word that, when placed on the end of these words, will produce new words.

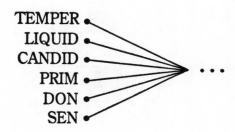

TEMPER
LIQUID
CANDID
PRIM
DON
SEN

. . .

(Solution 8)

43 Horse Race

In a 5-horse race, a bookmaker laid the following odds on four of the horses:

No.	Odds
1	2 to 1 against
2	3 to 1 against
3	4 to 1 against
4	5 to 1 against
5	?

What odds should he give on horse No. 5 in order to give himself a 15 percent margin of profit?

(Solution 12)

44 Three Too Many

Delete three of the letters in each 4-letter box to solve the crossword.

L S T R	E	T D S V	I	P R N L	E	L D M N
E		A		E		E
D C B R	I	D L G M	I	T P S R	A	T N L P
U		E		I		U
L D N C	A	T N P C	E	R S D L	E	D N T R
E		E		E		E
S D R L	E	M N S P	I	R S D T	E	L N D G

(Solution 16)

26

45 Symbols

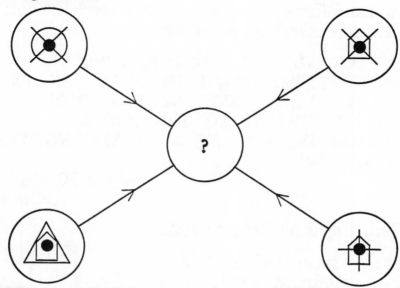

Each line and symbol that appears in the four outer circles is transferred to the center circle according to these rules:

If a line or symbol occurs in the outer circles:

once	it is transferred
twice	it is possibly transferred
three times	it is transferred
four times	it is not transferred

Which of the circles A, B, C, D, or E, shown below, should appear in the center of the diagram?

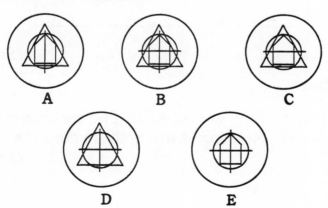

(Solution 20)

27

46 Cryptogram II

This is a straightforward cryptogram in which each letter of the quotation has been replaced by another.

IDWWDXQZ XH KXJBZ GJN KJDPPNQ
GQQSGWWR, FSJFXJPDQM PX PNAA VXK PX
YNGP PVN JGUNZ, KVNJNGZ PVN YNZP
FXZZDYWN GBEDUN XQ PVN ZSYLNUP
DZ HXSQB DQ PVN PVJNN IXQXZRWWGYWNZ:
'BX QXP PJR.'

—BGQ FGJANJ
(Solution 23)

47 Rectangle to Greek Cross

A Greek cross is one in which all sides are equal (as illustrated). Divide a rectangle measuring 6″ × 3″ into three pieces that can be assembled into the shade of a Greek cross.

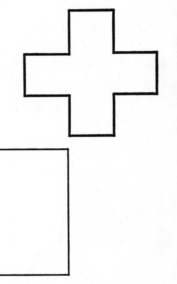

(Solution 28)

48 Motors

Out of ten motors, three are defective. Two are chosen at random. What are the chances that both are defective?

(Solution 32)

49 Word Circles

Place the letters in the correct boxes in each quadrant to obtain two 8-letter words, one reading clockwise and the other counter-clockwise. The two words are antonyms.

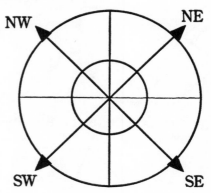

NE	:	EBUI
NW	:	BOGY
SW	:	RINN
SE	:	LTDS

Now use the same method to find two synonyms.

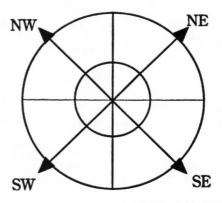

NE	:	TANN
NW	:	PINT
SW	:	HOIG
SE	:	ANGU

(Solution 36)

50 Number-Crunching Squares

The number 65 can be expressed as the sum of two squares in two different ways:
$$8^2 + 1^2 \ (64 + 1) \text{ and } 7^2 + 4^2 \ (49 + 16).$$

What is the smallest number that can be expressed in twelve different ways as the sum of two squares?

(Solution 41)

51 Sequence

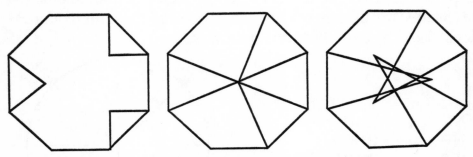

Which option below continues the above sequence?

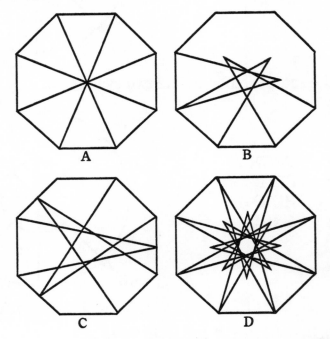

(Solution 45)

52 Do-It-Yourself Crossword

Place the pieces in the grid to complete the crossword.

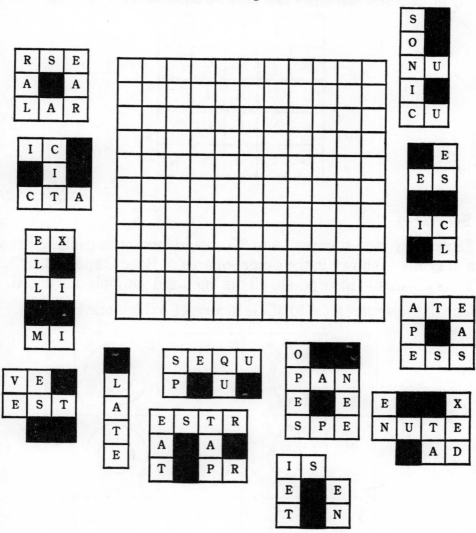

(Solution 48)

53 Longest Word

Find the longest word by moving from letter to adjacent letter in any direction. Each letter can only be used once.

R	E	F	P	C
W	T	G	O	V
H	D	A	I	J
K	N	L	U	Y
B	S	M	X	Q

(Solution 52)

54 Grid

Each of the nine squares 1A to 3C should incorporate all the lines and symbols shown in the outer squares A, B, or C and 1, 2, or 3. Thus 2B should incorporate all the lines and symbols in 2 and B.

One of the squares, 1A to 3C, is incorrect. Which one is it?

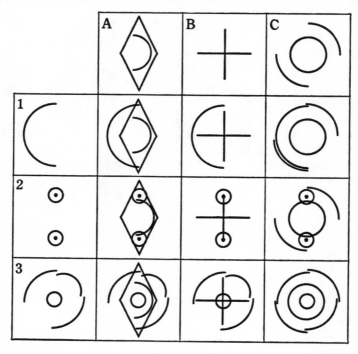

(Solution 56)

55 The Paradox of the Unexpected Gift

This is our presentation of a famous paradox which is more of an exercise in logic than a puzzle. Like all good paradoxes, it is designed to provide food for thought and philosophical discussion.

For the sake of argument, I am retiring next week and am to be presented with a gift. However, the day of presentation is meant to be a surprise; in other words, although I know I am to receive the gift, I do not know whether it is to be presented on a Monday, Tuesday, Wednesday, Thursday, or Friday.

The question to consider is: Can such a surprise gift be given? I know that it cannot be given on a Friday, the last day, for if it was left until then, the only day left, it would not be a surprise. So it must be on a Thursday. But then Thursday has in effect become the last day left, so it wouldn't be a surprise on that day either. The logic continues right back to Monday. Thus an unexpected gift is impossible.

Are there any other ways of solving the paradox? We make several suggestions in the solutions section, some of which you may think better than others.

At first, when you read the paradox with a clear mind, you may think the argument propounded ridiculous. But, like all good paradoxes, it is designed to confuse, and the more you think about it the more unclear your mind is likely to become about it.

(Solution 60)

56 Cross-Alphabet

Insert all twenty-six letters of the alphabet into the grid once each to form a crossword. Clues are given, but in no particular order.

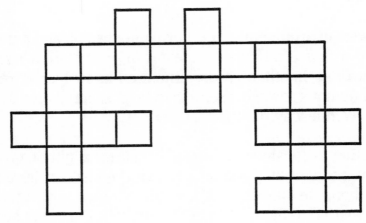

Clues:
- An opening in a house roof
- A valuable collection
- To spring into the air
- A Japanese sect of Buddhism
- Close at hand
- Bovine animal
- To make firm
- Small group of military personnel

(Solution 64)

57 Odd One Out

Which is the odd one out?

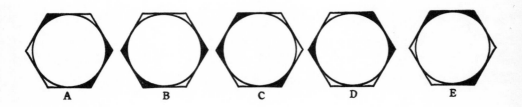

(Solution 67)

58 Directional Crossword

Answers run horizontally, vertically, or diagonally, either to the right or left. Each solution starts on the lower number and finishes on the next higher number, i.e., 1 to 2, 2 to 3, etc.

1 5							4
10		13		12		7	
	17				15		
					14		
			16				
11	8			9	6		
3						2	

Clues:

1. Make worse
2. Illegal behavior
3. Pain along a nerve
4. Wing or lifting surface
5. Embrocation
6. A rich confection
7. Small part
8. Thesis
9. Comes out
10. Specious argument
11. Wed
12. Canines
13. Grain storage containers
14. Result of addition
15. Shift
16. Ages
17. Steep in liquid

(Solution 72)

35

59 Lawns

My garden has two square lawns. Each has a whole number of feet along the sides. The total area is 8,845 square feet.

What are the sizes of the lawns if one lawn has a side that is one foot longer than the other lawn?

(Solution 76)

60 Same Word

Place a word in the parentheses that means the same as the two words or phrases outside the brackets.

1. Blockhead   (_____)   Pasta
2. Pot   (_____)   Decrepit person
3. Vessel   (_____)   Baseball thrower
4. Line of people   (_____)   Braid of hair
5. Set of three   (____)   Aquatic bird
6. Cask   (_____)   Post supporting roof
7. Goblin   (____)   Ice hockey disc
8. One who staggers (_____)   Crossed greyhound and collie
9. Grease over   (_____)   Tack in sewing
10. Small hound   (_____)   Spy or informer

(Solution 80)

61 The Train in the Tunnel

A train traveling at a speed of 75 m.p.h. enters a tunnel that is $2\frac{1}{2}$ miles long. The length of the train is $\frac{1}{4}$ mile. How long does it take for all of the train to pass through the tunnel, from the moment the front enters to the moment the rear emerges?

(Solution 84)

62 Links Jigsaw Puzzle

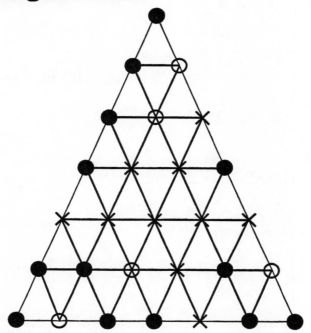

Place the twelve segment links below over the triangular grid above in such a way that each link symbol is covered by exactly the same symbol. The connecting segments must not be rotated. Note that not all the connecting lines will be covered.

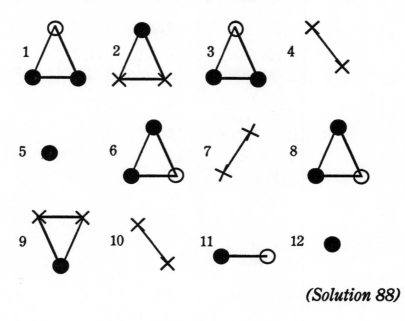

(Solution 88)

63 Plan In Works

A. Change one letter in each word of each grouping to make a well-known phrase. For example,

GO PAT OUR FEEDERS will become TO PUT OUT FEELERS.

    1. TAN ANY TOY
    2. O PUCK ON LIPS
    3. IF PULL TRY
    4. SO TREAT GUSS
    5. PUT ON POINT
    6. CHEER MY FOWL
    7. PINE TOWN
    8. PLAN SALE
    9. LAD COLD ON
    10. JIVING DOLT

B. The following are more difficult because the order of the words has also been changed:

OUR FEEDERS PAT GO will become TO PUT OUT FEELERS.

    1. ANDS ADDS ANY
    2. OLDER I TALK
    3. BEAST PAY SHE GO
    4. GOWN SHIPS ACE SHE THEN
    5. LIE ON SO
    6. ON SAND GLOBE
    7. I RUSH AS
    8. SHE STEAM SHOP
    9. MY FAKE STORY
    10. WAVE IN SHE

(Solution 93)

64 Piecemeal Quotation

A quotation has been divided into letter groups and arranged in alphabetical order. For example, FIND THE QUOTE would be presented as EQ, FI, ND, TE, TH, UO (4, 3, 5). Rearrange the following letters to find a quotation by Goethe (2, 5, 4, 7, 6, 2, 2, 4, 3, 2, 7, 2, 8, 3, 7).

AN, BE, DK, EA, ER, ER, IF, IO, KI, LE, MB, ND,
NO, NO, NO, NX, OA, ON, RE, RE, SE, TH, TO,
TS, TT, UL, US, WE, WE, WE, WO, WM.

```
__/_____/____/_____/_____/
__/__/____/___/__/_____/__/
_____/___/_____
```
(Solution 95)

65 Birds

Solve the clues, then change one letter to find the name of ten birds. The asterisk represents the letter to be changed.

	Answer	Birds
1. Stray away	* • • • • •	• • • • • •
2. Rolled up	• • • • • *	• • • • • •
3. Four-leafed is lucky	* • • • • •	• • • • • •
4. Best toasted with butter	* • • • • •	• • • • • •
5. Type of flag	* • • • • •	• • • • • •
6. What a dropped catch is	• • • • • *	• • • • • •
7. Animal found in rivers	* • • • • •	• • • • • •
8. Muffle	* • • • • •	• • • • • •
9. Type of fish	• • • • • *	• • • • • •
10. A lie	• • • • • *	• • • • • •

(Solution 100)

66 Matrix

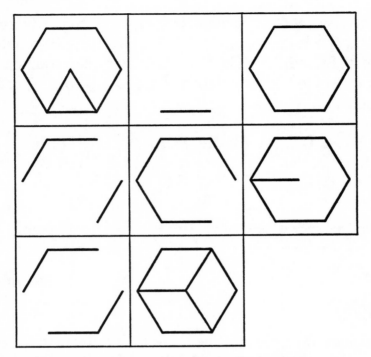

Find the missing tile from the choice below:

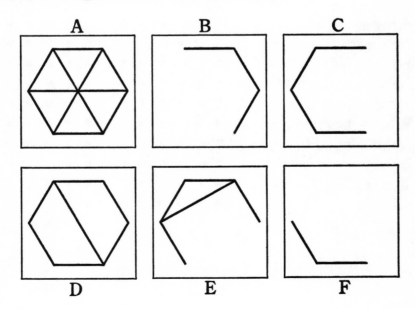

(Solution 104)

67 Links Jigsaw Puzzle

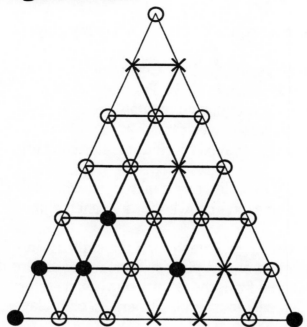

Place the twelve segment links below over the triangular grid above in such a way that each link symbol is covered by exactly the same symbol. The connecting segments must not be rotated. Note that not all the connecting lines will be covered.

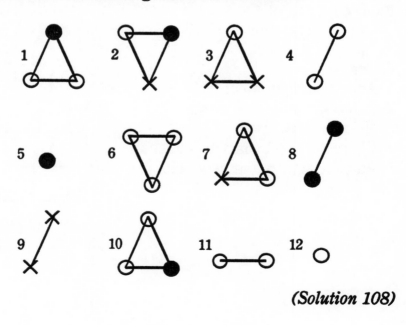

(Solution 108)

68 World Cup

A national soccer squad consisted of twenty players:

> Five players played for Germany
> Four players played for France
> Three players played for Italy
> Two players played for Spain
> Six players played for South American clubs

The squad only included one goalkeeper, who played for an Italian club. The captain played for a French club.

Assuming that the goalkeeper and the captain were included in every selection of eleven players, how many different teams could be selected from the twenty players, irrespective of positions, if at least four South American club players were included in each selection?

(Solution 113)

69 Pyramid Word

Solve the five clues, enter the correct words in the pyramid, and then rearrange all the answer letters to find one 15-letter word.

Clues:
1. An indefinite number
2. In the same manner or way
3. Holds a possession
4. Characterized by facility and skill
5. An ox less than four years old

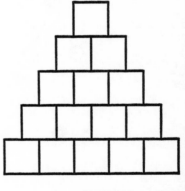

(Solution 116)

70 Two Quick Teasers

1. By what fractional part does four-fourths exceed three-fourths?

2. Write down quickly in figures the sum of 13 thousand and 13 hundred and 13.

(Solution 120)

71 Clueless Crossword

Delete three letters in each 4-letter box to solve the crossword.

FP SA	JC LT	RN EA	ET SA	OT SA	TC EL	HR MD
PL OT	■	AE NI	■	TR LN	■	IR EA
IO AS	MO NL	AE NS	TE ZC	PE IO	EN AY	DG SR
NI OE	■	PE AL	■	AE UO	■	AE NT
LT GI	RI NE	ED SX	NA PE	RP TN	TA OE	RY SE

(Solution 124)

72 Birds

My friend asked me the ages of my three daughters. I said:
"If you multiply their ages it equals 90, and they are all under 15.
If you add their ages then it equals the number of birds in that tree."

So my friend counted the birds in the tree, but he still did not know how old my children were!

How many birds were there in the tree?

(Solution 128)

73 Hexagons and Triangles

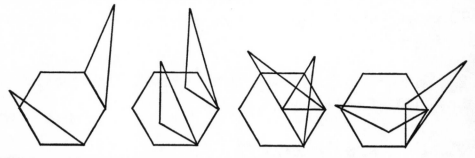

Which option below continues the above sequence?

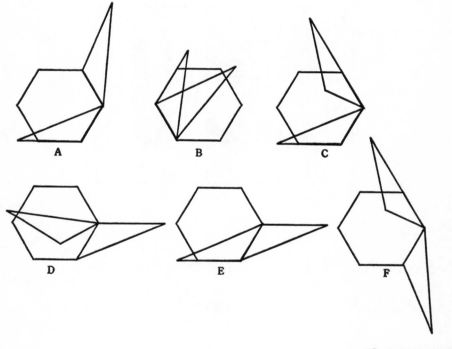

(Solution 132)

74 Decadice

With a pair of 10-sided dice, what are the odds of scoring at least 13 in one throw of the pair?

(Solution 137)

75 Hexagram

Solve the six anagrams of WEAPONS and ARMOR. Transfer the six arrowed letters to the key anagram boxes and solve this anagram to discover a key seventh term.

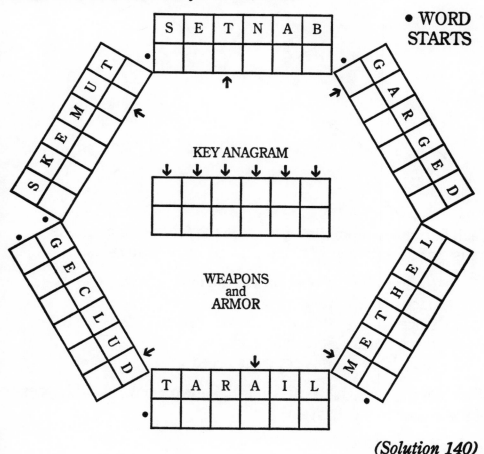

• WORD STARTS

KEY ANAGRAM

WEAPONS and ARMOR

(Solution 140)

76 Symbols

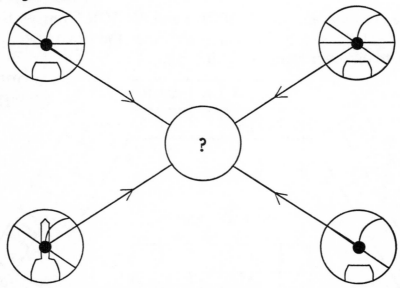

Each line and symbol that appears in the four outer circles is transferred to the center circle according to these rules:

> If a line or symbol occurs in the outer circles:
>
> once — it is transferred
> twice — it is possibly transferred
> three times — it is transferred
> four times — it is not transferred

Which of the circles A, B, C, D, or E, shown below, should appear at the center of the diagram?

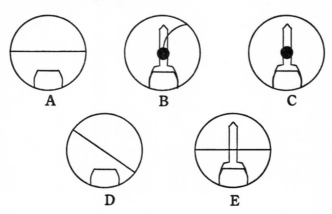

(Solution 144)

77 Odd One Out

Below are a number of car license plates. Which is the odd one out?

A   76 MON C

B   68 GRE F

C   12 STO S

D   56 MEL A

E   92 BAR S

(Solution 148)

78 Anagrammed Synonyms

In each of the following groups of three words your task is to discover which two of the three words can be paired to form an anagram of one word that is a synonym of the word remaining. For example: LEG – MEEK – NET. The words LEG and NET are an anagram of GENTLE, which is a synonym of the remaining word MEEK.

1.   LAP – APE – PLEA
2.   SIMPER – POSE – ATONE
3.   DIM – LIKE – ARE
4.   SAY – NOT – MINE
5.   TRADE – SIN – TAUT
6.   CLUES – KISS – OAT
7.   RED – COY – SEVER
8.   UNDER – RID – NUB
9.   ADD – GAUNT – ME
10.   NO – RULER – CHARM

(Solution 152)

79 Bars

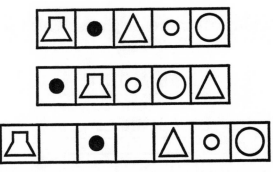

Which option below continues the above sequence?

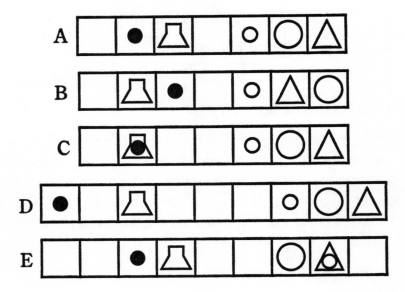

(Solution 156)

80 Palindromic

Rearrange these numbers to make the sequence in some way palindromic:

1, 3, 4, 9, 9, 12, 13, 14, 15, 16, 18

(Solution 160)

81 Cards

Select twelve cards, note the letters, and find a 12-letter word. Each card can be used only once.

Score the highest score that you can—the maximum is 160.

										(11)	(12)	(13)	(15)	
CARDS	2	3	4	5	6	7	8	9	10	J	Q	K	A	CARDS
♡	C	R	U	Y	B	X	V	H	D	V	T	I	N	♡
♣	S	Y	G	C	W	D	P	K	R	J	A	L	P	♣
◇	F	Z	O	L	G	Q	B	Q	M	W	O	T	A	◇
♤	S	U	E	Z	H	X	K	E	J	F	M	I	N	♤
SCORE	2	3	4	5	6	7	8	9	10	J	Q	K	A	SCORE
										(11)	(12)	(13)	(15)	

Example: MACHINATION

M	QS	12
A	QC	12
C	5C	5
H	9H	9
I	KH	13
N	AH	15
A	AD	15
T	KD	13
I	KS	13
O	QD	12
N	AS	15
		134

(Solution 1)

49

82 Saying

This saying has had all of its vowels removed. The consonants are in their correct order but have been broken up into groups of four.

Replace the vowels and reconstitute the saying.

THST RNGT KFRM THWK
THRC HTKF RMTH PRND
THGV RNMN TTKF RMVR
YN

—GLMM SLW

(Solution 5)

83 Synonym Circles

Read clockwise to find two 8-letter synonyms. You have to find the starting point and provide the missing letters.

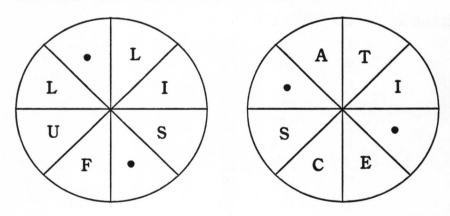

(Solution 9)

84 Nine Digits

The multiplication sum 51,249,876 × 3 uses the nine digits each, only once, producing the answer 153,749,628, which also uses the nine digits each, only once.

Can you find a multiplication sum using 6 as your multiplier that has the same property?

(Solution 13)

85 Grid

Each of the nine squares 1A to 3C should incorporate all the lines and symbols shown in the outer squares A, B, or C and 1, 2, or 3. Thus 2B should incorporate all the lines and symbols in 2 and B.

One of the squares, 1A to 3C, is incorrect. Which one is it?

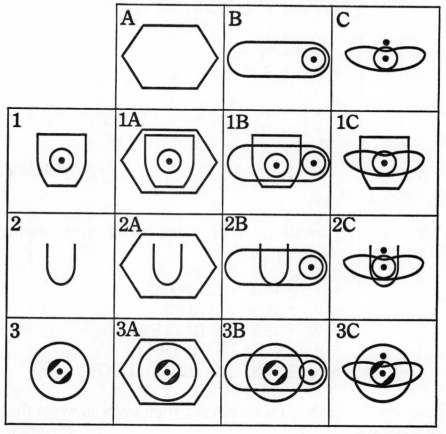

(Solution 17)

86 Alphametics

Replace the letters with numbers:

```
    THE
    TEN
+   MEN
  MEET
```

(Solution 21)

87 Languages

Fill in the missing alternate letters to spell the names of nine languages. For example, • N • L • S • represents ENGLISH. Then rearrange the initial letters of each language to find a tenth language.

```
• E • M • N
• C • L • N • I •
• A •
• M • A • I •
• O • A • I • N
• R • U
• E • G • L •
• R • B • C
• E • A • I
```

(Solution 25)

88 Book Titles

All the following are anagrams of famous books written during the twentieth century:

1. FIEND MAN COME
2. ANGRY MELTER
3. THEY GAG BATTERS
4. FATHER'S WINDOW
5. TIRING DIM BLACK LOOK

When you have solved them, can you then say who wrote them?

(Solution 29)

89 Triangle Matrix

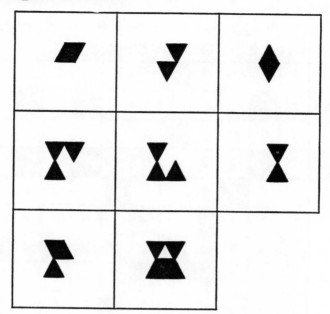

Find the missing tile from the choice below:

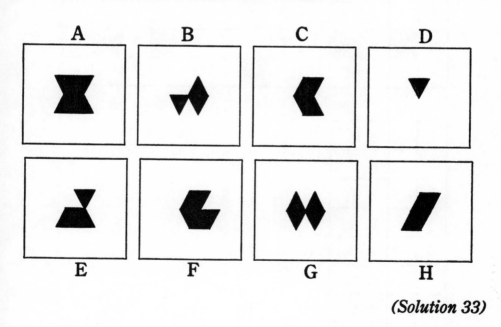

A   B   C   D

E   F   G   H

(Solution 33)

90 Alternative Crossword

The number in each square represents a letter, but you have to select one from a choice of three each time.

7	5	6	2	3	2	■	1	5	7	7	2	7
7	■	2	■	4	7	5	1	6	■	2	■	3
7	5	2	5	4	2	■	5	2	7	7	4	2
1	■	3	■	7	2	2	2	7	■	7	■	5
1	1	5	7	■	7	1	9	■	1	2	2	2
5	6	2	6	1	■	6	■	7	6	2	2	7
■	1	■	3	5	4	■	2	3	2	■	4	■
2	6	6	2	2	■	6	■	7	2	1	7	7
7	7	7	2	■	6	5	6	■	2	6	1	8
7	■	5	■	2	5	7	2	7	■	1	■	5
1	5	1	4	2	7	■	2	7	7	7	2	6
9	■	4	■	1	7	7	1	6	■	2	■	2
7	7	2	2	6	7	■	4	2	5	7	2	7

1	A B C
2	D E F
3	G H I
4	J K L
5	M N O
6	P Q R
7	S T U
8	V W X
9	Y Z –

(Solution 37)

91 Fore and Aft

Find a 3-letter word that completes all three words on the left and prefixes all three words on the right.

FORE ——— · · · ——— HOOD
WORK ——— · · · ——— DRAKE
MARKS ——— · · · ——— KIND

(Solution 38)

92 Odd One Out

Which is the odd one out?

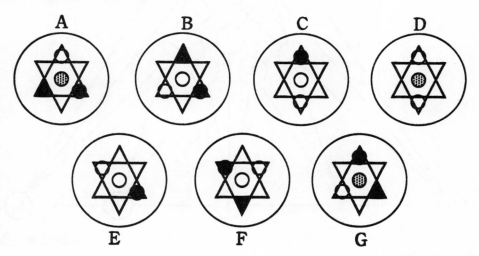

(Solution 44)

93 Sequence

What number comes next in this sequence?

12, 23, 35, 47, 511, 613, 717, 819, 923, 1029, ?

(Solution 49)

94 Network

Find the starting point and travel along the connecting lines in a continuous path to adjacent circles to spell out a 14-letter word. Every circle can be visited only once.

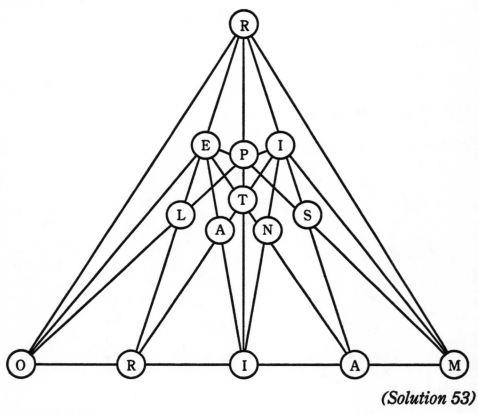

(Solution 53)

95 Odd One Out

Which is the odd one out?

        A. Got
        B. Car
        C. Seals
        D. Trips

(Solution 57)

96 Sequence

Which option below continues the sequence above?

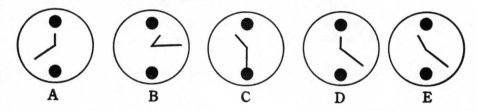

(Solution 61)

97 "D" Puzzle

Using the first and last letters already inserted, place the fifteen letters of the five words at the bottom anywhere in the grid to form five new 5-letter words reading across.

D				T
D				A
D				L
D				O
D				N

JEW
HIS
SIC
LAC
DIN

(Solution 65)

98 Fish Farm

A fish farmer had to visit a different fish lake each day. Where should he build his house in order to minimize his total walking distance?

(Solution 69)

99 Magic Number Square

Insert the remaining numbers from 1 to 16 so that each horizontal, vertical, and corner-to-corner line totals 34.

(Solution 73)

100 Trite Saying

Select the words in order to produce a trite saying.

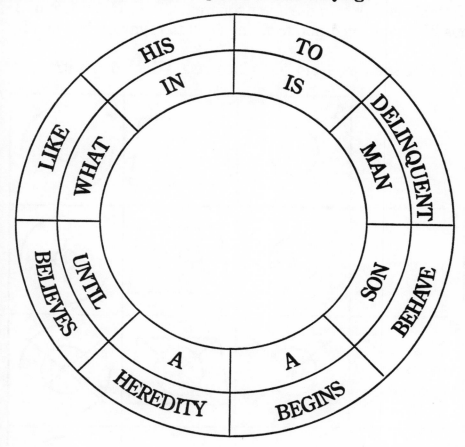

(Solution 77)

101 Cryptogram III

This is a straightforward cryptogram in which each letter of the quotation has been replaced by another.

IVAM UZ ZV HVHLAJB ZUKHAX PTEJLZT UY
UZ YST PTZY IJKT UQ YST FVBAC JY
FSUES YV PT PJC.

—J. J. KUAQT
(Solution 81)

102 Grid

Each of the nine squares 1A to 3C should incorporate all the lines and symbols shown in the outer squares A, B, or C and 1, 2, or 3. Thus 2B should incorporate all the lines and symbols in 2 and B.

One of the squares, 1A to 3C, is incorrect. Which one is it?

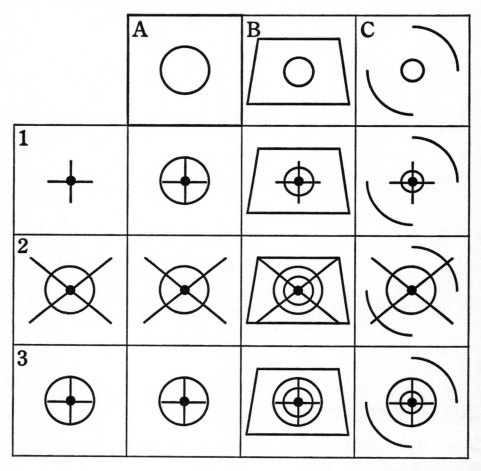

(Solution 85)

103 Anagram Theme

Arrange the sixteen words in pairs so that each pair is an
anagram of another word. The eight words produced have a
linking theme. For example, if the words TRY and CREASE
appeared in the list they could be paired to form the word
SECRETARY and the theme could be PROFESSIONS. (Words
are not necessarily one from each column.)

AM	AMINE
BY	EMU
FARM	FAT
FINE	FORT
HE	RACK
RAG	RAIN
ROMP	SO
SWORE	TRACE

(Solution 89)

104 Analogy

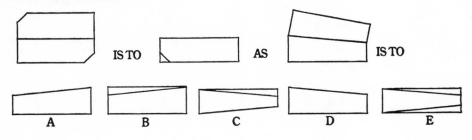

(Solution 92)

61

105 "Y" Puzzle

Find twenty-seven words that each contains at least one "Y."
Move from letter to letter along the lines. Letters may be used
more than once.

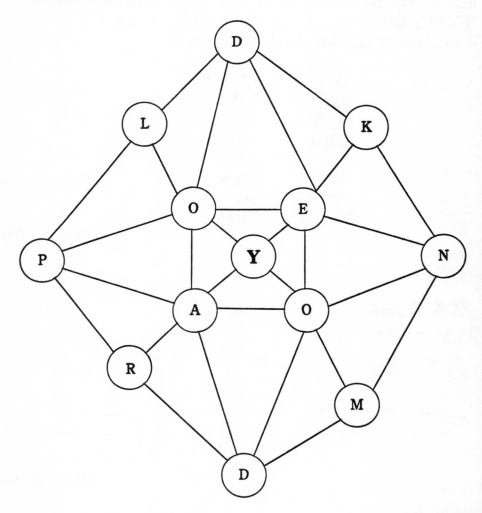

(Solution 97)

106 Rectangle

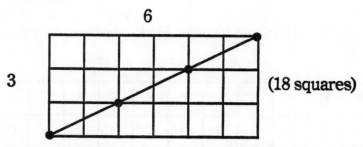

6

3

(18 squares)

In the example the diagonal crosses four points that are corners of squares.

How many points will be crossed in a rectangle 36 × 24 (864 squares)?

(Solution 101)

107 Alphabet Clueless-Crossword

Insert the remaining nineteen of the twenty-six letters of the alphabet to complete the crossword.

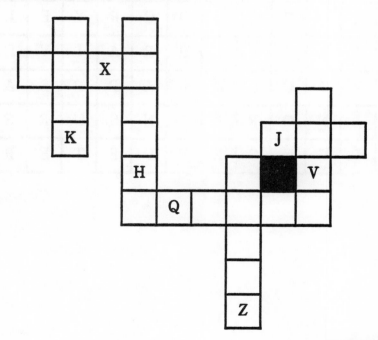

(Solution 105)

108 No Blanks

All the blank squares have been omitted and replaced with letters. See if you can find the blanks to form a symmetrical crossword.

P	L	A	N	E	T	S	F	A	T	H	E	R
U	A	R	O	R	O	T	O	R	N	O	V	A
F	R	I	D	A	Y	A	R	U	N	L	E	T
F	U	S	E	S	E	R	U	M	A	D	R	H
I	C	E	D	I	D	I	M	I	M	E	R	E
N	O	S	E	D	A	M	A	B	O	R	E	R
E	B	B	C	O	S	A	M	A	R	O	B	E
C	R	O	O	N	I	L	O	G	A	S	E	S
H	A	I	R	E	C	O	G	R	Y	E	L	P
A	I	L	O	Z	E	B	R	A	I	V	E	E
S	P	I	C	E	D	L	A	P	P	E	A	L
E	A	N	O	R	A	I	N	S	U	R	E	L
S	I	G	N	O	R	P	D	E	T	E	R	S

(Solution 109)

109 Logic

Logically, which circle fits the pattern?

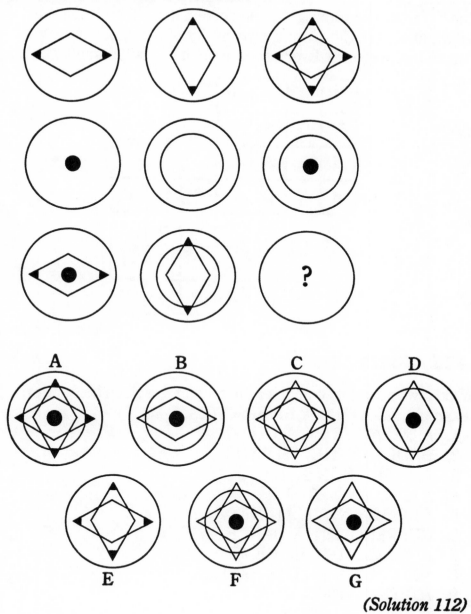

(Solution 112)

110 An Irish Proverb

Starting from the "N" in the top left-hand corner and ending with the "T" in the bottom right-hand corner, move from square to adjacent square (horizontally, vertically, and diagonally) to spell out an Irish proverb. Every square must be visited only once.

N	G	D	I			
T	O	N	D			
H	E	A	D			
H	E	O	D	S	N	E
			E	O	H	B
			T	O	T	O
			R	W	A	T

(Solution 117)

111 Containers

Find a word and its container for each of the clues below. For example, MEAT IN A RIVER = T(HAM)ES.
1. A RELATIVE IN A GLOVE
2. HADES IN THE ISLANDS
3. A BORDER IN A TOPIC
4. A COLOR IN A SHIP
5. DEPART IN A HATCHET
6. CURRENCY IN A DANCE
7. A NOBLEMAN IN GEMS
8. AN INSECT IN THE LARDER
9. AT THAT TIME IN A CAPITAL
10. FOLD IN A STATE

(Solution 121)

112 Connections

Insert the numbers 0–9 in the circles so that, for any particular circle, the sum of the numbers in the circles connected directly to it equals the value corresponding to the number in that circle, as given in the list.

Example: $1 = 14\ (4 + 7 + 3)$
$\quad\quad\quad 4 = 8\ (7 + 1)$
$\quad\quad\quad 7 = 5\ (4 + 1)$
$\quad\quad\quad 3 = 1$

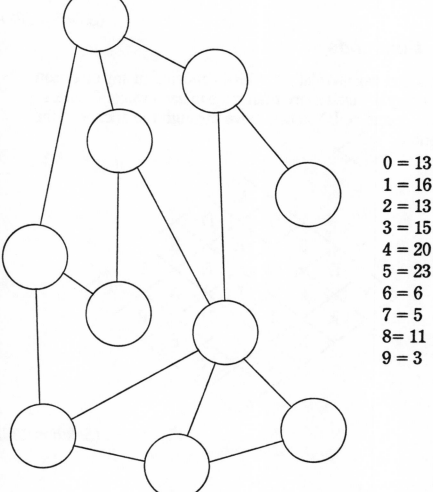

$0 = 13$
$1 = 16$
$2 = 13$
$3 = 15$
$4 = 20$
$5 = 23$
$6 = 6$
$7 = 5$
$8 = 11$
$9 = 3$

(Solution 125)

113 Trade

If the symbols above represent the word TRADE, what word is represented by the symbols below?

(Solution 129)

114 Diamonds

Find sixteen words relating to birds, moving in any direction. Letters may be used more than once in each word. Corners count as connected. You can move through the apexes of the diamonds:

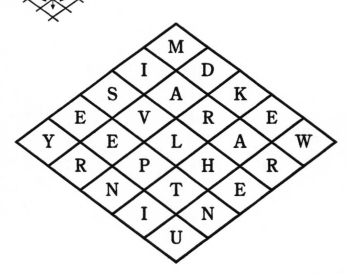

(Solution 133)

115 Cement

"How heavy is this bag of cement?" asked the builder.

"Five thousand pounds divided by half its own weight," said the merchant.

How much did the bag of cement weigh?

(Solution 136)

116 Words

Hostility
Intermezzo
Joyfully
Heifer
Fiddlesticks
Lockjaw

Logically, which word comes next?

Publisher
Racehorse
Tormentor
Galantine
Cantabile
Whimsical

(Solution 141)

117 Bracket Word

Place two letters in each pair of brackets so that they finish the word on the left and start the word on the right. Reading downward in pairs, the letters in the brackets will spell out a 10-letter word.

```
SO  (——)  AL
AR  (——)  IN
BE  (——)  D
 T  (——)  ON
ME  (——)  L
```

(Solution 145)

118 Circles

Which of these fits into the blank circle to carry on a logical sequence?

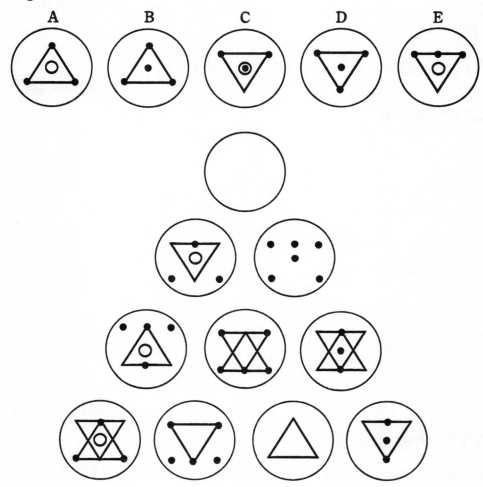

(Solution 149)

119 Roman Numerals

The year 2000 will have just two Roman numerals, MM. Which year in the previous 2000 had the most Roman numerals?

(Solution 153)

120 Porky Pies

How good are you at trivia? Each of the following presents three statements, one of which is a fabrication; the other two are true. Can you spot the untruth in each case?

1. a) Maloney was the name of actor John Barrymore's pet vulture.
   b) Raoulle was the barking dog in the 1978 movie *The Buddy Holly Story.*
   c) Herman was Maxim de Winter's pet cocker spaniel in the 1940 movie *Rebecca.*

2. a) The 31st president of the United States, Herbert Hoover, was a Quaker.
   b) John Edgar Hoover, head of the FBI, was married twice.
   c) Irwin H. "Ike" Hoover was the first chief usher at the White House.

3. a) Duke Ellington's real first name was Edmund.
   b) Dizzy Gillespie's real first name was Desmond.
   c) Jelly Roll Morton's real first name was Ferdinand.

4. a) Elvis Presley once recorded the song "I'll Take You Home Again, Kathleen."
   b) "I'm Forever Blowing Bubbles" was the theme song of the 1931 movie *Public Enemy.*
   c) "I Cried for You" was the song that Ginger Rogers sang to a photo of Mickey Rooney in the 1939 movie *Babes in Arms.*

5. a) In 1978, golfer Jack Nicklaus landed a 1,358-pound marlin, the biggest fish caught off Australia that year.
   b) Jockey Billy Pearson once won $64,000 on TV answering questions about art.
   c) Hurricane Mills was a heavyweight boxer who was once a member of the USA bobsled team.

(Solution 161)

121 The Hexagonal Circle

What should be the contents of the top hexagon?

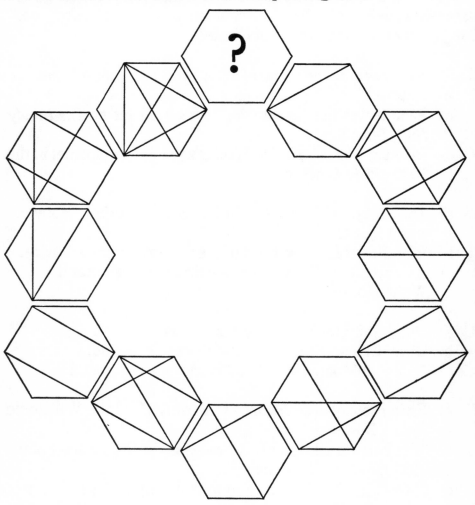

(Solution 2)

122 Logic

What number should follow next in this sequence to create a definite pattern?

$$4 - 6 - 6 - 6 - 4 - 2 - 4 - 8 - 2 - 6 - 1 - 8 - ?$$

(Solution 6)

123 Diamond

Find the longest word, moving to adjacent diamonds in any direction indicated in the diagram below.

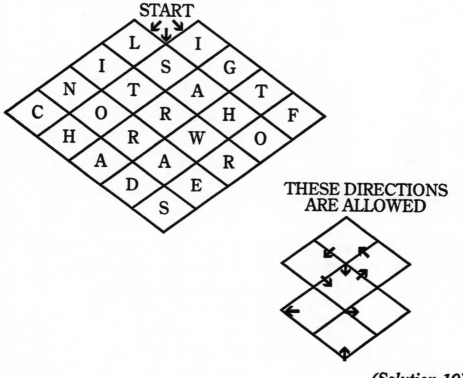

START

THESE DIRECTIONS
ARE ALLOWED

(Solution 10)

124 Common

What do these words have in common?

Rain
Mark
Land
Tine
Pore
Wait
Pain

(Solution 14)

125 Symbols

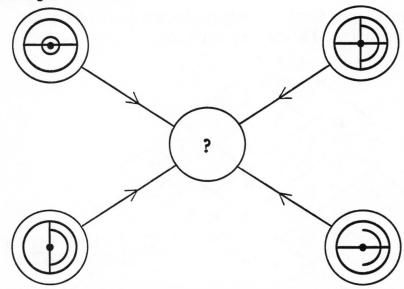

Each line and symbol that appears in the four outer circles is transferred to the center circle according to these rules:

If a line or symbol occurs in the outer circles:

once	it is transferred
twice	it is possibly transferred
three times	it is transferred
four times	it is not transferred

Which of the circles A, B, C, D, or E, shown below, should **appear** at the center of the diagram?

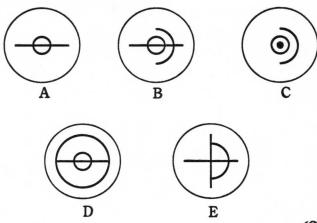

(Solution 18)

126 Division

Divide the grid into four equal parts, each of which is the same shape and contains the same sixteen letters, which can be arranged into a 16-letter word.

E	A	A	D	I	A	I	F
I	L	L	T	I	N	B	Y
F	I	N	T	D	I	E	G
B	T	I	G	Y	A	I	T
G	D	Y	E	I	A	I	I
N	I	B	F	T	D	A	I
Y	L	I	E	T	B	L	T
T	F	A	I	I	A	G	N

(Solution 24)

127 Sequence

What is the next number in this sequence?

199, 280, 344, 360, 396, ?

(Solution 26)

128 Synonyms

In each of the following, a number of synonyms of the keyword are shown. Take one letter from each of the synonyms to find a further synonym of the keyword. The letters appear in the correct order.

1. Keyword: HOMOGENEOUS
   Synonyms: Unvarying, Analogous, Kindred, Akin, Cognate

2. Keyword: PURITANICAL
   Synonyms: Narrow, Disapproving, Strict, Severe, Austere, Bigoted, Fanatical

3. Keyword: GARRULOUS
   Synonyms: Gossiping, Verbose, Talkative, Chatty, Loquacious, Gushing, Babbling

4. Keyword: GROOVE
   Synonyms: Furrow, Hollow, Gutter, Indentation, Trench

5. Keyword: PROPULSION
   Synonyms: Drive, Momentum, Pressure, Power, Thrust, Push, Impulse

(Solution 30)

129 Hexagonal Sequence

Which hexagon below continues the above sequence?

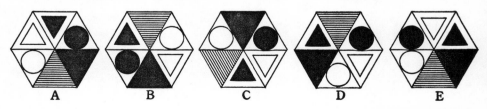

(Solution 34)

130 Word Power

Working from the top down solve the clues and place the letters in the circles of the pyramid. Each answer is the previous answer rearranged, with one letter added. Clues are given in no particular order.

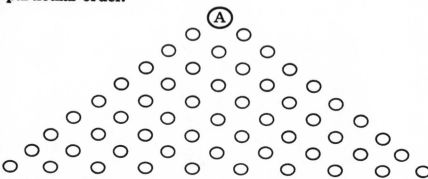

1. Shopkeepers
2. Singers
3. Look carefully
4. Manuscripts
5. Receptacle
6. Measure of fish
7. Article
8. Lifting machines
9. Deep sleeps

(Solution 39)

131 Odd One Out

Which is the odd one out?

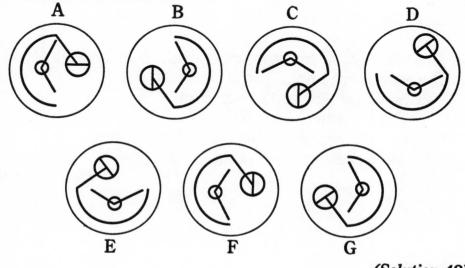

A   B   C   D

E   F   G

(Solution 42)

132 Ball

A ball is dropped to the ground from a height of twelve feet. It bounces up half of the original height, then falls back to the ground. It repeats this, always bouncing back half of the previous height.

How far does the ball travel?

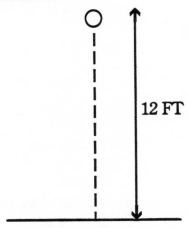

12 FT

(Solution 46)

133 Hidden Fish

Hidden in the sentences are the names of five fish and one sea mammal. See if you can find them.

1. This summer linger a little longer on the beach.
2. The girls have a skipping rope race.
3. Will the bursar dine at the restaurant?
4. They dug on ground that was too wet.
5. Eradicate the vermin now or you will be too late.
6. Dogs often chase cats and birds.

(Solution 50)

134 Anagram Phrases

Each of the following is an anagram of a well-known phrase. For example: SO NOTE HOLE = ON THE LOOSE

1. AH! LOVING FATE
2. SHOOT TENDER GREEN FLOWER AT GUESTS
3. TO NOTE FEET IN MINUS
4. HONE KEY OUR STRIP
5. USE DRAM OR FOE GO

(Solution 54)

135 Grid Logic

Insert the missing letters in the top left-hand corner square.

	TO	TO	FO	FO
OT	TT	TT	FT	FT
OT	TT	TT	FT	FT
OF	TF	TF	FF	FF
OF	TF	TF	FF	FF

(Solution 58)

136 Margana

If we presented you with the words MAR, AM, and FAR and asked you to find the shortest English word that contained all the letters from which these words could be produced, we would expect you to come up with the word FARM.

Here is another list of words: JOLT, ROUT, STAR, SIN

What is the shortest English word from which all these words can be produced?

(Solution 62)

79

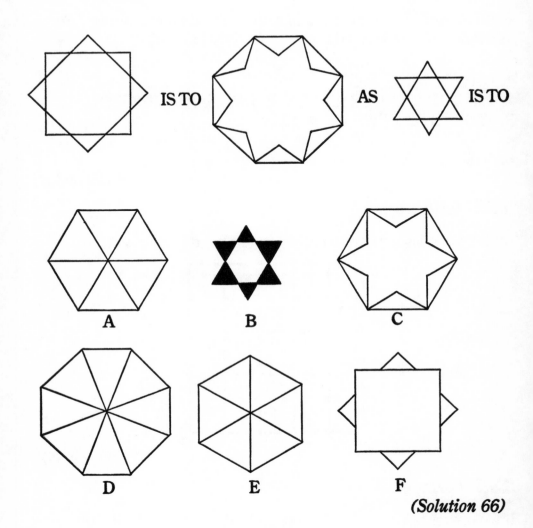

IS TO ... AS ... IS TO

A   B   C

D   E   F

(Solution 66)

138 Four Letters

Each of these sets of four letters forms part of a longer word.
Some of the words are hyphenated. What are the twelve longer
words?

SHBO
YEBR
NGPL
GHFL
RKSM
EE-QU
TLEB
GSPR
HY-WA
GONL
CHHO
NWRI

(Solution 70)

139 Initials

What do these initials stand for? For example:

16 – O in a P = 16 Ounces in a Pound

6 – P on a P T
32 – P on a C
6 – S on a S
3 – F in a Y
1 – G T D A
3 – C in the F
13 – M in a L Y
12 – S on a D

(Solution 75)

140 Word Search

Find 31 NAUTICAL TERMS. Words run horizontally, vertically, or diagonally, but only in a straight line. Every letter is used at least once.

R	S	T	O	W	A	W	A	Y	R
E	E	O	S	A	L	V	O	E	E
T	O	R	N	A	D	O	G	D	T
A	S	P	O	R	T	G	I	K	A
W	R	E	N	H	E	T	H	C	W
K	A	D	W	L	S	C	R	O	H
A	T	O	T	E	T	E	E	L	S
E	B	O	H	E	W	E	R	W	E
R	O	C	K	E	T	E	P	O	R
B	A	R	N	A	C	L	E	R	F

(Solution 78)

141 Magic Prime Square

Using prime numbers only, complete the square so that each horizontal, vertical, and corner-to-corner line totals the same.

	73	

(Solution 82)

82

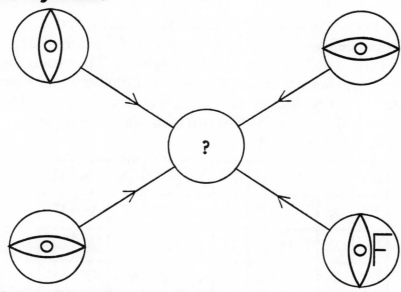

Each line and symbol that appears in the four outer circles is transferred to the center circle according to these rules:

If a line or symbol occurs in the outer circles:
once	it is transferred
twice	it is possibly transferred
three times	it is transferred
four times	it is not transferred

Which of the circles A, B, C, D, or E, shown below, should appear at the center of the diagram?

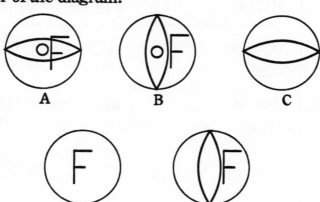

(Solution 86)

143 Ten-Letter Words Boggle

Work from square to square horizontally, vertically, and diagonally to spell out twenty 10-letter words. All letters are in pairs, and every pair of letters is used only once. Thus each 10-letter word occupies five squares. It does not matter which word you identify first, providing you make the correct turnings. The twenty words will eventually take you through the complete pattern of all 100 pairs of letters.

HY	OP	IL	PH	HW	RT	WO	TR	LE	IL
PR	OS	LE	HI	AT	ED	AF	IP	AR	EV
UD	ON	DR	AM	LI	FI	AL	TI	VA	UD
EN	TI	TA	UL	AT	IC	BI	MO	TE	NG
NC	TI	EX	AL	IC	ST	LE	TO	AU	HI
IL	CO	AL	AC	JE	MA	ER	EV	ER	YT
IA	RY	RV	EO	AU	OV	RC	RI	TA	VE
IO	CU	FI	US	UL	SP	DE	AN	GE	ON
US	IT	CT	TF	IO	IC	UN	TI	TR	TI
TH	OU	GH	US	EX	HI	BI	ON	AJ	EC

(Solution 90)

144 Two Coins

I have two old coins, one is marked George I and one is marked Edward VII. One is genuine, but one is a forgery. Which is the forgery?

(Solution 94)

145 Hexagons

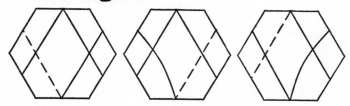

Which hexagon below continues the above sequence?

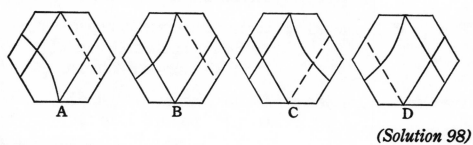

A   B   C   D

(Solution 98)

146 Star

Find the 12-letter word by going into each of the compartments only once.

(Solution 102)

147 Silent Order

What 8-letter word links these words?

Knoll
Heifer
Indict
Knew
Doubt
Toast
Nascent
Knickers

(Solution 106)

148 Journey

Three hitchhikers traveled along a road. They all left the hostel at the same time — twelve noon.

Traveler A journeyed by car for 1 hour at 30 m.p.h.
foot for 3 hours at $3\frac{1}{3}$ m.p.h.
cart for 4 hours at 10 m.p.h.

Traveler B journeyed by cart for 2 hours at 10 m.p.h.
car for $1\frac{1}{2}$ hours at 40 m.p.h.
foot for 3 hours at $3\frac{1}{3}$ m.p.h.

Traveler C journeyed by foot for 3 hours at $3\frac{1}{3}$ m.p.h.
cart for 3 hours at 10 m.p.h.
car for 2 hours at 30 m.p.h.

Who overtook whom and at what time?

(Solution 111)

149 Magic Word Square

The answers to the five clues are all 5-letter words that, when placed correctly in the grid, will form a magic square in which the five words can be read both horizontally and vertically.

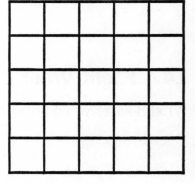

Clues (in no particular order):
Rhythmical effects
Existing in a particular place
In pieces
Short-necked giraffelike animal
Watercourse

(Solution 114)

150 Sequence

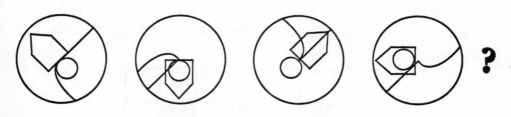

Which option below carries on the above sequence?

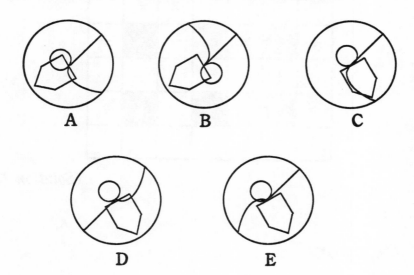

A B C

D E

(Solution 118)

151 People

In a set of 100 people, 63 have a height of over 5'6" and 75 have a weight of more than 140 pounds. What are the greatest and least possible numbers of people over 5'6" and more than 140 pounds? Each person has at least one of these features.

(Solution 122)

152 Brain Strain

Insert numbers into the spaces so that the calculations are correct across and down. All numbers to be inserted are less than 10.

	÷		+		=	9
×	■	+	■	+	■	×
	−		+	3	=	
÷	■	×	■	−	■	÷
	+	3	−		=	
=	■	=	■	=	■	=
4	+		−		=	

(Solution 126)

153 Common

What do these words have in common?

Rifles
Mugging
Tundra
Mural
Precaution
Emily
Boracic
Resort

(Solution 130)

154 Complete the Quotations

Each of the following is an anagram of one word. Solve the anagrams and then place the ten words into the correct quotations.

A. NOR I SHAME
B. CHEER SIR
C. O TIDY CRIME
D. MOTH PAN

E. PIN CASH
F. COVER ON SAINT
G. PRISES OPEN A TRAP
H. ROOT WORM

I. REACH IT CUTER
J. SEAL A PUP

1. "It is far harder to kill a _____ than a reality."
   —*Virginia Woolf*
2. "_____ is often the busiest day of the week."
   —*Spanish Proverb*
3. "After all, the only proper intoxication is _____."
   —*Oscar Wilde*
4. "The _____ of bound books are like the flowers of the field."
   —*Hilaire Belloc*
5. "Gave up _____ for lent."   —*F. Scott Fitzgerald*
6. "The excellence of a gift lies in its _____ rather than its value."   —*Charles Dudley Warner*
7. "_____ obtains more with application than superiority without it."   —*Baltasar Gracián*
8. "_____ is the beginning of abuse."   —*Japanese Proverb*
9. "_____ is a sort of oratory of power by means of forms."
   —*Friedrich Nietzsche*
10. "He who likes _____ soon learns to climb."
    —*German Proverb*
    (Solution 134)

155 A Long Time

Substitute numbers for letters in this multiplication problem. Each letter represents a different number from 1 to 9. There are two possible answers.

$$A \times LONG = TIME$$

(Solution 138)

156 Shields Matrix

What symbol should logically appear on the bottom right-hand shield?

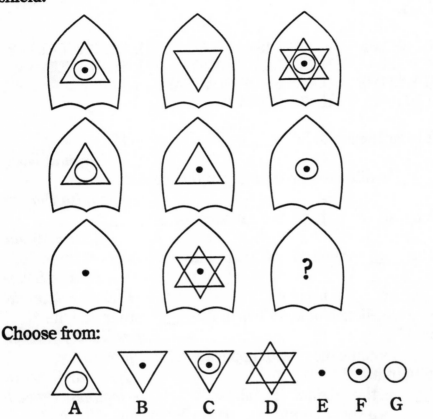

Choose from:

A   B   C   D   E   F   G

(Solution 142)

157 Animals

Hidden in the sentences are the names of five animals. See if you can find them.

1. Give the imp a large brandy.
2. You will soon age really quickly.
3. Watch out for he suspects trouble brewing.
4. Put the saucepan there on the table.
5. Drive a car a calculated distance.

(Solution 146)

158 Comparison

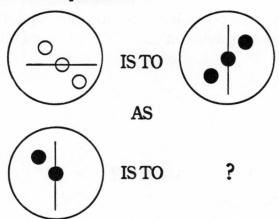

IS TO

AS

IS TO ?

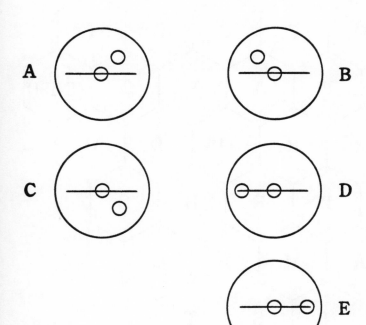

(Solution 150)

159 Honeycomb

Work from start to finish, from adjoining letter to adjoining letter in any direction, to spell out a quotation. Each letter is used only once.

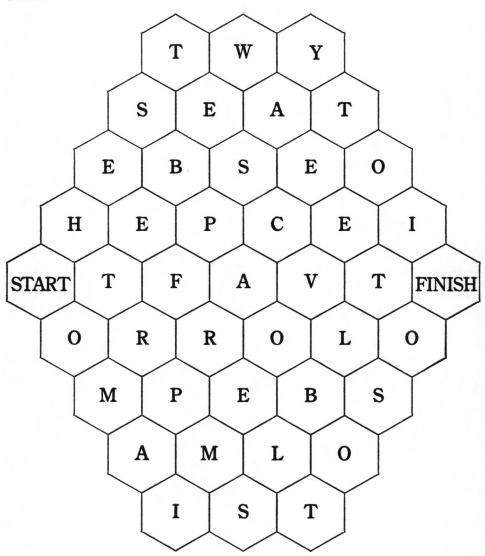

(Solution 154)

160 Word Cycle

Complete the twelve words below so that the same two letters that end the first word also start the second word; the two letters that end the second word also start the third word; etc. To complete the cycle, the two letters that end the twelfth word are also the first two letters of the first word.

```
• •   E E   • •
• •   N I   • •
• •   I G   • •
• •   S I   • •
• •   I G   • •
• •   L I   • •
• •   L L   • •
• •   C A   • •
• •   S T   • •
• •   T H   • •
• •   L U   • •
• •   T A   • •
```

(Solution 157)

161 Analogy

 IS TO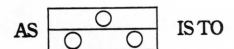

AS 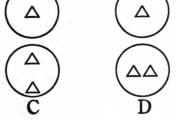 IS TO

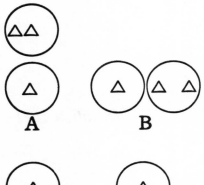

A   B

C   D

(Solution 158)

The Solutions
3

(Solutions are presented out of numerical sequence so that reading the answer to one puzzle will not inadvertently reveal the answer to the next.)

1 Cards

IMPLANTATION:

I	KH	13
M	QS	12
P	AC	15
L	KC	13
A	AD	15
N	AS	15
T	KD	13
A	QC	12
T	QH	12
I	KS	13
O	QD	12
N	AH	15
		160

(Puzzle 81)

2 The Hexagonal Circle

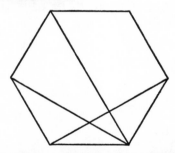

Start at the bottom hexagon and work upward. Every third hexagon in a straight line contains the contents of the two below it. When two lines appear in the same position they cancel each other out.

(Puzzle 121)

3 Knight's Saying

That man is great who can use the brains of others to carry out his work.

by *Don Piatt*
(Puzzle 1)

4 Triple Choice

1. (b)	6. (a)
2. (b)	7. (c)
3. (a)	8. (a)
4. (a)	9. (c)
5. (c)	10. (a)

(Puzzle 41)

5 Saying

"The strong take from the weak, the rich take from the poor, and the government take from everyone."

—*Glomm's Law*

(Puzzle 82)

6 Logic

7:
Each number represents the number of letters in each word of the question.

(Puzzle 122)

7 Center Word

TEN:

Rotten	Tenant
Batten	Tendon
Fatten	Tenon

(Puzzle 2)

8 Link Words

ATE.

(Puzzle 42)

9 Synonym Circles

Blissful
Ecstatic

(Puzzle 83)

10 Diamond

Straightforward.

(Puzzle 123)

11 Pulleys

A to **B** gives a clockwise direction at a speed of 10, but **B** to **C** halves the speed and **C** to **D** reverses the direction, so **E** revolves counterclockwise at a speed of 5.

(Puzzle 3)

12 Horse Race

4 to 1 against:

No.	Odds	Stake to Win $100	Returned $ (including stake)
1	2 to 1	33.33	100.
2	3 to 1	25.00	100.
3	4 to 1	20.00	100.
4	5 to 1	16.67	100.
5	4 to 1	20.00	100.
		115.00 Total stake	
		100.00 Pay out	
		$15.00 Profit	

$$\frac{15}{100} = 15\%$$

(Puzzle 43)

13 Nine Digits

$32,547,891 \times 6 = 195,287,346$

(Puzzle 84)

14 Common

They are all endings of the names of COUNTRIES:
bahRAIN
denMARK
finLAND
palesTINE
singaPORE
kuWAIT
sPAIN

(Puzzle 124)

15 Poser

P	O	S	E	R
S	E	R	P	O
R	P	O	S	E
O	S	E	R	P
E	R	P	O	S

(Puzzle 4)

16 Three Too Many

R	E	T	I	R	E	D
E		A		E		E
D	I	G	I	T	A	L
U		E		I		U
C	A	T	E	R	E	D
E		E		E		E
D	E	S	I	R	E	D

(Puzzle 44)

17 Grid

1C.

(Puzzle 85)

18 Symbols

B.

(Puzzle 125)

19 Grid

1A.

(Puzzle 5)

20 Symbols

B.

(Puzzle 45)

21 Alphametics

```
    490
    407
+   107
   ────
   1004
```

(Puzzle 86)

22 Cryptogram I

"Be bold. If you're going to make an error, make a doozy, and don't be afraid to hit the ball."

—*Billie Jean King*

(Puzzle 6)

23 Cryptogram II

"Millions of words are written annually, purporting to tell how to beat the races, whereas the best possible advice on the subject is found in the three monosyllables: 'DO NOT TRY.'"

—*Dan Parker*

(Puzzle 46)

24 Division

Indefatigability:

E	A	A	D	I	A	I	F
I	L	L	T	I	N	B	Y
F	I	N	T	D	I	E	G
B	T	I	G	Y	A	I	T
G	D	Y	E	I	A	I	I
N	I	B	F	T	D	A	I
Y	L	I	E	T	B	L	T
T	F	A	I	I	A	G	N

(Puzzle 126)

25 Languages

German, Icelandic, Lao, Amharic, Romanian, Urdu, Bengali, Arabic, Nepali
Anagram: BULGARIAN.

(Puzzle 87)

26 Sequence

477:
Square the middle digit each time and add this to the number.
For example:

$$396 + 9^2 = 477$$

(Puzzle 127)

27 Pentagon Figures

4:
$3 \times 9 \times 9 = 243$, or 3^5
$1 \times 2 \times 16 = 32$, or 2^5
$32 \times 8 \times 4 = 1024$, or 4^5

(Puzzle 7)

28 Rectangle to Greek Cross

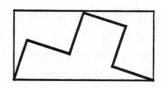

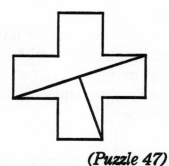

(Puzzle 47)

29 Book Titles

1. *Of Mice and Men* (John Steinbeck)
2. *Elmer Gantry* (Sinclair Lewis)
3. *The Great Gatsby* (F. Scott Fitzgerald)
4. *The Winds of War* (Herman Wouk)
5. *To Kill a Mockingbird* (Harper Lee)

(Puzzle 88)

30 Synonyms

1. Alike   3. Prating   5. Impetus
2. Ascetic   4. Flute

(Puzzle 128)

31 Wot! No Vowels?

By, Slyly, Ply, Spy, Hymn, Tryst, Wry

(Puzzle 8)

32 Motors

$$\frac{3}{10} \times \frac{2}{9} = \frac{6}{90} = \frac{1}{15}$$

Chances are 1 in 15.

(Puzzle 48)

33 Triangle Matrix

C:
Looking both across and down, the contents of the third square are formed by combining the contents of the first two squares, except that where two triangles coincide in the same position in the first two squares, they are then canceled out in the third square.

(Puzzle 89)

34 Hexagonal Sequence

D:
The black segment moves 2 counterclockwise, 1 clockwise, etc.
The white circle moves 1 clockwise, 2 counterclockwise, etc.
The black circle moves 2 counterclockwise, 1 clockwise, etc.
The white triangle moves 2 counterclockwise, 1 clockwise, etc.
The black triangle moves 2 counterclockwise, 1 clockwise, etc.
The striped segment moves 1 clockwise, 2 counterclockwise, etc.

(Puzzle 129)

35 Sequence

A.

A moves 45° clockwise at each stage.
B moves 90° clockwise at each stage.
C moves 90° clockwise at each stage.
D moves 45° clockwise at each stage.

Note: In stage 3, D is hidden by B.

(Puzzle 9)

36 Word Circles

Antonyms: Yielding, Stubborn
Synonyms: Haunting, Poignant

(Puzzle 49)

37 Alternative Crossword

S	O	R	D	I	D	■	C	O	S	S	E	T
T	■	E	■	L	U	N	A	R	■	E	■	H
U	N	F	O	L	D	■	N	E	S	T	L	E
C	■	I	■	S	E	E	D	S	■	T	■	M
C	A	N	T	■	S	A	Y	■	C	E	D	E
O	P	E	R	A	■	R	■	T	R	E	E	S
■	A	■	I	N	K	■	D	I	E	■	L	■
E	R	R	E	D	■	P	■	S	E	C	T	S
S	T	U	D	■	P	O	P	■	D	R	A	W
S	■	M	■	D	O	T	E	S	■	A	■	O
A	M	B	L	E	S	■	D	U	S	T	E	R
Y	■	L	■	A	T	T	A	R	■	E	■	D
S	T	E	E	R	S	■	L	E	N	S	E	S

(Puzzle 90)

38 Fore and Aft

MAN:

Foreman	Manhood
Workman	Mandrake
Marksman	Mankind

(Puzzle 91)

39 Word Power

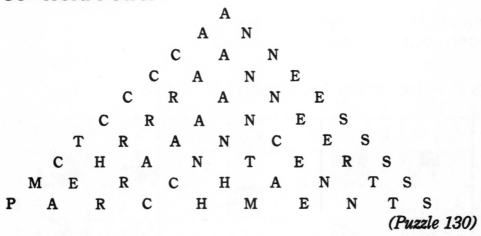

(Puzzle 130)

40 Children

To solve this problem use a Venn diagram:

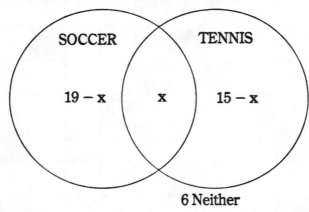

The area where the circles overlap indicates children who play both table tennis and soccer.

19 − x represents those who can play soccer but not table tennis.
15 − x represents those who can play table tennis but not soccer.

Now we have:
$$19 - x + x + 15 - x + 6 = 30$$
$$40 - x = 30$$
$$x = 10$$

Ten children can play table tennis and soccer.

(Puzzle 10)

41 Number-Crunching Squares

160,225:

$400^2 + 15^2$	$399^2 + 32^2$	$393^2 + 76^2$
$392^2 + 81^2$	$384^2 + 113^2$	$375^2 + 140^2$
$360^2 + 175^2$	$356^2 + 183^2$	$337^2 + 216^2$
$329^2 + 228^2$	$311^2 + 252^2$	$265^2 + 300^2$

(Puzzle 50)

42 Odd One Out

D:
A is the same as C.
B is the same as F.
E is the same as G.

(Puzzle 131)

43 Magic Word Square

D	A	V	I	T
A	R	O	M	A
V	O	C	A	L
I	M	A	G	E
T	A	L	E	S

(Puzzle 11)

44 Odd One Out

D:
A is the same as G.
B is the same as F.
C is the same as E.

(Puzzle 92)

45 Sequence

C:
There are three triangles that always have their bases on sides **A**, **B**, and **C** of the hexagon. The height of the three triangles increases by one quarter of the diameter of the hexagon at each stage.

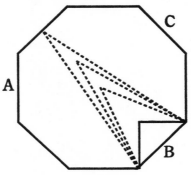

(Puzzle 51)

46 Ball

36 feet:
$12 + 2 (6 + \frac{6}{2} + \frac{6}{4} + \frac{6}{8} + \frac{6}{16} + \frac{6}{32} + ...)$
$= 12 + 2 (12) \text{ ft} = 36 \text{ ft}.$
(12 is equal to the series $6 + \frac{6}{2}$, etc.)

(Puzzle 132)

47 Magic "65"

20	11	13	4	17
6	24	7	23	5
22	18	1	14	10
2	9	25	8	21
15	3	19	16	12

(Puzzle 12)

48 Do-It-Yourself Crossword

S	E	Q	U	E	S	T	R	A	T	E
P		U		A		A		P		A
E	X	I	S	T		P	R	E	S	S
L		E		E	V	E				E
L	I	T		N	E	S	T	L	E	S
		E			X			A		
M	I	N	U	T	E	S		T	I	C
O				A	D	O		E		L
P	A	N	I	C		N	U	R	S	E
E		E		I		I		A		A
S	P	E	C	T	A	C	U	L	A	R

(Puzzle 52)

49 Sequence

1,131:
Each number describes consecutive prime numbers:
    12 = first prime number 2
    23 = second prime number 3, etc.

The eleventh prime number is 31, or 1131.

(Puzzle 93)

50 Hidden Fish

1. Merling
2. Groper
3. Sardine
4. Dugong
5. Minnow
6. Tench

(Puzzle 133)

51 Twelve Letters

1. MUDDLE HEADED
2. HORROR STRUCK
3. BUTTER SCOTCH
4. BREATH TAKING

(Puzzle 13)

52 Longest Word

Quatrefoils.

(Puzzle 53)

53 Network

Proletarianism.

(Puzzle 94)

54 Anagram Phrases

1. To have a fling
2. To let the grass grow under one's feet
3. Nine times out of ten
4. Keep your shirt on
5. For good measure

(Puzzle 134)

55 Odd One Out

Stella Strong.
In all the other name-pairs the second word is the definition of
the first:

> Ethel means Noble.
> Cyril means Lord.
> Clive means Cliff.
> Lloyd means Gray.

Stella actually means Star.

(Puzzle 14)

56 Grid

3C.

(Puzzle 54)

57 Odd One Out

D. Trips:
The others, if the preceding letter is included, form anagrams of an astrological feature:

        A. Got = Goat (Capricorn)
        B. Car = Crab (Cancer)
        C. Seals = Scales (Libra)

(Puzzle 95)

58 Grid Logic

OO = one across, one down:
TT, for example, represents two across, two down; or three across, three down; or two across, three down, and vice versa.

(Puzzle 135)

59 Grid

1B.

(Puzzle 15)

60 The Paradox of the Unexpected Gift

1. The Greek philosopher Zeno suggested that in the last few seconds of Thursday you see someone approaching with the gift. "Here is the gift," he says, and looks at his very precise watch. You claim that it's not unexpected for the reasons previously outlined. "But," says your friend, "Thursday is ending and Friday is about to begin," and hands you the present at the precise instant of the change—the moment between Thursday and Friday.

2. You receive the gift outside working hours—surely this would be unexpected as you would have expected the presentation to be made in the office during working hours.

3. A colleague comes to your house on the Saturday or Sunday immediately prior to your last working week and presents you with the gift on one of the very two days you did not expect to receive it.

4. Five boxes are placed in the office. Four have weights precisely the same as the present and one contains the present. You are to pick one box each day when given the word. The gift will, therefore, be unexpecte — unless, of course, you haven't picked the correct box by Thursday (when the odds are even) or Friday (when the odds are a certainty).

5. On Monday a colleague asks, "Are you expecting to receive the gift today?" You say "No." Your colleague then gives you the gift.

(Puzzle 55)

61 Sequence

E:
Starting at 6 o'clock the time advances 1 hour and 20 minutes at each stage:

    6:00, 7:20, 8:40, 10:00, 11:20.

(Puzzle 96)

62 Margana

Journalist.

(Puzzle 136)

63 Do-It-Yourself Diamond Crossword

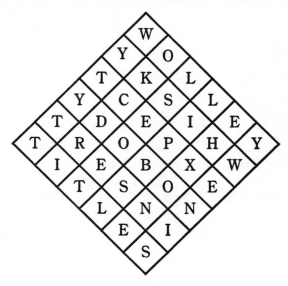

(Puzzle 16)

112

64 Cross-Alphabet

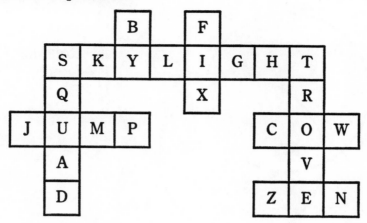

(Puzzle 56)

65 "D" Puzzle

Didst
Dacha
Dwell
Disco
Djinn

(Puzzle 97)

66 Analogy

A:
The outer triangles are folded into the internal part of the figure and the whole shape is then enlarged.

(Puzzle 137)

67 Odd One Out

E:
All the others are the same figure rotated.

(Puzzle 57)

68 Survey

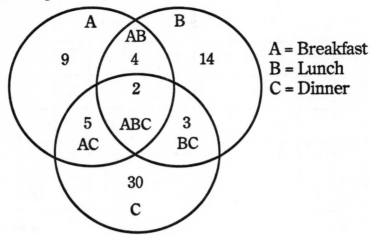

A = Breakfast
B = Lunch
C = Dinner

One meal eaten = 9 + 14 + 30 = 53.

(Puzzle 17)

69 Fish Farm

The center point between ten lakes north/south and ten lakes east/west.

	A	B	C	D	E	F	G	H
1								
2								
3								
4								
5								
6								
7								
8								

(5) LAKES

(5) LAKES   (5) LAKES

(5) LAKES

(Puzzle 98)

70 Four Letters

A number of answers are possible. Here is a sample:
Washbowl
Eyebright
Gangplank
Highflier
Marksman
Three-quarter
Turtleback
Wingspread
Wishy-washy
Wagonload
Watchhouse
Wainwright

(Puzzle 138)

71 Pyramid

The number of sides in the figure on the top row is determined by multiplying the number of sides in the two figures beneath it.

The number of sides in the two figures on the second line are each determined by dividing the sides in the two figures directly below them on the third line.

The number of sides in the three figures on the third line are determined by multiplying the number of sides in the two figures directly below them in the fourth line. So:

Hexagon = six sides
Triangle = three sides
Semicircle = two sides
Circle = one side

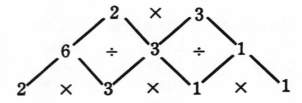

(Puzzle 18)

72 Directional Crossword

1. Aggravate
2. Extortion
3. Neuralgia
4. Aerofoil
5. Liniment
6. Truffle
7. Element
8. Theme
9. Emerges
10. Sophism
11. Married
12. Dogs
13. Silos
14. Sum
15. Move
16. Eras
17. Sop

¹A	⁵L	I	O	F	O	R	E	⁴A
¹⁰S	G	I	¹³S	G	O	¹²D	I	⁷E
O	E	G	N	I	E	G	L	L
P	¹⁷S	G	R	I	L	E	¹⁵M	F
H	O	A	R	A	M	O	U	F
I	P	R	R	E	V	E	¹⁴S	U
S	A	U	N	¹⁶E	M	A	N	R
¹¹M	E	⁸T	H	E	M	⁹E	T	⁶T
³N	O	I	T	R	O	T	X	²E

(Puzzle 58)

73 Magic Number Square

10	5	16	3
8	11	2	13
1	14	7	12
15	4	9	6

(Puzzle 99)

74 Honeycomb

Marmalade	Margarine	Melba
Rice	Crab	Lamb
Gravy	Liver	Lard
Veal	Bran	Brawn
Beef	Egg	Gigot
Tart	Roll	Loaf

(Puzzle 19)

75 Initials

6	Pockets on a Pool Table
32	Points on a Compass
6	Sides on a Snowflake
3	Feet in a Yard
1	Good Turn Deserves Another
3	Coins in the Fountain
13	Months in a Lunar Year
12	Sides on a Dodecahedron

(Puzzle 139)

76 Lawns

$8,845 = 66^2 + 67^2$

(Puzzle 59)

77 Trite Saying

"Heredity is what a man believes in until his son begins to behave like a delinquent."

(Puzzle 100)

78 Word Search

Bootlegger	Freshwater	Breakwater
Barnacle	Foreshore	Water
Shore	Fore	Stowaway
Torpedo	Port	Tornado
Rocket	Rope	Ketch
Row	Rowlock	Lock
Dog	Chest	Tide
Lee	Crew	Sleet
Wren	Bow	Tot
Tars	Salvo	Rock
Stow		

(Puzzle 140)

79 Find a Word

Featherweight.

(Puzzle 20)

80 Same Word

1. Noodle
2. Crock
3. Pitcher
4. Queue
5. Tern
6. Puncheon
7. Puck
8. Lurcher
9. Baste
10. Beagle

(Puzzle 60)

81 Cryptogram III

"Golf is so popular simply because it is the best game in the world at which to be bad."

—*A. A. Milne*
(Puzzle 101)

82 Magic Prime Square

103	79	37
7	73	139
109	67	43

(Puzzle 141)

83 No Repeat Letters

Designator.

(Puzzle 21)

84 The Train In the Tunnel

$(2.5 + 0.25) \times \dfrac{60}{75} = 2.2$ minutes or 2 minutes 12 seconds.

(Puzzle 61)

85 Grid

2C.

(Puzzle 102)

86 Symbols

E.

(Puzzle 142)

87 Symbols

A.

(Puzzle 22)

88 Links Jigsaw Puzzle

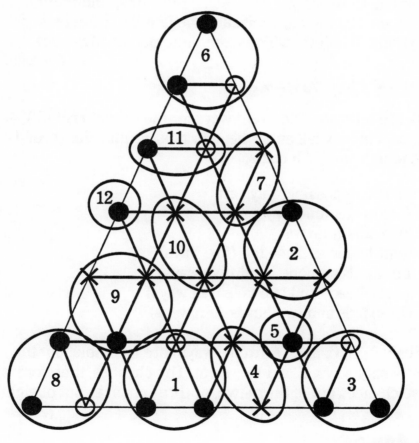

(Puzzle 62)

89 Anagram Theme

All COMPUTER TERMS:

Interface (Fine Trace)　　Hacker (Rack He)
Program (Romp Rag)　　Mouse (So Emu)
Format (Fort Am)　　Software (Swore Fat)
Binary (By Rain)　　Mainframe (Amine Farm)

(Puzzle 103)

90 Ten-Letter Words Boggle

Exultation, Dramatical, Affiliated, Worthwhile, Philosophy, Prudential, Conciliary, Curvaceous, Fictitious, Thoughtful, Auspicious, Exhibition, Trajection, Vegetarian, Undercover, Everything, Vaudeville, Tripartite, Automobile, Majestical.

(Puzzle 143)

91 The Five Pennies

There are thirty-two different ways for the coins to fall (2^5), as the first coin may fall either head or tails, as may the second, third, fourth, and fifth coins.

The thirty-two possible ways are:
    A. Five heads (one way)
    B. Five tails (one way)
    C. Four heads and one tail (five ways)
    D. Four tails and one head (five ways)
    E. Three heads and two tails (ten ways)
    F. Three tails and two heads (ten ways)

Of these, A, B, C, and D (twelve ways) are favorable, but the other twenty ways, E and F, are not. The chances, therefore, are twelve chances out of thirty-two, or three chances out of eight.

(Puzzle 23)

92 Analogy

D:
The top half is folded along the middle line onto the bottom half.

(Puzzle 104)

93 Plan In Works

A.
1. Man and boy
2. A pack of lies
3. In full cry
4. Go great guns
5. Out of joint
6. Cheek by jowl
7. Pipe down
8. Play safe
9. Lay hold of
10. Living doll

B.
1. Odds and ends
2. A tall order
3. To say the least
4. When the chips are down
5. Do or die
6. Hand in glove
7. At a push
8. Steal the show
9. Take by storm
10. On the wane

(Puzzle 63)

94 Two Coins

George I: A coin would not be marked George I because at the time it was produced it would not be known whether there would be a George II. The first Elizabeth did not become Elizabeth I until the second Elizabeth became Queen. Similarly, Victoria is Queen Victoria and not Queen Victoria I.

(Puzzle 144)

95 Piecemeal Quotation

"We would know mankind better if we were not so anxious to resemble one another."

— Goethe
(Puzzle 64)

96 Hexagon Logic

A = ⬭   B = ◇

Each straight row of four hexagons will then contain a circle, diamond, triangle, and ellipse.

(Puzzle 24)

97 "Y" Puzzle

Key	Doyen	Monkey
Money	Day	Rayon
Dray	Ray	Aye
Pray	Prayed	Pay
Ploy	Donkey	Yard
Yon	Yen	Yap
Yeo	Keyed	Eye
Eyed	Yoyo	Monkeyed
Moneyed	Ployed	Yenned

(Puzzle 105)

98 Hexagons

B:
The dotted line moves around each of the four positions in turn. Any dotted line becomes curved in the next option only.

(Puzzle 145)

99 Links

1. ROW
2. UP
3. AND
4. BOARD
5. FOX
6. SAIL
7. HEAD
8. SWORD
9. OR
10. HELL

(Puzzle 25)

100 Birds

1. Wander – Gander
2. Curled – Curlew
3. Clover – Plover
4. Muffin – Puffin
5. Banner – Lanner
6. Missed – Missel
7. Beaver – Weaver
8. Baffle – Yaffle
9. Barbel – Barbet
10. Canard – Canary

(Puzzle 65)

101 Rectangle

Express as fractions:

$$\frac{24}{36} = \frac{22}{33} = \frac{20}{30} = \frac{18}{27} = \frac{16}{24} = \frac{14}{21} = \frac{12}{18} = \frac{10}{15} = \frac{8}{12}$$

$$= \frac{6}{9} = \frac{4}{6} = \frac{2}{3}$$

= 12 points, plus 1 at start = 13.

(Puzzle 106)

102 Star

Dodecahedral.

(Puzzle 146)

103 Pentagram

Foray
Decoy
Cadre
Corps
Truce
Key = PEACE

(Puzzle 26)

104 Matrix

F:
This is a magic square of lines. The number of lines in each horizontal, vertical, and corner-to-corner line totals 15.

(Puzzle 66)

105 Alphabet Clueless-Crossword

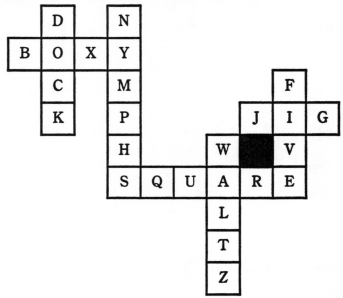

(Puzzle 107)

106 Silent Order

Kickback:

Ⓚ N O L L
H E Ⓘ F E R
I N D I Ⓒ T
Ⓚ N E W
D O U Ⓑ T
T O Ⓐ S T
N A S Ⓒ E N T
Ⓚ N I C K E R S

Each word has a silent letter. Taken in order they spell KICKBACK.

(Puzzle 147)

107 Three to Choose

1. (c)   6. (a)
2. (b)   7. (b)
3. (a)   8. (a)
4. (a)   9. (a)
5. (b)   10. (a)

(Puzzle 27)

108 Links Jigsaw Puzzle

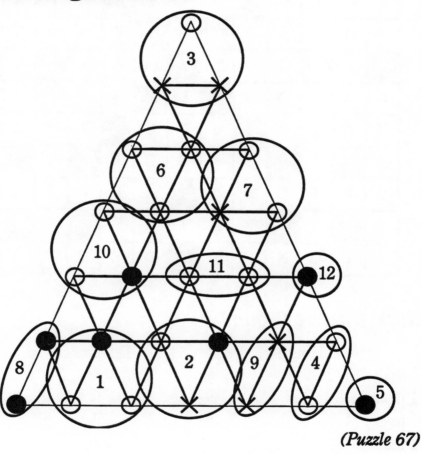

(Puzzle 67)

109 No Blanks

P	L	A	N	E	T		F	A	T	H	E	R
U		R		R	O	T	O	R		O		A
F	R	I	D	A	Y		R	U	N	L	E	T
F		S		S	E	R	U	M		D		H
I	C	E	D		D	I	M		M	E	R	E
N	O	S	E	D		M		B	O	R	E	R
	B		C	O	S		M	A	R		B	
C	R	O	O	N		L		G	A	S	E	S
H	A	I	R		C	O	G		Y	E	L	P
A		L		Z	E	B	R	A		V		E
S	P	I	C	E	D		A	P	P	E	A	L
E		N		R	A	I	N	S		R		L
S	I	G	N	O	R		D	E	T	E	R	S

(Puzzle 108)

110 Cricket Ground

	Hours	Reciprocal	Decimal
1 man	2	$\frac{1}{2}$	.500
1 man	3	$\frac{1}{3}$	.333
1 man	4	$\frac{1}{4}$	.250
1 man	5	$\frac{1}{5}$	.200
1 man	6	$\frac{1}{6}$	.167
			1.450

Take reciprocal again:

$$60 \left(\frac{1 \text{ hour}}{1.450} \right) = 41.4 \text{ minutes}$$

(Puzzle 28)

126

111 Journey

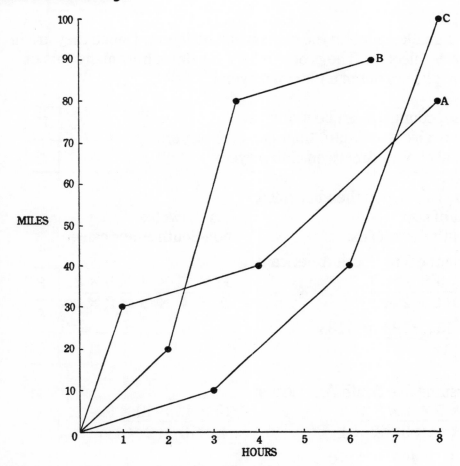

1. B overtook A at approximately 2:20.
2. C overtook A at approximately 7:00.

(Puzzle 148)

112 Logic

A:
The contents of the first two circles in each row and column are combined to form the contents of the third circle.

(Puzzle 109)

113 World Cup

15,070:

The goalkeeper and the captain can be ignored since they are in every selection. The problem then becomes how many sets of nine players out of eighteen players?

Also, countries can be written as:

    twelve non-South American club players
    six South American club players

The calculation then becomes:

out of six South Americans:

out of twelve non-South Americans:

Assume four South Americans:

$$\frac{6 \times 5 \times 4 \times 3}{4 \times 3 \times 2 \times 1} \quad \times \quad \frac{12 \times 11 \times 10 \times 9 \times 8}{5 \times 4 \times 3 \times 2 \times 1}$$

$$= \frac{15}{1} \times \frac{792}{1} = 11880$$

Assume five South Americans:

$$\frac{6 \times 5 \times 4 \times 3 \times 2}{5 \times 4 \times 3 \times 2 \times 1} \quad \times \quad \frac{12 \times 11 \times 10 \times 9}{4 \times 3 \times 2 \times 1}$$

$$= \frac{6}{1} \times \frac{495}{1} = 2970$$

Assume six South Americans:

$$\frac{6 \times 5 \times 4 \times 3 \times 2 \times 1}{6 \times 5 \times 4 \times 3 \times 2 \times 1} \quad \times \quad \frac{12 \times 11 \times 10}{3 \times 2 \times 1}$$

$$= \frac{1}{1} \times \frac{220}{1} = 220$$

Total 15,070

(Puzzle 68)

114 Magic Word Square

L	O	C	A	L
O	K	A	P	I
C	A	N	A	L
A	P	A	R	T
L	I	L	T	S

(Puzzle 149)

115 Word Circles

Synonyms: Despotic, Arrogant
Antonyms: Vivacity, Lethargy

(Puzzle 29)

116 Pyramid Word

1. N
2. So
3. Has
4. Deft
5. Steer
15-letter word: SOFTHEARTEDNESS

(Puzzle 69)

117 An Irish Proverb

"Nodding the head does not row the boat."

(Puzzle 110)

118 Sequence

C:
In each circle

○   moves 45° clockwise

╲   moves 180° clockwise

▷   moves 225° clockwise

╱   moves 90° clockwise.

(Puzzle 150)

119 Circles

Each pair of circles produces the circle above it by carrying forward only those elements that are different. Similar elements are canceled out.

For example:

D

Answer:

(Puzzle 30)

120 Two Quick Teasers

1. By one third: Three of anything, if increased by one third, becomes four.

2. 14,313: 13,000 + 1300 + 13

(Puzzle 70)

121 Containers

1. G(aunt)let
2. Seyc(hell)es
3. T(hem)e
4. D(red)ger
5. C(leave)r
6. Fa(rand)ole
7. P(earl)s
8. P(ant)ry
9. A(then)s
10. Ken(tuck)y

(Puzzle 111)

122 People

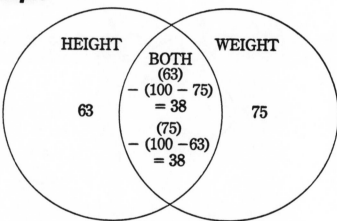

Use a Venn diagram to show detail:
Greatest = 63
Least = 38

(Puzzle 151)

123 Eggs

$$\frac{6}{100} \times \frac{5}{99} = \frac{30}{9900} \text{ or } \frac{1}{330}$$

One chance in 330 or 329 to 1 against.

(Puzzle 31)

124 Clueless Crossword

F	L	A	T	T	E	R
L		I		R		I
I	N	S	T	E	A	D
N		L		A		E
G	R	E	A	T	E	R

(Puzzle 71)

125 Connections

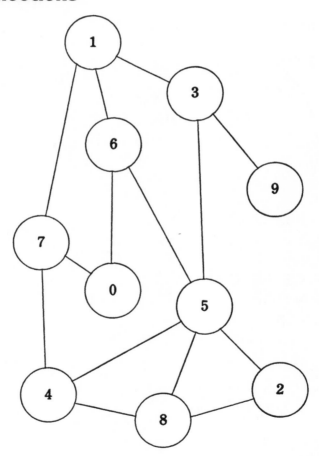

(Puzzle 112)

126 Brain Strain

8	÷	2	+	5	=	9
×		+		+		×
2	−	1	+	3	=	4
÷		×		−		÷
4	+	3	−	1	=	6
=		=		=		=
4	+	9	−	7	=	6

(Puzzle 152)

127 Number-Crunching Series

1,680: $1681 = 41^2$
$841 = 29^2$

(Puzzle 32)

128 Birds

Factorizing 90, with no
factors as high as 15:   Add factors:
$90 = 1 \times 9 \times 10$ 20
$90 = 2 \times 5 \times 9$ 16
$90 = 3 \times 5 \times 6$ 14
$90 = 3 \times 3 \times 10$ 16

As my friend still did not know the girls' ages, there must have
been 16 birds in the tree, giving two possible answers: 2, 5, and 9
years old, or 3-year-old twins and a 10-year-old.

(Puzzle 72)

129 Trade

Peer:

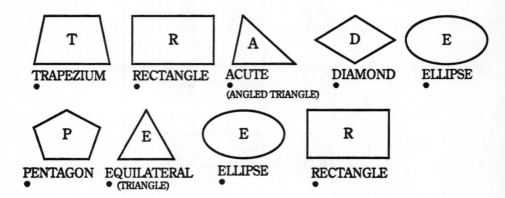

(Puzzle 113)

130 Common

They all contain names of TREES, FLOWERS, or SHRUBS spelled backward.

Fir
Gum
Nut
Arum
Acer
Lime
Carob
Rose

(Puzzle 153)

131 Pyramid

Instrumentalist.

(Puzzle 33)

E:

The two triangles, **A** and **B** remain pivoted on corners **C** and **D**. Triangle **A** pivots clockwise at each stage with its shortest side pointing to one of the corners of the hexagon at each stage in turn. Triangle **B** pivots in the same way but counterclockwise.

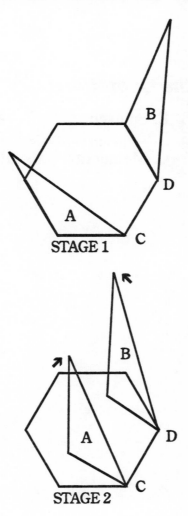

STAGE 1

STAGE 2

(Puzzle 73)

135

133 Diamonds

Mallard	Hen
Lark	Raven
Mavis	Wren
Drake	Pen
Tit	Pern
Tui	Reeve
Kaka	Veery
Rhea	Pipit

(Puzzle 114)

134 Complete the Quotations

1 - D. Phantom   5 - E. Spinach   8 - J. Applause
2 - H. Tomorrow   6 - G. Appropriateness   9 - I. Architecture
3 - F. Conversation   7 - C. Mediocrity   10 - B.Cherries
4 - A. Harmonies

(Puzzle 154)

135 Track Word

Incommensurable.

(Puzzle 34)

136 Cement

$$x = 5000 \div \frac{1}{2}x = \frac{5000}{\frac{x}{2}}$$

$$\frac{x^2}{2} = 5000$$

$$x^2 = 10,000$$

$$x = 100 \text{ pounds}$$

(Puzzle 115)

137 Decadice

Lose

1-1	2-1	3-1	4-1	5-1	6-1	7-1	8-1	9-1	10-1
1-2	2-2	3-2	4-2	5-2	6-2	7-2	8-2	9-2	10-2
1-3	2-3	3-3	4-3	5-3	6-3	7-3	8-3	9-3	10-3
1-4	2-4	3-4	4-4	5-4	6-4	7-4	8-4	9-4	10-4
1-5	2-5	3-5	4-5	5-5	6-5	7-5	8-5	9-5	10-5
1-6	2-6	3-6	4-6	5-6	6-6	7-6	8-6	9-6	10-6
1-7	2-7	3-7	4-7	5-7	6-7	7-7	8-7	9-7	10-7
1-8	2-8	3-8	4-8	5-8	6-8	7-8	8-8	9-8	10-8
1-9	2-9	3-9	4-9	5-9	6-9	7-9	8-9	9-9	10-9
1-10	2-10	3-10	4-10	5-10	6-10	7-10	8-10	9-10	10-10

Win

Lose		Win
10		–
10		–
9		1
8		2
7		3
6		4
5		5
4		6
3		7
2		8
64	to	36

or 16 to 9 odds against.

(Puzzle 74)

138 A Long Time

$4 \times 1,738 = 6,952$
$4 \times 1,963 = 7,852$

(Puzzle 155)

139 Sequence

B:

The bottom symbol moves to the middle and then to the top in turn. That is, in Stage 1 the symbol ⌂ is at the bottom, in Stage 2 it is in the middle, and in Stage 3 at the top. Since that sequence is now complete, in Stage 4 it is the turn of symbol ⌂ to move up in the same way.

(Puzzle 35)

140 Hexagram

Basnet
Dagger
Helmet
Lariat
Cudgel
Musket
Key = SHIELD

(Puzzle 75)

141 Words

Galantine:
Each word starts with the letter whose position in the alphabet coincides with the number of letters in the preceding word.

Lockjaw has seven letters, therefore, the next word starts with the seventh letter of the alphabet.

(Puzzle 116)

142 Shields Matrix

D:
Looking both across and down, the contents of the third shield are formed by merging the contents of the first two shields, but matching symbols are canceled out.

(Puzzle 156)

143 Missing Number

4:
$$15 \div 12 = 1.25 \ (\times 8) = 10$$
$$24 \div 16 = 1.5 \ \ (\times 8) = 12$$
$$5 \div 10 = 0.5 \ \ (\times 8) = \ 4$$

(Puzzle 36)

144 Symbols

E.

(Puzzle 76)

145 Bracket Word

Mechanical.

(Puzzle 117)

146 Animals

1. Impala
2. Onager
3. Rhesus
4. Panther
5. Caracal

(Puzzle 157)

147 Wot! No Vowels?

Crypt	Slyly	Sly
Fly	Try	Fry
Dry	Pyx	Cry
Pry	Wynd	Sync
Lych	Fyrd	Ply
Shy	Wry	

(Puzzle 37)

148 Odd One Out

The license plates represent the year, followed by the first three letters of the city, followed by the first letter of the country of venues of Olympic Games of the twentieth century:

76 MON C =	1976, Montreal, Canada
68 GRE F =	1968, Grenoble, France
12 STO S =	1912, Stockholm, Sweden
56 MEL A =	1956, Melbourne, Australia
92 BAR S =	1992, Barcelona, Spain

68 GRE F is the odd one out because it represents winter Olympic Games; the others were all summer Olympic Games.

(Puzzle 77)

149 Circles

C

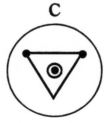

Each pair of circles produces the circle above it by carrying forward the elements, but similar elements are canceled out. For example:

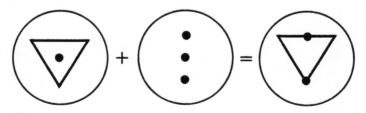

(Puzzle 118)

150 Comparison

A.

(Puzzle 158)

151 Consonants

1. Yardstick, Benchmark, Standard, Criterion
2. Recalcitrant, Obstinate, Wayward, Intractable
3. Enchant, Bewitch, Delight, Mesmerize
4. Locution, Articulation, Intonation, Accent
5. Allegory, Parable, Apologue, Fable
6. Guileful, Cunning, Underhand, Deceitful

(Puzzle 38)

152 Anagrammed Synonyms

1. Plea – Appeal
2. Pose – Impersonate
3. Like – Admire
4. Say – Mention
5. Taut – Strained
6. Kiss – Osculate
7. Coy – Reserved
8. Rid – Unburden
9. Add – Augment
10. Ruler – Monarch

(Puzzle 78)

153 Roman Numerals

1888 = MDCCCLXXXVIII

(Puzzle 119)

154 Honeycomb

"The best way to escape from a problem is to solve it."
—*Brendan Francis*

(Puzzle 159)

155 Grid

2C.

(Puzzle 39)

156 Bars

C:
The symbols move as follows:

⏢   one right, two left, one right, two left, etc.

●   one left, one right, etc.

△   two right, one left, two right, one left, etc.

○   one left, two right, one left, two right, etc.

◯   one left, two right, one left, two right, etc.

(Puzzle 79)

157 Word Cycle

Cheese, Senior, Origin, Insist, Stigma, Malice, Cellar, Arcane, Nestle, Lethal, Allude, Detach.

(Puzzle 160)

158 Analogy

D:
The rectangle splits into two circles and the small circles become triangles.

(Puzzle 161)

159 Analogy

B:
The diamond turns upside down (it appears the same both ways). The base of the rectangle moves down from the top point to the bottom point of the diamond. The small triangle rotates clockwise through 90°.

(Puzzle 40)

160 Palindromic

Arrange the digits in this sequence:

16, 1, 12, 9, 14, 4, 18, 15, 13, 9, 3

Now convert the numbers into their corresponding letters in the alphabet:

P A L I N D R O M I C

(Puzzle 80)

161 Porky Pies

1. (c) Maxim de Winter's pet cocker spaniel was named Jasper.
2. (b) John Edgar Hoover was a lifelong bachelor.
3. (b) Dizzy Gillespie's real first name was John.
4. (c) It was Judy Garland, not Ginger Rogers, who sang "I Cried for You."
5. (c) Hurricane Mills is a town north of Nashville.

(Puzzle 120)